PASTORING
EVOLVING FAITHS

PASTORING
EVOLVING FAITHS

Guiding Spiritual Seekers in the Messy Process of
Faith Deconstruction and Reconstruction

STEPHEN D. SCHMIDT

the
Abbey Press

Oklahoma City

2026

the Abbey Press

The Abbey Press
PO Box 21684 • Oklahoma City, OK 73156

The names and identifying characteristics of some individuals mentioned herein have been changed to protect their privacy.

Printed in the United States of America

LCCN 2026910612 (paperback)
ISBN 979-8-9958109-0-2 (paperback)
ISBN 979-8-9958109-1-9 (ebook)

*To Neill Spurgin Coffman, my pastor, friend,
fellow sojourner, brother in the Kingdom and in ministry*

to the beautiful and entertainingly neurotic saints who participated with me in the Evolving Faiths Discussion Group at The Abbey, and to those in the book groups who continue to keep those conversations alive. I thank God for bringing such a rich and diverse collection of people into my life. I am truly richer because of all of you

and to Jake, my partner in life, who brings so much extroverted energy, music, and beauty to my otherwise introverted world

Contents

Preface

"These conversations are important. They may well be the front lines of the faith these days." I keep coming back to this phrase over and over. That's why I wrote this book.

Those sentences paraphrase Bishop Robert Baron speaking to a group of young Jesuits addressing the contemporary crisis of faith in the Church, encouraging them to get back into their churches and classrooms, and start taking the questions of their students and parishioners seriously. And as I moved through the first year of our Evolving Faiths Discussion Group, I came to see just how true those statements are.

This book began as a project thesis for my doctor of ministry degree at the Virginia Theological Seminary. As part of the degree program, we were required to initiate some sort of project or "act of ministry" within our church setting, and then write about it. Simple enough. And since my area of concentration was Christian Spirituality, I imagined hosting a cozy group of people meeting on Wednesday or Thursday evenings to practice some set of spiritual disciples. I hoped that by regular practice of prayer and meditation, perhaps accompanied by some physical act of "praying with our bodies," we would experience a deeper encounter with the Spirit.

As I explain in the first chapter, that didn't happen. Instead, we were faced with a situation involving a number of our congregants. They were undergoing crisis-level transformations of their beliefs, and we wanted to figure out a way to help them. Turns out, what was happening was nothing unusual. It was happening in churches all across America. They were "deconstructing." Some, very painfully. And most were doing it alone. Suddenly, my ministry project changed from quiet time in a dimly lit room in our church to a time of laughter and intense discussion, sometimes over food and drinks, at private rooms in restaurants and in community club houses.

And those conversations, where we talked about everything related to being an evangelical or fundamental Christian, were life changing.

Many of us rediscovered God. And I found my place in ministry like I had never experienced in the years preceding serving in the church.

Those 12 months of meetings, of profound and sometimes silly discussions, became the focus of that doctoral project. And when I was finished describing the experience in my thesis, I realized that I was walking away with a handful of principles, new perspectives, that other pastors and congregational leaders might also find useful for guiding their people through the messy process of faith deconstruction and reconstruction.

I've revised that thesis, toning down some of the academic language and scaling back some of the sections that addressed academic requirements I presumed would be of little interest to most pastoral readers—my new audience.

What you have in your hand is the result. It still reflects the gene-pool of academic research. You'll still find scholarly quotations and tons of notes and references. Not much more could be done about that short of gutting it entirely and starting from scratch. But I think it's readable and informative. And readers should feel free to skip sections that might be less relevant to their concerns, and focus on the ones that speak more to their interests.

For leaders interested in helping those going through deconstruction, and considering starting a discussion group in your own houses of worship, I want to especially point out those "Learnings" at the end of Chapter 4, "The Act of Ministry: Launching the Evolving Faiths Discussion Group", and the "Closing Thoughts." For those interested in biblical theology, you may find the discussion enlightening about how Jesus and the early church "deconstructed" in Chapter 3, "A Biblical Theology of Deconstruction." Some practical considerations about starting a group are included in Chapter 4. And, as someone involved in an evangelical-related ministry, I found the recent history of American evangelicalism and the study of the spiritual habits of current younger generations to be eye-opening and attention-grabbing. You'll find that in Chapter 2, "Deconstruction in American Christianity." Chapter 5 contains some snapshots of certain conversations we had over some hot-topic issues we were rethinking (like God, the bible, and sex).

I walked away from this project, the first iteration of the Discussion Group, a changed minister. My faith and my own sense of mission were clarified. And virtually everyone who participated in the group commented how their relationship with God had been improved through the process. I pray that you experience similar outcomes.

1

Introduction: The Situation

There is a "distinction between being rooted in your tradition and being stuck in it. The point is to have roots that nourish, rather than a desperate clinging that chokes off real spiritual vitality."

~ WAYNE TEASDALE[1]

The Problem

We sat almost in the dark in the living room of my co-pastor, Neill, the four of us, holding coffee in hand while the book we were ostensibly to discuss sat in our laps. It was the first (maybe the second) Thursday evening gathering of our book discussion group which we hoped would become a dynamic ministry of our new church, The Abbey. But instead of discussing Ken Shigematsu's *God In My Everything*, we talked about our pasts, how we got here.

Matthew's story changed everything.

Matthew* is a 22-year-old man of God and social activist. He grew up in the United Pentecostal Church (UPC), a strict

* Not his real name. All names referenced in this work, except mine and my co-pastor Neill's, have been changed to protect the anonymity of

holiness denomination that had prescribed his behavior as a Christian man down to even the clothes he could wear. Matthew went to a UPC bible college, studied "apostolic doctrine" and even helped plant churches in Oklahoma. But Matthew is also now proudly and openly gay. His former church's doctrines no longer made sense to him. He left the church; he left God. But he didn't stay away from God long. Little by little, Matthew is in the process of redefining his faith: what he believes, what he can accept, what he refuses to believe about God, and how he can fulfil the call to ministry he feels.

He spoke about the hurt he felt from his former pastor, how he'd begun leading bible studies in a nearby Assisted Living Center, and yet his pastor was not interested unless those in the bible study could contribute to the Sunday offering. His pastor knew of Matthew's sexual orientation and reaffirmed the church's position on the matter: he would need to remain celibate and suppress any "unnatural or ungodly" attraction. Matthew's enthusiasm quickly waned and his cynicism grew. On top of this, weekly he heard sermons laced with a legalism and judgmentalism that he intuitively knew was misplaced. He told us of his turning point, when he took all of his old college theology notes and textbooks, "tubs full of them" (his words), and threw them in the dumpster. He was done.

But that Thursday evening, he was on his way back. He still didn't know how to do it yet, but he could feel the pull of the love of God, and he could now separate his former church, his former doctrine, from the Loving God he felt.

Aaron is a 24-year-old trans-male. Born into a Native American Baptist family, Sarah Ann had been involved in church worship since childhood. When Sarah Ann became

---

the participants, as agreed in their signed Letters of Information and Consent (sample attached as Appendix A).

Aaron, his theology also underwent transformation. Aaron feels the calling of a prophetic psalmist, a worshipper and song-writer. Aaron attended our church and led the praise team. But unlike Matthew, Aaron did not re-embrace Christianity. Instead, he found more welcome, more sense, in Judaism and began the conversion process. But Aaron still lingers somewhere between his Christian and Jewish faith, and his journey is far from over.

Kevin and Analise are a straight, married couple in their early-30s. Analise did not grow up in the church; her parents were not religious at all, and she knows almost nothing about the bible. Kevin grew up in the church, the son of a Southern Baptist pastor and missionary, he knows his bible and his theology well. But he could no longer stomach the close-minded, homophobic and bigoted views of his church. The day he first walked into The Abbey, he told me he was deconstructing (he actually used the word) and was looking for a safe place for him and his wife.

Jordan is a young man, recently graduated from a conservative Christian university in Oklahoma affiliated with the Church of Christ. He has a quirky sense of humor (as many of his fellow Gen Z'ers do), a deep love for God and Christianity, and a desire to serve in the church. He is also gay—something his denomination does not approve. He came to terms with his sexuality in his final years of college, coming out to his closest friends, but not yet to his family. He was looking for a church that honored the God of his faith and also accepted and affirmed him in his sexuality. He and his roommate Michael (straight) have agile minds and enjoy exploring esoteric topics. They already had a book club they had formed with other former college friends, and met weekly on Zoom to discuss topics of faith. They aren't content with simply attending church or with a Sunday-sermon kind of faith. They are hungry for more.

Lauren and Eric saw one of The Abbey's ads on Facebook, and they were curious. The church typically reposts an image of a church stained-glass window (our logo) with the questions, "LGBTQ+ and love God? Got faith, but also lots of questions? Rethinking everything? Come join us!" They had two teenaged children who were pushing them to greater inclusivity, to a more generous view of humanity, and their former church was anything but that. The previous U.S. presidential elections had brought out an ugly side of Christian nationalism in their church leadership, and Lauren and Eric could no longer tolerate being there. They were looking for a new church home where they could ask questions, explore faith outside the box of their former church doctrine, and find an inclusive place that more reflected a God of love.

These stories, and others, have similar themes: people who sensed inconsistency and discordance with the faith they inherited from their parents. Whether it was because they were directly excluded for being LGBTQ or simply because the teachings they grew up with no longer fit the God they know, they have rejected some or all of traditional evangelical Christianity and are looking for something "better," something that fits in the modern world, with a progressive, inclusive, socially generous sensibility. Some are embracing spirituality, some questioning its place in their lives, but everyone is rethinking theology and redefining community.

They are all deconstructing and reconstructing their faith.

The problem is that each has gone, or is going, through the deconstruction process alone. And that process can be spiritually and emotionally devastating. As Matthew expressed to me, there was no place and no one to talk with about these feelings and frustrations. The Church has avoided, and often suppressed, active engagement with the doubts, struggles, and evolving sensibilities of its people. He also mentioned having no time or opportunity (being too busy) to explore alternative theologies on his own, and no idea of resources—where to look for answers. In short, no place, no time, no resources, and no guide or mentor to help navigate the process. And the result is one of the leading factors in the dramatic loss of faith in post-Boomer generations, and the rapid decline in American church membership in the past 50 years.

It was Matthew's complaint that gave voice to the problem and sparked the idea for this ministry experiment. The other witnesses confirmed the urgency in rapid-fire successive conversations. Could we, as a small, independent church, provide a solution? Could a church-sponsored series of encounters, essentially an ongoing support group, meet the needs of this generation of spiritual seekers?

Exploring the Problem: The Bigger Picture

What each of these people expressed was some type of dissatisfaction and disagreement with the evangelical form of Christian faith they possessed. And it was a soul-crushing experience.

During preliminary conversations and subsequent group discussions, several common themes emerged as the primary culprits in these people's dissonance. Some problems were theologically based, and others were due to behaviors inside the Church that they found disturbing and un-Christlike.

Issues that fell in the "church behavior" category generally can be described as "repressive or misogynistic," "exclusive," "dogmatic/certain," and "politically unloving." None of these were particularly surprising—each of us had witnessed them in our various church backgrounds—and most have been previously noted extensively in existing books about contemporary church life.[2] These, we could explore and discuss, but there was no solution to "fix" other churches; we could only examine our own.

Issues that were caused by troublesome or problematic doctrine—such as images of a wrathful God, Hell or eternal conscious torment, penal substitutionary atonement and blood sacrifice theories, Christian exclusivism, gender roles, sexism in the church, and purity culture, etc.—we could (and would) discuss among ourselves. Hopefully, we could arrive at more palatable theologies, perspectives we could accept and embrace personally. Theologies and practices based in love. But if not, at least we would be able to point to the specific doctrines, and in naming them, render them less potent in our lives.

The Act of Ministry

The experiment I proposed to the pastoral team at The Abbey was to implement a support and discussion group as a ministry of the church that would meet on a regular (weekly or monthly) basis to act as a "safe space" to engage people in the Deconstruction/Reconstruction (D/R) process. Since I was wrapping up my studies in the Doctor of Ministry program at Virginia Theological Seminary at the time, with the approval of the faculty and dean this would also serve as my doctoral thesis research project. And I hoped that tracking the process and the results of forming the group might ultimately be helpful to other church leaders facing similar situations.

The aim, then, was to provide a regular time and place where congregants' concerns and questions could be voiced without critique, where they would feel heard, and where productive dialogue could occur. I intended to address with those wrestling with deconstruction the particular theological and practical issues that cause the discordance, and then try to engage those points to help construct a healthier faith in which they could feel at home. In response to the initial problem voiced so poignantly by Matthew, this experiment would attempt to provide the place, the time, the resources, and the guide to help navigate the Deconstruction & Reconstruction process.

The goal of this act of ministry, however, was not simply theological reconciliation—not simply finding "better answers"—but engendering deeper personal relationship with God. In effect, to inspire a more active and personally satisfying spirituality. And in the process, I hoped it would create a more vibrant spiritual community within our church.

The support group would be actively facilitated by myself and other church leadership. We didn't envision this new activity to be a permanent ministry of the church: it was a targeted project. And we estimated the project duration would run approximately 6–9 months, or unless otherwise terminated. (At the completion of the initial project, the group had been meeting for about a year. It proved to be one of the central ministries—the heartbeat—of the church. Topics that arose in group discussions regularly became fodder for Sunday sermons, and it was not unusual to hear participants reflect on comments made months earlier—something that rarely occurred with those Sunday sermons!)

The "unless otherwise terminated" stipulation was a deliberate inclusion and highlights the ambivalence with which church staff viewed the project, myself included. We all felt it had great potential, both as a type of counselling and therapy for those who were going through the difficult passage from theological certainty into the uncharted territory of the Unknown God (as the Apostle Paul might have called it). It could be a great instrument in spiritual formation and maturity for the participants, our people. At the same time, though, we recognized the volatility of openly entertaining potentially "heretical" ideas concerning God, the work of

Christ, the Church, other religions, and fundamental doctrines of the faith. There was a legitimate fear of offending some people's religious sensitivities, and that we might lose congregants in the process—something our church, only months old, could ill-afford. But the perceived need overrode our fears. The need was clear. So was the challenge: Would we respond or back away from it?

To meet the requirements of my doctoral program, the project couldn't just be a haphazard, impromptu type of bible study. It would need to be well-defined, and would have to align with the goal and practices of practical theology:

- it would be a communal activity (faith relating to others);
- it would be a spiritually formative activity (faith shaping identity);
- it would be a critical activity (faith seeking understanding);
- and lastly, it would lead to public activity (faith expressing itself in the marketplace and in real life).[3]

The Context of Ministry and the Minister

No church ministry or group spiritual activity exists in a vacuum. It would be shaped by the people, of course, but also by our particular context. And my own religious background (and baggage!) would certainly play a role in how it all worked out. So for the sake of clarity and specificity, it would be helpful here for me to paint the bigger picture.

• The Church

The Abbey Church in Norman, Oklahoma was a relatively new inter-denominational church, and at the time of initiating this project, was approximately six months old. The founding pastoral team consisted of myself and Neill Coffman, both formerly of Expressions Church in Oklahoma

City, the only non-denominational LGBTQ+ affirming church in the city at the time. Neill, a former Assemblies of God pastor, had been the founding pastor of Expressions in 2007, and had for years dreamt of starting a sister church in neighboring Norman. After struggling with chronic health issues, he stepped down as Senior Pastor at Expressions in 2020, and the dreaming and planning for The Abbey began shortly thereafter.

He and I spent countless hours at a local bistro discussing what the outlook and mission of this new church would be, along with new leadership and discipleship paradigms. The Abbey would be led by a pastoral team, initially Neill and myself as elder co-pastors, with plans to bring on two associate pastors to handle other aspects of ministry. Our callings were unique and complementary, he with a more pastoral gifting, and me with more of a teaching, spiritual formation focus. Neill was the type to hold your hand through personal crisis or visit you in the E.R. at 3:00 AM, while I was more inclined to sit with you for hours over coffee discussing the nature of the universe. We branded the church with the motto "A Safe Place to Grow Deeper." This would be our chief role in the community: a safe place for spiritual growth and exploration. Looking back, I see now more clearly how this project was a natural out-working of the church's primary mission, though at the time it was less obvious.

The church was situated in the historic, somewhat bohemian end of Main Street, not far from the University of Oklahoma, and we hoped it would attract students and the liberally-minded population associated with the university. We would be (and were) a blended congregation, bringing together elements of liturgical and contemporary (evangelical-friendly) worship styles. And even as small as the church was (around twenty at the time the project began), congregants come from at least ten different denominations, representing both high- and low-church traditions, ranging from Roman Catholic and Episcopal churches on the one end to Pentecostal and Southern Baptist backgrounds at the other.[4] The "official doctrines" posted on the church website were deliberately broad in order to be inclusive and accepting, while being "united in our confession of faith in Jesus Christ as Lord, our common love for God, humanity and creation, and our commitment to do good in the world." Our mission was to form a spiritual community that would worship and grow together, and serve the community and world around us.

Both elder co-pastors recognized the evolution of faith that had occurred in our own spiritual journeys and wanted to create a sacred community that encouraged growth, both in expanding theological perspectives and in deepening spiritual experience with God. With the plurality of doctrinal beliefs and practices within the church, we hoped the potentially explosive nature of the Discussion Group would be well-tolerated. But both Neill and I had experience in our former church with how dogmatic and defensive people from fundamentalist and evangelical backgrounds could be about what they believed, especially when it was questioned. Our small congregation was barely affording rent each month on the building we occupied. Loss of congregants due to offense could be devastating. We prayed we were discerning God's will correctly as He led us into this potential field of landmines.

- **Hermeneutical Autobiography: Where I'm coming from**

My role in the Discussion Group project would be integral to the experience, not just as co-participant (discussed further below) but as facilitator and researcher. It would be careless not to recognize that my own theological and religious background (and triggers) would be a major influence in the operation of the group. As professor of education, Lynn Butler-Kisber puts it, "in qualitative inquiry, no apologies are needed for identity, assumptions, and biases; just a rigorous account of them."[5]

In seminary, we were sometimes required to begin our biblical studies papers with a statement of "hermeneutical perspective." It was a way of keying the professor in to how we, as students, would be interpreting the biblical texts. A Southern Baptist, for example, might read a passage differently than, say, an Episcopalian or Roman Catholic. Mine typically read something like:

> The writer of this paper claims the classification of: Charismatic, Evangelical, Conservative. That is, I hold to the inspiration and infallibility of Scripture; given by the Spirit of God, and fully authoritative in all that it asserts as true. I also recognize a heightened awareness of the power of the Holy Spirit to illuminate the meaning of Scripture. It serves as a stable and God-given guide for all things that pertain to life and godliness; it is a standard for life and practice. Reason and Experience play the major roles in interpreting Scripture.

Ministers will recognize the distinctly evangelical and charismatic tone of that position, tempered by the "Wesleyan Quadrilateral" sources of doctrinal authority (Scripture, Tradition, Reason, and Experience), notably omitting "Tradition" which was highly suspect to our evangelical mentality.

At the time of launching the Discussion Group, I was decades out of seminary and had been on my own spiritual journey long before I'd ever heard the term "deconstruction." I came to this project as a self-identified post-evangelical, still leaning on those four sources of authority, but with a much greater emphasis on reason and (spiritual) experience.

I had been raised in a conservative evangelical church and family since the cradle. The bible was part and parcel to our daily life and faith. From my earliest memories, I recall sitting on my father's lap, attempting to recite memorized verses from the King James version of the bible. This was part of our spiritual formation: my brothers and I had a weekly list of verses to memorize. Scripture was to be "hidden in our hearts" from childhood, and prayer was an essential part of the day. I would routinely wake up for school to find my mother sitting on the living room couch with her coffee, her bible open on her lap, talking with her Lord. My father also began his day kneeling at his bed, bible open before him. And church attendance was a given; Sunday morning and evening, and sometimes on Wednesday nights. My father was a blue-collar worker at General Motors from the time he was 18 years old until he retired in his mid-fifties, and his ambition had always been to become a minister. Being an elder at our home church was the closest he came, so his dream was that at least one of his sons would be in ministry. (As it turned out, four of his five children would become ordained ministers.)

Steeped in Scripture as we were, with a conservative and largely literal interpretation of it, my family became part of the charismatic renewal movement that swept through the evangelical church world in the 1980s. It provided me that "transcendent experience" I and so many people craved, an accessible and available encounter with the divine. It presented a God who was present and active in our daily lives—a significant change from the attitude of a somewhat distant if all-knowing God I'd grown up with. As a result of my encounter with the Spirit, my post-college plans changed from pursuing a career in computer technology to enrolling in a charismatic conservative evangelical seminary, where I earned an M.Div. and an M.A. in Biblical Studies and Languages. My academic knowledge expanded, as did my experience of the Spirit, but after four years of seminary, my theology had changed little. I still viewed the world and Christian life largely through a conservative evangelical, if charismatic, lens. That charismatic component, however, would be a key to later opening my eyes to broader, hopefully inspired, readings of Scripture, and allow the breathing space to deconstruct much of what had been instilled in me.

It was my decade-plus experience as Associate Teaching Pastor at Expressions that propelled me on my journey of rethinking everything I believed. The process had begun years earlier as I wrestled trying to reconcile my conservative faith with my identity as a gay man.[6] Typical evangelical theology insists that homosexuals will not inherit the Kingdom of God, yet I knew the presence of God in my life for as far back as I could remember. The two were in conflict. And it would take an encounter with God to settle the issue once for all: there was no denying my connection with God, my place was secure. My theology was not.

Sometime in 2012, when speaking with a non-Christian friend who practiced meditation, I had an eye-opening, theology-expanding, "ah-hah" moment. He had been describing his morning encounter with Ultimate Reality, and I was curious. As a charismatic, I could appreciate a divine encounter, but I felt I was mostly humoring him. My theology at that time still had not expanded enough to concede that his experience was "legitimate." I interrupted him as he related chanting his Om mantra. I asked what it meant, and he explained that, to his understanding, it was approximating the primal vibration of creation, the sound through which all things came into being. By repeating the Om, he was bringing himself into alignment with that creative force. He said the sound was derived from the Sanskrit root word meaning "to be." And in that moment, I had an epiphany. "You're uttering the Name of God," I nearly shouted, suddenly making a connection with Moses's encounter with the burning bush, with the revelation of God's name as YHWH, "I Am." And I *knew* in a moment of absolute clarity that my friend, and people for millennia, had been connecting with God—that God had been leaving bread crumb trails to Himself for all of humanity throughout history, for anyone who sought Him—even outside the chosen inner circle of Christians and Jews. That moment opened a door of pluralism and inter-spirituality that exploded my exclusivist theology with finality.

In the years that followed, I would have successive moments of insight and revelation that began systematically dismantling my well-constructed evangelical theologies. With new, broader perspectives on God and faith, I could no longer self-identify as evangelical. But I still held—and continue to hold—to the sacredness of Christian Scripture, even if I now read it differently. This is why I embrace the label "post-evangelical" over the equally common "exvangelical"—which to my mind reflects more my distancing from evangelical rigidity without making a complete break from it.* I recognize the continued imprint and influence of my evangelical roots even as I disregard much of the calcified conclusions and theologies of the evangelical church world.

I began the Christian Spirituality track of the Doctor of Ministry program at Virginia Theological Seminary in 2019,

* There is no precise difference between "post-evangelical" or "exvangelical," both being relatively new terms. However, in my experience, the latter is more often embraced by those who have had harsh or negative experiences within the evangelical church and retain a degree of hostility as a result, whereas "post-evangelicalism" is more often associated with a "less traumatic" separation caused by sincere self-examination and recognition of theological differences. Admittedly, this is a subjective distinction which may not be commonly shared.

a few years before launching this project, propelled by that hunger for deeper—bigger, broader—things of God, most recently fueled by reading Wayne Teasdale's *The Mystic Heart.*[7] Based on my personal fascination with mysticism and spirituality (an extension of my charismatic background), my original vision for the required D.Min. project had been to initiate some program or discipleship group focused on spiritual disciplines. I envisioned a group of post-evangelicals gathering weekly for meditation and prayer, perhaps even integrating some forms of yoga or Tai Chi to create a holistic body-spirit practice. I could see in my mind's eye the flickering of candles, the smell of incense, and perhaps even the singing of brass bowls as we practiced a communal form of spirituality. The sudden and immediate shift of focus to something as prosaic as creating a space to rethink Christian doctrine, triggered by the faith crises of my congregation, took me by complete surprise. But as someone several years into my own D/R journey, this felt right. I knew it would draw on the foundation of my deeply-rooted faith, my training in evangelical theology, my fascination with mysticism and spirituality, and my curiosity with other faiths and world religions. This project would be the confluence of many life-long interests, and the culmination of my ministry. And at the time of this writing, it continues to be one of the most rewarding things I've ever done.

Argument and Desired Outcomes

Based on the preliminary conversations I'd had, I theorized that even in a conservative state like Oklahoma, these Millennial and Gen Z people would not embrace any Christianity that is not in-tune with a more progressive, inclusive, socially relevant, and pluralistic-colored faith. The Church must evolve its theology and its practices to catch up with the dynamic spiritual life of its newest adult generations, or it will lose these generations perhaps permanently.

Although the Discussion Group would come to include participants with ages ranging from 19 to 65, I did not originally expect age to be a significant factor in how deconstruction was experienced. I expected sexual orientation and denominational background to be the primary predictors of crisis-level. Matthew, after all, came from a Pentecostal/Holiness background and was gay. And evangelicalism, as I'll explore in Chapter 2, provided sufficient negative stimulus to trigger a crisis of faith. However, early on I began to notice that age, conveniently typified by generational cohort, would be just as important. Gen Zs, for example, experience deconstruction entirely differently than Gen Xers or Boomers. (For this reason, whenever I refer to a particular individual or comment in this study, I will also note the person's age-group and its related characteristics.)

While the age brackets for each generational cohort are somewhat flexible, the Pew Research Center identifies the generally accepted birth-year ranges for each generation as follows:

- **Boomers** - those born between 1946–1964
- **Gen X** - those born 1965–1980
- **Millennials** - those born 1981–1996
- **Gen Z / Zoomers** - those born from 1997–2012
- **Gen Alpha** - those born from 2012–2025

Gen Alphas would be the first cohort born entirely in the 21st century, followed by Gen Beta (2025–2039), but none in these last two age groups were involved in our Discussion Group.[8] Fortunately, we had participants representing the four preceding age groups, which provided for a wide range of perspectives and made for some lively conversations.

Since faith deconstruction (and hopefully, subsequent reconstruction) is a process that occurs over an extended period of time, typically many years, we didn't expect absolute resolution to all the participants' questions. But this project would create a safe space for that process to occur, with the desired outcome of empowering people to be comfortable with questions and lack of definitive answers to the point that their spiritual sense of security with God is not threatened. Since the timeframe involved in the D/R journey is indefinite, the experiment would be more focused on *introducing* and *acclimating* participants, normalizing the ongoing questioning process.

A signal of success would be the cultivation of a life-habit that involves continued expansion and exploration, continued seeking and dissatisfaction with rigid, predetermined theology, and a continually expanding vision of God. The standard against which I would measure the success of this experiment can be neatly summarized by "Three C's." Will the participants *continue* with the process as a life-long journey of spiritual and theological exploration? Are they more *comfortable* with questions and uncertainty as a sign of spiritual health? Do they experience an enhanced sense of spiritual *connection* with God and the world? Ultimately, this last question was of greatest pastoral concern to me.

From an academic point of view, I sought to learn if a church-sponsored series of encounters, an ongoing support group, could satisfy the higher standards of younger generations to the degree that they would continue to identify as Christian, and what the church would look like if this succeeds. From a ministry point of view, I was genuinely interested in helping our people process their faith questions in a healthy way. The success or failure of this project would ultimately lead to the shaping of The Abbey Church in Norman, Oklahoma. Would it stimulate healthy growth or would it cause disruption and possible closure of this young church? In either event, I expected the outcome of this project to leave its imprint on the ethos of the church and on myself.

The intent of this intervention was to help guide those in the D/R process, but also for the church to be shaped by the spiritual identity of this generation of Christians; to create a spiritual community that assists in their spiritual formation and in turn be reshaped by them.

A Self-Implicating Methodology

The church staff had agreed to this project. We were going to do it. But to satisfy the requirements of my doctoral program, I had to approach it from an academic viewpoint. I needed to observe, record and participate according to some set of accepted research standards. There are many different research methodologies to pick from, but a few were obvious from the start.

For my thesis, I had to spell out the methodologies I would choose, so this section may get a little technical. Readers should feel free to skip this part and jump to the "Look Ahead" section at the end of the chapter if this topic isn't of interest to you.

• Action Research

As stated earlier, this project, almost by definition, engages in action research. It studies and addresses practical, real-world problems with the intent to not only add to a body of academic knowledge but also to enact change within the ministry context and in the lives of its participants.[9] The real-world problem, as mentioned earlier, was the state of spiritual disorientation caused by the conflict and discordance of lived experience against taught doctrines and lived religious encounters. This project developed in response to, and as a remedy for, that problem. Inherent in action research is also an underlying position that the researcher will be a participant to some degree in the project or experiment. I would be there with them, and we would be walking through the process together.

Jesuit scholar and action research instructor, David Coghlan, highlights four central characteristics of action research that will become readily apparent in the chapters to follow. First, there is a focus on practical issues, aiming to produce knowledge-in-action. Second, it is a participatory mode of doing research *with* people rather than *on* people. Third, it is carried out with an awareness that truth emerges over time, and that the process may be as important as the outcomes. Lastly, it holds central a concern that new knowledge should lead people into a dynamic of emancipation.[10]

These characteristics would emerge as key components of our experience: we discovered that the experience itself—both of specific issues that arose on the D/R journey and the Discussion Group to help process that experience—was vital to the desired outcome of deeper spiritual connection with God. This would become evident in some of the participants more than in others, but as a pastor seeking growth in his congregants, it proved to be rewarding.

The adaptive nature of the research was evident not simply in the discussions and choice of topics, but also in the structure of the group. Almost immediately from the decision to host the group, the participants played an active role in setting (and changing) the meeting times and location to suit their schedules and financial situations as we progressed. As will be explored in Chapter 4, "The Act of Ministry," the pastor/researcher sometimes wondered who was in charge, or if, in fact, anyone needed to be.

Action research, Coghlan further explains, also brings to this ministry experiment a conscious awareness of three different "audiences." Integral to this type of research is "First Person" inquiry-practice, the "I/me" focus. It keeps an eye always directed at what is happening to the individual researcher: "how am I being changed or influenced during this interaction and in this process?" This is often central to the researcher's motivation in pursuing the project; the research is birthed out of an inner drive, an important question, leading the researcher to this particular project. Phenomenological research and pedagogy specialist, Max van Manen, describes this as the "abiding concern" which seriously and persistently holds the researcher's interest.[11] In this case, the activity of the discussion/support group would be of direct, personal interest to me as a fellow deconstructor and participant.

"Second Person" inquiry-practice of action research centers on the quality of relationships being formed between the researcher and the participants. It is the "I-You" dynamic working throughout the project. Most, if not all, of the participants in the group would be members of The Abbey Church and I would be their pastor. What we said and how we interacted would not simply be one of impersonal engagement, scientist with test subjects, or even lecturer with students. It would directly impact how they viewed me as their congregational and spiritual leader, and influence my ability to serve them. An on-going, healthy and mutually respectful relationship was vital to my role as pastor—during and after this experiment.

Lastly, the "Third Person" audience, less relevant to the actual implementation of the project but of concern in my thesis and in this book, is about the dissemination of this research to the wider, non-involved community; the "them" that is always lingering in the researcher's mind.[12] This is where this book comes in: hopefully to encourage and inform other church leaders in similar efforts to engage seekers in small group communities. How do I communicate the *experience* of both deconstruction and participation in the group? What is the best means of presenting the living data?

Early on, I decided I wanted to approach the problem and the act of ministry from an experiential *and* a theological vantage point. It was also important to me to be a full participant in the group process and to be a fellow beneficiary of the experience.

To address the experiential components, I would apply aspects of phenomenological methodology.[13] Van Manen offered a helpful perspective here, voicing a caution about becoming a slave to objective method or technique. The tools are secondary to the work. They aid the researcher in his task; they do not dictate it. The method, or methods, chosen should serve the study, and "should maintain a certain harmony with the deep interest" of the researcher.[14]

That clarified my approach for me: the act of ministry would be implemented as an action research project, and interpreted through heuristic phenomenology.

• Heuristic Phenomenology

Phenomenological research is particularly suited for extracting common meaning from the lived experiences of several individuals of a particular experience. Professor of Practical Theology, John Swinton explains that "the aim of phenomenology is to determine what an experience means to a person quite apart from any theoretical overlay that might be put on it."[15] It is the study of an experience itself, and seeks to answer the foundational question, "What is this kind of experience like?" Van Manen qualifies it further: "It differs from almost every other science in that it attempts to gain insightful descriptions of the way we experience the world pre-reflectively, without taxonomizing, classifying, or abstracting it."[16]

There is a focus on a particular phenomenon to be explored, and the study usually involves a small group of participants (as few as 3 or 4 to as many as 10–15) who share in the lived experience. Data collection usually involves interviewing the individuals involved, and identifying significant phrases and sentences representative of the common experience. The data analysis then moves from the specific descriptions to more generalized statements of "what the experience was/is" and "how they experienced it." From that, an exhaustive description of the "essence" of the shared phenomenon is extracted. Finally, the conclusions are shared with the participants to validate the findings.[17]

While hermeneutical phenomenology focuses on "interpreting the 'texts' of life," allowing the researcher to make an interpretation of the meaning of the mutual experience or phenomenon shared by a group, heuristic phenomenological inquiry highlights the personal experience and insights of *the researcher*. With this latter approach, the foundational questions are, "What is *my* experience of this phenomenon and the essential experience of others who *also* experience this phenomenon intensely?"[18] or "How does it affect *me* and how do *I* see it?"[19] As van Manen writes,

> Phenomenology projects and their methods often have transformative effect on the researcher himself or herself. Indeed, phenomenological research is often itself a form of deep learning, leading to a transformation of consciousness, heightened perceptiveness, increased thoughtfulness.[20]

The appeal of this approach is that it directly brings myself into the study as participant-researcher and fellow-deconstructor. I wanted to be impacted, be transformed by our interactions as much as I wanted to help guide the others as they walk through their questions and crises.

Clark Moustakas, one of the leading proponents of heuristic research, takes this one step further. Not only is the researcher a participant and beneficiary, but he or she *must* have experienced the phenomenon personally in order to effectively contribute to the study and "own" the experience.

> In heuristic research the investigator must have had a direct, person encounter with the phenomenon being investigated. There must have been actual autobiographical connections. Unlike phenomenological studies in which the researcher need not have had the experience (e.g., giving birth through artificial insemination), the heuristic researcher has undergone the experience in a vital, intense, and full way...[21]

This personal-experience vantage point was immediately attractive to me. First, as already mentioned, the researcher not only becomes personally involved in the process, but has *already* been part of that process or phenomenon. This allows him or her to give up concerns over neutrality, and fully embrace the subjectivity of the experience. It also enables the researcher to look simultaneously at both the phenomenon and at him- or herself. In this way, "the researcher is invited to be an instrument through self-reflection and self-discovery," and the entire endeavor then is not merely an academic pursuit, but "a search for personal integration and realization."[22] Moustakas describes it as, "The self of the researcher is present throughout the process and, while understanding the phenomenon with increasing depth, the researcher also experiences growing self-awareness and self-knowledge."[23] This personal experience and understand ing would, at least theoretically, enable me to facilitate discussion as one who has already "been there, done that—let me help."

In my research, I also intended to explore some of the key evangelical theologies that proved so troublesome to many of us, myself included.

Thus, adapting phenomenological methodologies allows for describing the subjective realities experienced by the other participants combined with my own perception of the D/R phenomenon. It facilitates exploring central themes and makes space for discussion and dialogue as part of the restorative process. Ultimately, this will allow me to accomplish the goal of this project: to describe the common experience of faith/theological deconstruction and reconstruction among fundamentalist and evangelical Christians, and to provide a practical ministry outreach in response.

- **Self-Implication**

Those who choose to dip deeper into the well of spirituality, including those researching and writing about shared experiences and theological worldviews, usually do so out of great personal interest with implications for our own lives. This was certainly true in my case. Professor of New Testament Studies and Spirituality, Sandra Schneiders, echoes our thoughts earlier on deep personal involvement. Self-implication implies that "we are not really neutral or detached about what our research generates. Vital personal interest in the answers to one's questions can lead to skewing [or directing] one's research, consciously or unconsciously ... Conversely, it can also lead to a passionate honesty in the search for the truth no matter where that might lead."[24] It is the search for truth that resonates on a deeply personal level that sits at the heart of this project, making it an act of ministry as much to myself as to the other participants.

Again, this self-implicative nature of the research is part of what drew me to the heuristic approach. As Moustakas puts it, "the heuristic researcher is not only intimately and autobiographically related to the question, but learns to love the question. It becomes a kind of song into which the researcher breathes life, not only because the question leads to an answer, but also because the question itself is infused in the researcher's being. It creates a thirst to discover, to clarify, and to understand crucial dimensions of knowledge and experience."[25] This quest to explore together beyond the rigid and well-defined limitations of our evangelical faith would become the predominant focus of the next twelve months of my life.

Schneiders also reminds us of the personal risk inherent in touching the live wire of Spirit. "Self-implication also implies that research in the field of spirituality can be dangerous to the researcher. ... [W]hat if one's study leads to a conversion that leaves no aspect of one's life untouched?"[26] This seems the very definition of faith deconstruction. A significant reason I embraced this project was because I relished the idea of exploring a more generous (progressive?) theology and spirituality *with others*, not simply in my own personal reading and devotion. We could make this journey together. The cry I heard in the complaints and comments of Matthew and the others triggered my pastoral instinct and forced the idea out of the realm of wishful thinking into a practical ministry. But without having begun to travel my own D/R journey, and desiring the companionship of other fellow travelers, I might not have been as sensitive to respond in this fashion. I could have, perhaps, addressed the problem in a more impersonal, less interactive format, like a Wednesday topical bible study.

As a fellow deconstructor as well as researcher, I would help create the dynamic of the Discussion Group as much as that dynamic would inform my research and shape me. Because of this symbiotic interrelationship, the process of discovery and evolution would have direct implications for myself as well as those in the group, and ultimately our entire church.

• Bracketing

Some form of "bracketing" is typically employed in qualitative research whereby the researcher attempts to isolate—or, at least name—his/her own experience and perspective from the phenomenon being studied. Creswell and Poth put it this way: "investigators [attempt to] set aside their experiences, as much as possible, to take a fresh perspective toward the phenomenon under examination."[27] It is a nod of acknowledgment to an Enlightenment, positivist emphasis on objectivity, and reflects a legitimate desire to observe an object or phenomenon in its native state without contaminating it, or allowing personal experience or assumptions to influence one's research conclusions.

It is debatable to what degree this is realistically possible. Post-modern and post-positivistic perspectives recognize that current social contexts and places of privilege, as well as prior experience, shape one's consciousness and perceptions. Bracketing, then, would attempt to name that position and recognize the possible effects of the research writer's perspective and potential inherent bias. Richard Osmer suggests upfront acknowledgement of one's stance.

> Rather than pretending to bracket out all preunderstandings in the futile attempt to hold a neutral, objective point of view, scholars do better to acknowledge their interpretive starting point, the particular research tradition that guides their work. It was only the Enlightenment's "prejudice against

> prejudice" that led modern science and scholarship to deny the positive role of preunderstanding.[28]

Especially as it relates to the study of faith and spirituality, objectivity is not necessarily an asset. The depth of one's personal experience adds to the richness of the research, as long as it is identified as such.

In this project, I embraced the role of participant-researcher, and, as mentioned earlier in "Context of Ministry and Minister" section, I recognize that I bring a distinct viewpoint (and set of hermeneutical presuppositions) as a post-evangelical Christian pastor to the group discussion and the research. The research was as much about my own journey of discovery as much as it was about examining the experience of others. I was, and still am, undergoing deconstruction myself, and it would be difficult if not impossible to remove my experience from studying the experiences of those in the group. The heuristic approach, I contend, moves against a strict bracketing impulse. Again, quoting Moustakas, "The power of heuristics is in its recognition of the significance of self-searching and the value of personal knowledge as essential requirements for the understanding of common human experiences."[29] Rather than attempting to isolate my own experience and tacit knowledge, I bring them into the shared encounter—as one might expect of a pastor-teacher, beyond being solely a researcher.

My experience, then, engages the experience of others, and is influenced by them. It is a give-and-take, a mutual influence, that shapes us as a spiritual community. It is, in effect, a communal activity. No effort was made to isolate my background, preunderstandings, or experiences from group discussion; rather, they were often intentionally introduced to trigger, contribute, and at times guide the conversations.

As facilitator of the group (not just a participant), however, I did employ some self-limitation on my involvement; what I would call "pastoral engagement bracketing." That is, while I contributed personal thoughts and insights to the conversations, I endeavored to employ more "active listening" to encourage the engagement of the others without restricting or "stepping on" the interaction and contributions of the others. They'd already been filtered and critiqued enough. That's why this shared safe space was so important.

A Look Ahead

In the next two chapters, I will lay the groundwork for defining and implementing the act of ministry, the Evolving Faiths Discussion Group. The current phenomenon of deconstructing Christians as a social trend makes sense—and is justifiable—when understood in light of recent U.S. history and when Scripture is read with a particular mindset.

So, in Chapter 2, "Deconstruction in American Christianity," I will explore the social context that makes faith deconstruction such a popular issue in contemporary U.S. Christianity. I'll explore how the evangelical world's focus shifted from its original mission of evangelism to securing social and political clout to achieve its conservative agenda. The process exposed the ugly underbelly of the evangelical world that had until then been largely overlooked in 20th century United States. This shift also had the unintended consequence of driving people *away* from the Church, seeing it more as an aggressive and hostile force rather than a nurturing one. People, however, did not cease being spiritual; they did not lose their hunger for God (however they understood God) or the spiritual life. Instead, they turned away from the Church, specifically away from the evangelical world, and embraced alternative forms of spirituality. It sparked the explosive rise of the "spiritual but not religious."

Looking specifically at some of the spiritual proclivities of Millennials and Gen Z—those most likely to be religiously unaffiliated—will shed light on the worldview and religious practices expressed by some of the younger participants in the Discussion Group which might otherwise have seemed unusual or characteristically "unevangelical."

Since the word "deconstruction" has recently become as ubiquitous as the label "spiritual but not religious," in the last section of Chapter 2, I will attempt to declutter the messiness of defining what "deconstruction" means as a real-life practice.

In Chapter 3, "A Biblical Theology of Deconstruction," I will then present a biblical defense of faith deconstruction core practices: wrestling with God, challenging the faith, and reinterpreting Holy Scripture to include a broader, more loving meaning. This was important groundwork to facilitate the free-flowing conversations that would occur throughout the year.

In Chapter 4, "The Act of Ministry," I will describe the evolution of what would become the Evolving Faiths Discussion Group, the act of ministry at the heart of this project, including some problems that were worked out along the way. I'll also offer a few take-away lessons learned in the process that may be helpful for future group leaders to have in mind. The project became a virtual case study in action research, as the logistics, discussion format, and even leadership style of the group changed and adapted over time in response to the needs and preferences of the participants. As just mentioned, I chose to place this description of the act of ministry *after* the chapters exploring the social context and a biblical defense of deconstruction because so much of what occurred and what was spoken about by the participants makes better sense in light of that cultural environment and with a theological framework already in place.

Chapter 5, "Deconstructing Theologies & the Group Experience," will examine the reactions and statements of participants in this project, grouping them into themes—a handful of theological topics we processed as a group, and then describing the experience—with some interpretive comments as a glue holding participants' comments together. In the last section of this chapter, I will define a summary, composite description of what it is like to deconstruct one's faith, to wrestle with core elements of evangelical theology, and how working through the process together as a group helped or hindered that process.

In "Closing Thoughts," chapter 6, I will offer some final observations about my experience as a participant and as a pastor in the group, and suggest a few implications for the church at large, particularly the importance of creating a supportive community.

Lastly, in "Post Script," I add a few comments five years after the fact—the group is still going!

To conclude this introduction, I return again to the words of spirituality-researcher, Sandra Schneiders. "Studying the human experience of God is not viewing through a telescope a bush burning in a distant desert. It is taking a chance on hearing our name called at close range."[30] This is both my prayer and my earnest desire—for myself, this group, and for my church.

2

Deconstruction in American Christianity

"The fields are not filled with faithless people in need of the gospel. They are filled with people of deep spiritual integrity who simply cannot suffer the shallow message of the churches of their birth any longer."

~ David M. Felten & Jeff Procter-Murphy[1]

The Big Picture

We live in exciting times for the Christian faith. For all the hype and crosstalk about deconstruction, the anger and resentment over the unholy marriage of the conservative evangelical church world with far-right politics, the spotlight on internal corruption and scandals within big-named churches, and the disillusionment with hypocritical and hateful American-brand Christianity, I cannot help but be excited about the prospects of a faith returned to its core spiritual values, about people connecting with God on simpler, purer, and more mystical grounds—even at the expense of leaving their traditional form of religion. As popular Christian author, Kurtis Vanderpool, so aptly put it, "I believe deconstruction is the revival evangelicals have been praying for for centuries. Deconstruction is God's way of returning our hearts to the main point: Love. ... It will bring us back to a place of simple faith. ... Deconstruction will bring us back to the heart of God."[2] I am absolutely convinced Vanderpool is correct.

Every social or spiritual movement is birthed out of a particular historical context and set of catalytic circumstances. I contend that the whole deconstruction trend in the past two decades is the step-child of the decadence of the evangelical church world. To be sure, increased secularization in society and the ready availability of information and virtual global community found on the internet provided fertile ground for rethinking the bases of one's faith. But the catastrophic shifts occurring within the evangelical church world, including the Religious Right's dalliance with the politics of power and its moral hypocrisy, fed into a greater spiritual dissatisfaction marked by the rise of generations more comfortable identifying as "spiritual but not religious" than as "Christian." These two factors—the "fall" of American evangelicalism and the "rise" of the "spiritual/not religious"—intersect to create conditions ripe for a new movement of personal spiritual exploration and growth.

In this chapter, I will first explore those two dominant social factors, and then take a closer look at the outcome inside the Church, namely the Deconstruction/Reconstruction process virtually imposed on those who wish to maintain or reclaim their faiths. Then, because the topic is often linked in academic circles with the ideas of Jacques Derrida, who popularized the term, and Paul Ricoeur, who proposed a simple model of spiritual maturation, I will briefly examine how the experience rightly or wrongly corresponds with what they hand in mind. This is followed by a survey of various models of the D/R journey proposed by some recent sociologists and psychologists. Lastly, I will situate the wave of deconstruction happening in U.S. Christianity back into the social context out of which it was birthed.

The Fall of American Evangelicalism

There can be little doubt that Christianity in America has been experiencing a time of crisis and upheaval. It is surprising to virtually no one in American churches that the pews are becoming visibly more and more empty, those occupying those seats are becoming more and more gray, and that the younger generations are more and more cynical about institutional Christianity. Though the COVID-19 pandemic accelerated and intensified this church exodus, it is not a new phenomenon. For decades—for at least as long as I can remember, dating back into the 1970s, overhearing the "gray hairs" in my home church—church leadership has wrung their hands and lamented over the increasing secularization of our culture and the decline in church attendance.

In the past, this was largely blamed almost exclusively on liberal or anti-religious trends in higher education. Whether knowingly or not, many in church leadership adopted the secularization theories of 20th century sociologist Max Weber and even Karl Marx that as society became more educated, people would abandon religious ideas about life and the nature of the world. Weber described the process as the "disenchantment of the world" (*Entzauberung*, which might literally be translated, "de-magic-ation")—that people would view the world through the cold eye of science and rationality instead of through the warmer gaze of wonder, superstition, or as the activity of magical or spiritual forces.[3] Marx saw religion as an artificial structure created to control the masses by those holding power, and as a means for those oppressed to cope with the harsh conditions of their realities, "the opiate of the masses." When the proletariat became fully aware of this manipulative aspect of the class struggle, they would throw off their oppressors, and religion would lose its hold.[4]

Neither of those views has quite taken hold in American popular thinking, despite ecclesiastical fears and Marxist expectations. Notwithstanding a dramatic rise in atheism and agnosticism in recent years, most Americans remain convinced of the existence of God. Even with the explosion of scientific knowledge in the 20th and 21st centuries, and widespread access to that knowledge on the internet, 9 out of 10 Americans still believe in God or some other higher power.[5] Science and education have not killed the faith.[6]

More recently, the main reasons for a skeptical view of the faith and the Church, particularly the evangelical brand, appear to be doubts and questioning about religious teaching (which may be just another expression of the education argument), opposition to the positions taken by churches on social and political issues, dislike and distrust of religious institutions and leaders,[7] and, to no small degree, the perceived lack of authenticity, the moral rigidity, and lack of any real spiritual depth among church people and leadership.

This last aspect, lack of spiritual depth, is also not a new phenomenon, though it is especially relevant to Millennials and Gen Z/Zoomers these days. Thomas Keating, father of the Centering Prayer movement in Catholic and Protestant faith circles, reported this decades ago as a perennial issue. "There is a growing expectation that teachers of the Gospel [should] speak out of a personal experience of contemplative prayer. ... Until spiritual leadership becomes a reality in Christian circles, many will continue to look to other religious traditions for the spiritual experiences they are not finding in their local churches."[8]

These issues, particularly the ones touching social/political values and spiritual experience, cannot be overemphasized in their role in driving people, especially the younger generations, further away from the Church.

- **Politics and Power**

In pre-modern societies, virtually all governmental structures were intertwined with, and to some degree based upon, religious belief. In every aspect of society, not just political, the presence and activity of God or Ultimate Reality however perceived, was assumed, and, in fact, most seats of power (kings, rulers, emperors) were built on the foundation of some kind of divine claim. Social and political stability was derived from a sense of order rooted in the Divine. Thus, in pre-Enlightenment society, the idea of a "separation of church and state" was virtually inconceivable.[9]

However, this has not played well for the Christian Church. History, going back at least to the time of Constantine, testifies that whenever the Church has been bedfellow to politics of state, the relationship has been disastrous. The outcome is almost always uniform, resulting in both internal corruption within the Church and external resistance and rejection of the faith as hypocritical and oppressive by those outside it. Those whose beliefs or practices were found to be outside the favored theological position in power, often found themselves persecuted or excommunicated, deprived of spiritual and physical solace—in direct antithesis to the teachings of Christ.*

---

* As a matter of pastoral concern, whenever I find myself in a discussion about the role of the Church in politics, discussion of what Jesus did or did not do inevitably enters the conversation. Argument can be made on both sides. Jesus seems to have avoided political entanglements, outside of his "give to Caesar what belongs to Caesar" remark, yet he clearly addressed the religious leaders of his day on all manner of social issues—

In American history, the Church has been interwoven in local and national politics from the beginning. The Pilgrims landing at Plymouth Rock in 1620 were a group of Puritans who wanted to "purify" the faith from Roman Catholic influences and create a "Christian commonwealth" in the new world. Most of the original colonies early on established an official church, following the European paradigm familiar to them, and typically imposed church membership as a requirement for civil service and privileges, including voting. Most, with the exception of Rhode Island which was founded on the basis of religious tolerance, were inhospitable and even hostile to other sects, and nonconformists and dissenters were often punished or exiled. The Puritans of New England were particularly noted for their rigidity and harshness to those who did not comply. Over the early years of the country, attitudes vacillated between varying degrees of religious tolerance and hostility, but it is noteworthy that even Thomas Jefferson's Deism was weaponized against him by Federalists during his presidential campaign in 1800, claiming his belief was incompatible with a "Christian nation" and rendered him unsuitable as a national leader.[10]

While the influence of the Church in politics has ebbed and flowed over the decades, sociologists generally trace the rise of evangelical sway in more recent American history to its conservative commitment to racial segregation. After the humiliating defeat of conservative religionists after the Scopes Monkey Trial in 1925 and the repeal of Prohibition in

---

leaders who exercised extensive social power over people's lives. Ultimately, my argument goes not to whether Christians should vote their religious convictions or not, but to whether those convictions (and resulting laws) would be oppressive to the marginalized. If the imposition of a religious conviction as law contradicts the Law of Love, of doing no harm to one's neighbor, or imposes a control over others which one would not want imposed on oneself, then that exercise is ungodly and unchristian.

1933, fundamentalist influence receded from the public eye. Embarrassed by the "cultural separationist" and belligerent image that fundamentalism had acquired, in the 1940s some fundamentalist leaders rebranded themselves as "evangelicals." They were committed to orthodox Protestant theology and social outreach in the way of world missions and individual conversion ("soul-winning"), but, importantly, "they were not trying to foist their religion upon the nation by law."[11]

However, as Dartmouth College professor of religion Randall Balmer points out, that attitude quickly changed when the government interfered with the tax-exempt status of private Christian schools and universities that practiced racial segregation during the 1960s and '70s. Leading conservative religious figures began stepping up efforts to regain popular influence and restrain governmental encroachment on their "religious freedoms."[12] Recognizing, however, that the general public in the mid-1970s was no longer on their side of the segregation issue, Jerry Falwell, Sr, televangelist of nationally syndicated *The Old-Time Gospel Hour* and founder of Lynchburg Christian Academy, a "private school for white students," adopted abortion as the catalytic cause to marshal followers.[13]

Roe v. Wade, the landmark Supreme Court case which made abortion legal in all states in the U.S., had been settled in 1973 without much outcry from Falwell or conservatives. In fact, the Southern Baptist Convention in 1971 passed a resolution *recommending* "Southern Baptists to work for legislation that will allow the possibility of abortion under such conditions as rape, incest, clear evidence of severe fetal deformity, and carefully ascertained evidence of the likelihood of damage to the emotional, mental, and physical health of the mother." The conservative-leaning convention reaffirmed that position a year *after Roe*, in 1974, and again in 1976. Abortion was seen primarily as a Catholic issue.[14]

But Falwell and other conservatives recognized it could serve as the foundation for the "pro-family" platform, inflammatory enough to unite disparate fundamentalist and evangelical congregations in the cause.[15] Adding feminism (equal rights) and homosexuality (gay liberation) to their agenda completed the pro-family trifecta—conveniently intersecting to defend a "biblical view" of heterosexual male dominance in family and society. As historian Kristin Kobes Du Mez puts it, "the reassertion of white patriarchy was central to the new 'family values' politics, and by the end of the 1970s, the defense of patriarchal power had emerged as an evangelical distinctive."[16] Attacking those three civil rights issues (abortion, women, and homosexuals) allowed the Religious Right to appear the defenders of conservative—distinctly "white" and "patriarchal"—values, without having to explicitly mention racial segregation.

Together, these issues (race, women, gays) intersected at the focal point of conservative concern: disruption of the social order. Intermingling of the races and gender-role confusion threatened the stability of social order, with "family" as its core. Such order, conservative Christians believed and defended biblically, was ordained and implemented by God. Resisting "civil rights," then, assumed the fervor of a religious crusade.[17]

It was a strategy that proved successful, raising the threat level to "traditional family values" high enough to turn out conservative Christian voters in the 1980 election of Ronald Reagan, defeating fellow evangelical but left-leaning Jimmy Carter's bid for a second term.

That political power was later turned against liberal Democrat president Bill Clinton. In 1994, Falwell financed and promoted a smear "documentary" entitled *The Clinton Chronicles: An Investigation into the Alleged Criminal Activities of Bill Clinton*, which accused Clinton of murder and other financial misdealings. Clinton nonetheless won re-election in 1996, but the political clout of conservative Christians had forced him to go against his own progressive leanings and implement two historic anti-homosexual policies that would set LGBT rights back for decades: the 1994 "Don't Ask, Don't Tell" Department of Defense directive, which prohibited homosexuals from serving in the armed forces; and signing the "Defense of Marriage Act" (DOMA) into federal law in 1996, which banned federal recognition of same-sex marriages and legally defined marriage as the union of one man and one woman. The Religious Right may have lost the White House, but on the gay front, they won the social-morality war.

The former image of evangelicals being concerned with saving souls and defending biblical inerrancy was irreversibly exchanged in the eyes of the public for that of a manipulative, politically power-hungry, ruthless, and self-serving religious entity.

Not coincidentally—which is the main point of this historical survey—the percentage of religiously unaffiliated ("Nones") in the American population had been relatively steady at 5-8% for decades, but in the early 1990s suddenly took a dramatic swing upward (see graph "Americans With No Religious Affiliation, 1972–2024" on page 53 below).

The evangelical regressive push on social issues continued into the new millennium. Even during the George W. Bush presidency, in the early 2000s, David Kinnaman, president of the evangelical polling Barna Group, observed the profoundly negative perception of American Christianity among younger generations. His polling found that the faith, particularly its evangelical brand, was seen as strongly anti-homosexual, judgmental, and hypocritical (each scoring above 85% of those surveyed), followed by impressions of being "old-fashioned, too involved in politics, out of touch with reality, insensitive to others, boring, not accepting of other faiths, and confusing. When they [younger generations] think of the Christian faith, these are the images that come to mind"[18]—hardly surprising considering the decades of effort by Falwell and company.*

This image did not shift even under the next presidency of Barack Obama when many Americans hoped for a more tolerant turn in society. In 2011, Kinnaman would label chapters in his next book describing further disconnection from the faith, including "Overprotective" (sheltered), "Shallow," "Anti-science," "Repressive," "Exclusive," and "Doubtless" (certain, intolerant of questioning).[19] These same themes appear in the books and blogs of then-Millennial evangelical spokesperson Rachel Held Evans. Often asked to speak at pastoral conferences and address why Millennials were leaving the church *en masse*, she would recite these examples, and then report in frustration that the pastors would fail to hear the message. "Invariably, after I've finished my presentation and opened the floor to questions, a pastor raises his hand and says, 'So what you're saying is we need hipper worship bands.'"[20] (It is little wonder that Kinnaman's subsequent book, *Faith for Exiles* (2019),[21] would focus on how to recapture that lost audience.)

Kinnaman's original point, however, is still glaringly relevant. The most common reaction to Christianity among outsiders, and here I would include the latest generations, is

---

* Jerry Falwell, Sr. was not the sole influence behind the Religious Right or the "Moral Majority," though he was definitely among the most well-known. Others also deserve specific mention by name, including Paul Weyrich of the Heritage Foundation (who actually coined the phrase "moral majority"), Pat Robertson of the Christian Broadcasting Network, James Dobson of Focus on the Family and the Family Research Council, Franklin Graham, son of the famous evangelist Billy Graham, and later, Ralph Reed of the Christian Coalition.

that "they think Christians no longer represent what Jesus had in mind, that Christianity in our society is not what it was meant to be. ... They admit they have a hard time actually seeing Jesus because of all the negative baggage that now surrounds him." As one of his survey participants eloquently remarked,

> Christianity has become bloated with blind followers who would rather repeat slogans than actually feel true compassion and care. Christianity has become marketed and streamlined into a juggernaut of fear-mongering that has lost its own heart.[22]

Those same thoughts were echoed in the voices of some of the participants in this project's Discussion Group. Jack complained about his former church's internal self-focus, unconcerned about the welfare of even its home-bound congregants. Eric stated outright that the right-leaning politics among his church's leadership was a primary factor in his family leaving that church, particularly their stances in favor of Donald Trump and against the Black Lives Matter movement which arose after a national spate of brutal fatalities of people of color at the hands of law enforcement. The hearts of some evangelical churches seemed to have turned cold—and it is obvious to many.

The general disgust among outsiders and non-conservative faithful over continued evangelical support of President Trump particularly, and his regressive policies and MAGA-type politics, only serves to highlight these on-going issues. During the Trump campaigns and presidencies, it seemed as if the conservative evangelical world doubled-down on its social and political plays for power, all too easily throwing into the trash heap any values actually associated with Jesus. It escaped hardly anyone's notice that 77.5% of white evangelicals voted for Trump in the 2016 election, and after tasting four years of his morally-objectionable policies and antics as president, that number *increased* to 80.1% in the 2020 election, and to 81% in his 2024 victory at retaking the presidency.[23] Playing off evangelicalism's roots in fundamentalism, former Southern Baptist ethicist David Gushee comments, "The sense that card-carrying American evangelicalism now requires acquiescence to attitudes and practices that *fundamentally* (aha!) negate core teachings of Jesus is fueling today's massive external criticism, internal dissent, and youthful exodus from evangelicalism."[24] The anger and distrust against people who claim to represent a loving and compassionate God while actively supporting "hate thy neighbor" policies seem more than justified.

- **Sexual Scandals**

Political and social issues, however, were not the only factors in the decline of evangelicalism in the public view. Add to this distaste of the adulterous relationship of the church with politics of oppression, the long-term criticism over church sexual scandals—from Catholic priests and bishops abusing those under their care, to the forced resignations of evangelical celebrities and mega-church pastors over "inappropriate behavior," along with the exposure of shameful attempts to cover-up the sexual abuses—the world, churched and unchurched, has justifiably viewed evangelicalism as a whole with jaundiced eye.

More recently (at the time of first writing this in 2022), Southern Baptist mega-church pastor Matt Chandler of The Village Church in the Dallas area, who was a prominent voice in conservative, Reformed theological circles, was placed on indefinite leave for "inappropriate communications" with a woman not his wife.[25] In January 2022, Brian Houston, world-renowned leader of the Hillsong Church in Sydney, Australia and the global Hillsong Network of

Churches, also stepped down after multiple allegations of sexual and financial misconduct, including covering-up his late father's sexual abuse of a minor while pastor of the church. His Sydney-based school of ministry was reported riddled with sexual abuse of students by staff.[26] John Cameron, Pentecostal pastor of New Zealand's largest church, Arise, with 13 campuses and a membership of over 10,000, resigned in April 2022 over charges of intern abuse and sexual harassment.[27] Also earlier that year, Jeremy Foster, pastor of Hope City Church in Houston, once touted as "the fastest-growing church in American history," boasting as many as 14,000 attenders per weekend, was forced to resign after admitting to an extramarital affair.[28]

Perhaps worse, in May 2022, came the release of a 300-page report detailing a two-decades-long sexual abuse cover-up by the Southern Baptist Convention. The report detailed 703 cases of sexually predatory behavior involving 409 SBC clergy or church staff—including Johnny Hunt, former president of the SBC. The offenses listed child molestation and other sexual abuse, which were consistently met with attempts to bury the information, with little or no efforts made to protect the victims. The survivors' complaints and reports were treated "'time and time again, with resistance, stonewalling, and even outright hostility' by leaders who were concerned more with protecting the institution from liability than from protecting Southern Baptists from further abuse."[29] The cover-up reached to the top echelon of SBC leadership, including three past convention presidents, a former vice president, and the former head of the SBC's administrative arm.[30]

And that was all just in 2022. Looking back further just a few years, there was the scandalous resignation in 2018 of Bill Hybels, pastor of Chicago based Willow Creek Community Church (with its eight campuses and average Sunday attendance of 25,000), over sexual misconduct, nonconsensual fondling, and harassment claims spanning decades. This, while the independent, conservative church world was still recovering from the shock of headlines caused in 2014 by Mark Driscoll of Mars Hill Church in Seattle when he was removed from pastoral leadership by the church board after accusations of misconduct. In this case, however, the misconduct was not sexually-based. The church had a history of controversy over its rigid Calvinist, homophobic and complementarian (male-headship/female-submission) theologies, autocratic leadership style (accusations of bullying and intimidating behavior), unethical use of funds and manipulation of sales data (using $210,000 of church funds to purchase Driscoll's book to artificially bolster its place on the *New York Times* bestseller list), plagiarism by Driscoll in another of his books, mishandling of donations, etc, all culminating in a federal racketeering lawsuit in 2016.[31] The church, with its 15 satellite locations and average Sunday attendance of over 12,000, folded shortly after Driscoll's removal, leaving the evangelical world in shock at the loss of one its premier celebrity spokesmen and success stories.

These are among the more recent in a long line of scandals involving famous names in evangelical circles, including fundamentalist (and Trump endorser) Jerry Falwell, Jr. in 2021,[32] Ravi Zacharias (2021), Carl Lentz (2020), Bill Gothard (2014), Tony Alamo (2009), Richard Roberts (2007), Ted Haggard (2006), and others,[33] going back to the sexual scandals of Jimmy Swaggart (1988) and Jim Bakker (1987)—not to mention the innumerable cases of sexual abuse by Roman Catholic priests making national headlines in the 1990s and 2000s.

And, sadly, since the initial writing of my thesis in 2022, sexual scandals in the evangelical world have continued to plague the headlines and newsfeeds on a regular basis. In

2024, for example, Mike Bickle, founder of the International House of Prayer (IHOP) in Kansas City, was exposed for repeatedly sexually abusing his teenaged babysitter; and Trump spiritual adviser Robert Morris of Dallas-based Gateway megachurch, was forced to resign for abusing a 12-year-old girl, and spent 6 months in an Oklahoma county jail in 2025–2026, with a 10-year suspended sentence, after pleading guilty to child sex abuse charges.[34] And in October 2025, NBC News published a 50-year pattern of abuse and cover-up in the Assemblies of God, implicating nearly 200 pastors and leaders, involving more than 475 victims, most of whom were children.[35]

And, though not reported to be of a sexual nature, in 2026 an exposé was published of the toxic culture and abuse of spiritual leadership at Life.Church, the then-reported "largest church in the U.S.," boasting 46 locations and an average weekly attendance of 85,000.[36] Four hundred of its former employees formed a private Facebook group as a safe space to share their experiences and find mutual support. The church generally continues to enjoy favor in its home Oklahoma City, but it is yet another black-eye for the evangelical church as a whole.

Further listing just seems redundant. History repeats itself, especially when it comes to religious power and its sexual abuse. And the failure to in any way successfully deal with this crisis is an indictment against the Church at large and a constant trigger for faith disillusionment and deconstruction among the faithful.

In light of this decades-long resumé of a regressive social agenda, aggressive pursuit of political power, abusive behavior and sexual scandal, the outlook for the evangelical church is dismal, and its reputation seems beyond repair. The concern of the church "gray hairs" over shrinking church attendance in the late 20th century seems quaint in comparison, yet remains a well justified one—but not for the reasons they speculated. Secular education is not the enemy of faith, as they feared. But hypocrisy is. Hatefulness is. Lack of personal transformation is. And post-Boomer and -Gen X generations will no longer be persuaded to look the other way. Millennials, Gen Zs, and newer generations want something "real." If they can't find it in the Church, they'll look elsewhere.

And that, as far as this researcher and pastor is concerned, is *great* news. As Jesus once said, "I tell you, open your eyes and look at the fields! They are *ripe* for harvest" (John 4:35). The question is—and this project hoped to begin to answer—is the church ready to welcome in that harvest? Can we be a safe place for those seekers, the ones unsatisfied with what the evangelical church has been peddling since the mid-20th century? They are dismantling, breaking apart, everything they've been told, sometimes finding the gems of truth underneath, sometimes rejecting the whole enterprise. As patriarch of the emerging church movement, Brian McLaren, puts it, "Thank God more people are deconstructing their faith!"

> For many of us, faith deconstruction has been a quest to honestly examine our faith, to understand how it has changed over time, to face the harm done by and within our faith, and to acknowledge that its contemporary forms are neither its original form nor its ultimate form, which means that our faith is not static...[37]

For many of us, this dismantling and rethinking is not a sign of impending apostasy or agnosticism, but is actually evidence that our faith is still vibrant and alive.

The threat of openly examining the beliefs and practices of the Church, of questioning "unquestionable doctrine," unjustly terrifies some in the evangelical world. But it should, in fact, be viewed as a welcome invitation to engage the faith at the root level. This is why the so-called "rise of the Nones," those who claim no religious affiliation, can be viewed as an opportunity for rebirth for the Church. It strips away so much of the cultural accretion, the corruption of Western history and values, and begins again with the basics of the faith Jesus and the apostles taught. It invites a fresh look, and attempts once again to answer the basic questions of life.

The Rise of the Spirituals

Concomitant with the moral decline of the evangelical church is the consequential "Rise of the Nones and the Spiritual but not religious," reflecting the meteoric escalation in numbers of those who claim no religious affiliation. The term "None" is sometimes, somewhat mistakenly, used interchangeably with the description "spiritual but not religious." However, I found that while "None" had in the past often reflected Gen X and Millennial sentiments—seeing religion as something divisive, fixed and inflexible, unhealthy, and to be avoided—it was less and less appropriate to Gen Z sensibilities which were more embracive of religion in its positive aspects. Granted, traditional Christianity, especially the evangelical variety, was rarely among the acceptable religions,[38] but those in the younger generations tend to be more amendable to religious practices as an essential, physical/embodied means of practicing spirituality. In other words, there is no strict dichotomy between being "spiritual" and "religious," as had commonly been thought.[39]

To be sure, the younger generations show a marked distrust in institutions of religion, and to a lesser degree in religious leaders, but they show a conspicuous affinity toward spirituality in general, and particularly their own personalized eclectic set of spiritual practices.[40] What distinguishes these younger, spiritually-inclined people is their insistence on the right to define for themselves what they believe and how they practice, outside of any institutional control.[41]

As mentioned earlier, the percentage of "Nones" in the American population had been relatively stable at 5-8% at least as far back as the 1970s until the Religious Right began emerging in force. In the early 1990s, at the height of conservative evangelicalism's political interference and direct antagonism toward any progressive movement in society and specifically against president Bill Clinton, things began to change in these numbers. The percentages swing upwards, and, as political science professor Ryan Burge tracks, that escalation continued unabated for the next three decades:

> In 1972, just 1 in 20 Americans had no religious affiliation. That share inched up only marginally for the next two decades, before beginning its climb in the 1990s. The unaffiliated jumped about 4 percentage points between 1993 and 1996, up to nearly 1 in 6 (nearly 15%) by the new millennium. The number of respondents indicating they had "no religion" continued to grow, reaching 1 in 5 in 2012 (19.6%) and close to 1 in 4 (23.7%) in the most recent wave of the survey available [2021].[42]

Subsequent data from Pew Research updated those 2021 numbers, showing an even *higher* percentage, indicating 3 out of 10 Americans (29%) identified as "Nones," up 6 points from just 5 years earlier (before Trump's first presidency), putting a significant dent in the Christian majority. "Christians continue to make up a majority of the U.S. populace, but their share of the adult population is 12 points lower in 2021 than it was in 2011."[43] Those numbers apparently reached their peak following Trump's first administration at 28 or 29%, and began to dip during the Biden presidency, returning to their earlier 1-in-4 levels, perhaps suggesting that the rapid decline in religious affiliation had begun to stabilize. But the change in percentage of self-identified Nones—from 1 in 20 in 1978 increasing to nearly 1 in 3 in 2021—is simply staggering.

The question that comes immediately to mind is, Why? What accounts for this meteoric rise?

Like charting the fall of evangelicalism, the reasons are multiple—and I would claim, congruent. As the Religious Right began to manipulate social factors to their political and social advantage, those on the opposite side of those issues were driven further and further away from traditional Christianity. Burge puts it this way: "What can be observed is clear and unmistakable—disaffiliation is directly related to

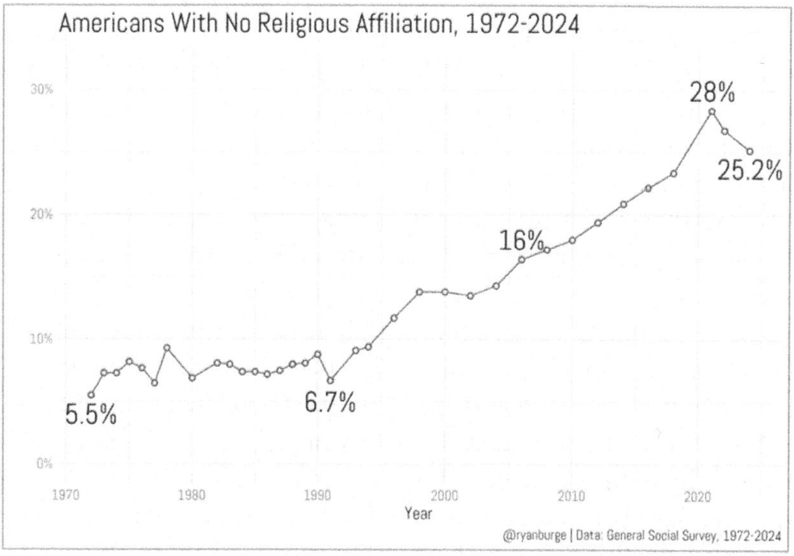

Chart 1 – Source: Ryan Burge, "America Got a Little More Religious. No, Really." Mar 28, 2026, www.graphsaboutreligion.com

political ideology." "As evangelicals have become more linked to one political party [and its conservative agenda], that has naturally led to the alienation of a lot of people who think differently about politics."[44] In short, evangelicalism traded souls, including its own, for political influence.

Burge examines a number of social factors in attempting to explain the movement in religious disaffiliation. First, he looks at secularization as a possible factor in the move away from religion, highlighting the theories of Max Weber, Emile Durkheim and Karl Marx, as mentioned earlier. But the United States does not behave like Europe where the number professing faith has decreased dramatically since World War II. The U.S. has consistently clung to its religious moorings despite increased educational and economic advancement: "secularization theory doesn't work in the case of the United States."[45]

Burge then looks at "social desirability bias" (the impulse of people wanting to present themselves favorably in others' eyes), yet despite U.S. culture clinging to some form of civil religion (the common sensibility that people "ought" to believe in God or attend church), numbers of unaffiliated seem immune to this social pressure.

He then looks at internet accessibility, where one might find a larger community of like-minded skeptics, and he argues that the polarizing impact of the internet likely does play some part. Referencing Robert Putnam's influential 2000 book, *Bowling Alone: The Collapse and Revival of American Community*, Burge credits social isolation as another factor likely involved: as technology, the internet, and especially cable television became more wide-spread, people became less interested and involved in group social activity, and this decline in church socialization facilitated the separation from established religion. (This correlates with Kinnaman's identification of "digital Babylon" as his designated bogeyman for the latest social influence to be overcome by the young generation of faithful.[46])

Loss of trust in social and religious institutions—directly related to the Church's abuse of public trust described in the section above—no doubt is also a contributing factor. For example, Burge cites an ABC News poll from 2002 indicating that nearly 80% of those polled disapproved of the Catholic Church's handling of the then-headline sex scandals. But he concludes that the evidence does not point to lack of trust in institutions being the main contributor in the rise of the Nones.

Burge lastly studies changes in family structure from the mid-1970s onward as a possible explanation, and while it remains true that unmarried people and those without children are more likely to be religiously unaffiliated, the percentage of Americans without children has stayed relatively the same, at 24% in the 1970s to 28% from the 1990s to the present. Lack of children cannot explain this stunning rise of religiously unaffiliated.

Ultimately, Burge contends, it was the conservative shift in politics in the 1980s and '90s that was the most significant factor. "In every graph that looks at American religion, something unmistakable happens in the early 1990s. ... The biggest religious trend occurring at that moment was the *rise of evangelicalism and the religious right.*"[47] When the Church invests its energy in what is viewed by significant portions of the community as regressive or oppressive politics, progressive-leaning people will leave—as confirmed by a number of participants in this project's Discussion Group—and the Church ultimately suffers. This negative perception and resultant exodus, contributes to and corresponds with a rise in "Nones."

• Nones and Spirituality

The terms "None" and "spiritual but not religious" (SBNR) are closely related but not exactly synonymous. "None" includes three distinct subcategories of religious non-affiliation: those who identify as atheist, agnostic, or "nothing in particular."[48] Historically, the words "religious" and "spiritual" have been used somewhat interchangeably. However, as antipathy toward organized religion increased in the late 20th century, exacerbated by the Religious Right, there became a clear need to differentiate between the two. In 2000, Sven Erlandson published his book *Spiritual but not Religious*, coining the phrase that would become the self-identifier of a generation who affirmed their claim on spirituality, in whatever form they chose, while asserting their independence from the trappings of organized religion. The label "None," however, gives no indication of whether one identifies as spiritual, while SBNR clarifies that position. That subtle distinction, however, is mostly lost, and the two terms become functionally indistinguishable.

Thus, the dramatic rise of the Nones emphatically does *not* mean that people are increasingly rejecting belief in God or some higher power. Americans in general remain spiritually inclined, whether they associate that with a traditional religion or not. Even while as many as 1 in 3 Americans may not identify with a particular religion, 9 in 10 Americans still claim to believe in some kind of God.[49] This holds true even of Gen Z. Findings from Springtide Research Institute (2022) show that 68% of young people ages 13–25 say they are at least "slightly religious," and 77% self-identify as at least "slightly spiritual," with almost half claiming to believe in the existence of a higher power.[50] Put another way, over three-quarters of Gen Zs claim to be either spiritual, religious, or both.

Despite the impression cast by the startling "rise of the Nones," "None" does not necessarily mean atheist or agnostic. Of the 29% of the U.S. population in 2021 labeled "None," only 4% identified as atheist (5% identified as agnostic). Twenty percent of the population simply claimed to be "nothing in particular."[51] As Burge points out, "while many people have walked away from a religious affiliation, they haven't left all aspects of religion and spirituality behind."[52] This suggests that people across the generational spectrum continue to maintain some kind of personal belief and/or practice that connects them to a higher power.

More to the point, a related survey in July 2022 in the U.K. found that the younger generation was *more likely* to pray than their older counterparts (though "prayer" was not specifically defined). Of the 2073 adults surveyed, a majority—56%—of the 18 through 34-year-olds reported that they have prayed during their life, with a third (32%) claiming to have prayed in the past month. By contrast, in the 55+ age group, only 41% admitted to having ever prayed, and only 25% saying they had prayed in the last month. Stephen Hance, National Lead for Evangelism and Witness for the Church of England, explained: "These findings really challenge the all-too-common assumption that young people are not interested in faith or spiritual things. In fact, they show us that—more than simply being interested in spirituality—they are already exploring it in practice, to a greater extent than their elders."[53] The survey confirms the overall impression that people—particularly the younger generations—continue to seek connection with a higher power beyond themselves.

Pew Research Center surveys tend to confirm a persistent spiritual inclination even among the "Nones." In a study released in 2026, they noted that many Nones believe in a Deity of some kind (about 45% in the U.S.), and even among self-identified atheists and agnostics, many believe in life after death (about a fifth or more), or believe in "something spiritual beyond the natural world," even if it can't be seen. Many believe that animals or parts of nature, like mountains, rivers, trees, can have spirits or spiritual energies (about 54%). And despite generally avoiding religious services, a small segment of Nones still engage in religious practices, such as praying and fasting, lighting incense or candles for spiritual reasons, visit fortune tellers, consult horoscopes, or wear religious symbols.[54]

Though it may seem counter-intuitive, the rise of the Nones actually corresponds with a *rise* in spiritual seekers, even if they insist on defining that spirituality for themselves. This leads us to conclude that these Nones are mostly disillusioned with institutional religion—not faith, belief or spirituality in general—and prefer a more personalized, non-dogmatic, and inclusivist experience.

- **What Kind of Spirituality?**

So, what kind of spirituality are seekers engaged in these days?

The term "spirituality" generally is viewed as the *interior* life of faith, while "religion" is typically associated with the *exterior*, communal or organizational aspects of faith. As the Barna Group explains it, in the common current mindset, "to be religious is to be institutional—it is to practice one's spirituality in accordance with an external authority. But to be spiritual *but not religious* is to possess a deeply personal and private spirituality. Religions point *outside* oneself to a higher power for wisdom and guidance, while a spirituality divorced from religion looks *within*."[55] This association with institutions bears out with the sentiments of Gen Zs as well. Sociologist and director of the nonsectarian Springtide Research Institute, Josh Packard, summarized the difference based on the institute's 30,000 surveys of 13 through 25-year-olds. "For Gen Z, being religious aligns with brick-and-mortar places of worship and practices associated with traditional religion. Being spiritual applies to those sacred experiences that happen outside of traditional settings and can include feeling connected to something other than a higher power."[56] "Religion," then, implies what is done communally, while "spirituality" is seen as a personal thing.

These distinctions are clearly imprecise and subjective, since there is considerable overlap, and spirituality and religion each may involve internal/personal and external/organizational aspects,[57] but the contrast between personal versus institutional experience will serve as a convenient, if fuzzy, working definition for the terms. (This was the case in our group with Matthew, who despite his negative experience in church and his ultimate (but temporary) rejection of Christianity, nonetheless embraced a personalized form of spiritualized ethical humanism.)

Like the Nones, those identifying as Spiritual but Not Religious tend to avoid communal or organizational worship, while still maintaining a rich variety of spiritually edifying practices. Barna's polling indicated that approximately 60% of SBNRs maintain spiritual practices comparable to practicing Christians and evangelicals, including reflection in nature, meditation, practicing silence and/or solitude, prayer, journaling, yoga, reading books on spiritual topics, Scripture reading, and attending groups or retreats.[58] "They [SBNRs] are distinct among their irreligious peers in their spiritual curiosity and openness. ... [They] display an uncommon inclination to think beyond the material and to experience the transcendent."[59] Yet despite recognizing an almost unique spiritual thirst among SBNRs, Barna's data did not include non-traditional spiritual practices, which perhaps illustrates an evangelical blind spot in what comprises "spirituality."

Other sources are quick to note the SNBRs' inclination—particularly among Gen Zs—toward exploring other religions and alternative means of connecting with the Divine, including New Age practices, Reiki healing techniques, use of crystals, yoga, meditation and mindfulness, horoscopes, astrology, Tarot cards, witchcraft, Wicca, neo-pagan spiritualities, or weaving together practices from various religions to their personal taste.[60] Springtide's research, for example, showed that 51% of the 13–25-year-olds surveyed engage in "tarot cards or fortune telling" on a regular basis.[61] This was confirmed in our Discussion Group, as well. A number of our Gen Z participants admitted to "playing with" Tarot, and one Millennial regularly wears a crystal to protect him from negative energies. These are interwoven into their Christian faith. The comment by the Barna researchers that this generation has an "uncommon" curiosity and openness seems an understatement.

The eclectic tendency of the younger generations is particularly noteworthy. They do not feel the same social pressure to "pick one" of the major religions and settle there. They have a remarkable ability to selectively choose whatever elements they find personally attractive or fulfilling from the wide range of religious and spiritual options available. Elaborating on the phenomenon Springtide Research calls "faith unbundled"—the cherry-picking approach to religious and spiritual belief and practice—one Gen Z writer wrote, "Unlike 20 years ago [before the advent of social media], '...we don't live cut off from other systems of belief...' as the Dalai Lama puts it.... Young people today know: there's not just 'another side to the story' we're told when raised in a given tradition, but thousands of other perspectives!"[62] This is a distinctly 21st century interfaith perspective made possible by electronic globalization.

Ready worldwide access affects how newer generations see the world and themselves. "Our relationships with ourselves are enhanced. The center of our lives is redirected to our individual hearts. Instead of measuring ourselves against a system of belief, we measure those systems against ourselves—what makes us whole and human."[63] This independent attitude explains how Christian Gen Zs can also read Tarot, practice Reiki, or take note that "Mercury is in retrograde," without any sense of internal conflict. The freedom to select from a smorgasbord of religious options and to "measure them against themselves," as will be noted in chapters ahead, also allows Gen Zs within the Church to experience deconstruction with much less psychic trauma than their older counterparts. They feel freer to question or discard even core aspects of their faith as best suits their sensibilities. This innate prerogative is built into their worldview.

The characteristic spiritual curiosity and openness of the latest generations is not simply based on a few exaggerated claims in isolated online platforms. Gen Z members of the Evolving Faiths Discussion Group in this project confirmed that not only had they and their closest friends read Tarot as a means of personal guidance, but that some of their friends were self-identified witches. They are quick to point out that "witch" does not mean what older generations typically imagine. These are people embracing a magical, "re-enchanted" worldview—the very thing Max Weber feared the modern life would stifle and Charles Taylor bemoaned the loss of in an overly-rationalized, demysticized Christianity—one that holds a deep reverence for nature, sees the universe alive, and everything in it connected. They hold to a strict code of doing no harm, to others or to the world, and have embraced the existence of the supernatural and higher power(s).[64] And during the Gay Pride festival the summer our group was in session, one of the group took me to a booth to get my cards read, and there was a line of people waiting to receive spiritual guidance. I went mostly out of curiosity, wanting to understand the underlying assumptions to Tarot reading (were the cards directed by a higher power, or were they simply a tool for self-interpretation of life events?). Regardless of my personal views on the matter, I recognized the interest as a reflection of Gen Z's desire to connect with the supernatural—something the largely non-metaphysical and doctrinally-focused Church has failed to help them do.

How All This Fits

People, especially the younger generations, are still seeking connection with the Divine. They want God, or at least God as they would like to understand God—*not* as God has been presented by traditional religions in the past. This is especially true for those coming out of fundamentalist and evangelical backgrounds. The politicking and scandals, the hypocrisy and unloving behavior toward the marginalized by the evangelical world—the misogyny, racism, and homophobia—have irreparably damaged the evangelical brand, perhaps even the reputation of Christianity in general. The "rise of the Nones," especially those who adopt the label "Spiritual but not religious," proves that Americans are *still* a religious-leaning people. Perhaps even more so now than before. They are simply exploring other options.

For those who stay in the faith, who still hold to some form of evangelical belief, deconstruction is one of those alternatives. It opens the doors to questions, to a freedom to explore, to challenge, to rethink, and ultimately to choose for oneself the set of beliefs and practices one wants to embrace. Deconstruction allows the opportunity to break free from the stale, predefined structures and restrictions of a faith inherited, and to redefine what it means to be Christian. It is an "insider's" approach to reclaiming a vital faith nearly destroyed by organized religion.

So, what is faith deconstruction really all about?

"Everybody's Deconstructing"

Deconstruction in the life of faith is simply the dismantling of some or all of the elements of one's belief system, examining them piece by piece, and either discarding as false or no longer useful, or retaining as essentially sound and to be recycled back into one's system of belief. It is an apt term since it summons images of the disassembling, in some cases demolition, of a constructed edifice. Just as one constructs an object from various multiple elements over a period of time—as one's faith or belief system normally is—so one *de*constructs in the same manner, by removing doctrines or practices, usually one or two at a time, inspecting them closely, and deciding if or how to retain them.

Deconstruction for the Christian is, as Brian McLaren describes, a kind of quest, a digging and sifting through "layers and layers of practice, piety, and theology" sorting between the "something real" and the "something wrong," between that which resonates deep inside as "right" and good, and that which doesn't feel right.[65]

The process may span years of a person's life, but it universally results in one of two outcomes: either a reconstructed, revived faith, or deconversion where the faith is abandoned.

• More Ricoeur than Derrida

Conventional academic thinking embraces the idea that the process and the term came out of a literary analysis developed by French philosopher Jacques Derrida in the 1960s which highlights the tension between text and meaning. This theory suggests that words or texts cannot hold objective truth or meaning in themselves; they are merely signs pointing to other signs. Thus, it is impossible to discover from a text any "true" meaning. What is only possible is uncovering the assumptions and motives of the creator of the text, what the author *meant* or intended to construct, but never being able to ascertain or define the underlying truth itself. Derrida's deconstruction attempts to expose the hidden assumptions and cultural worldviews behind a text. It is primarily concerned with literary analysis—not exactly how it generally experienced in popular religious culture.

As Jon Bloom, a Reformed Baptist theologian, summarizes, this kind of deconstruction "asserts that human language at best communicates, not absolute truth, but how a certain individual conceives of truth at a certain moment in time, in the contexts of his cultural, political, religious, environmental and experiential influences." Therefore, "philosophers (or theologians) consult written works of the past in vain to discover absolute truth or meaning, since all they're encountering are other authors' constructs of truth or meaning."[66] Renowned religious writer Phyllis Tickle locates Derrida's theory squarely in the era influenced by Heisenberg's Uncertainty Principle, claiming there is no absolute truth, only relative truth. "All writing—be it sacred or secular—has no innate meaning until it is read and, therefore, has no meaning outside of the circumstances and disposition of the reader."[67]

There are superficial similarities between Derrida's literary deconstruction theory and the internal work of religious seekers in that there is a re-examination and questioning of traditional ways of thinking and notably a rejection of appeals to voices of spiritual or traditional authority. Faith deconstructors insist on their individual, personal right to accept or reject constituent components of their faith.

But, as mentioned, faith deconstruction is *not* primarily or exclusively a literary exercise, nor is it focused on the use of language. It is much broader, more inclusive and comprehensive. It focuses attention, as Brian McLaren puts it, on "the questions that are simmering in our souls." It is "careful and loving attention to the construction of ideas, beliefs, systems, values, and cultures."[68] *Everything* involved in one's spiritual or religious life becomes subject to re-examination, re-evaluation, and subject to the individual's right to accept, re-position, or reject. Faith deconstruction is the disassembling of theological presuppositions and religious practices in order to reconstruct (or reject) those beliefs and practices under a new paradigm, typically resulting in significant alteration. It is not just challenging a particular interpretation of Scripture (a text), although for evangelicals that will likely be part of the process. It is a redefining of the structures of one's faith life.

In this sense, the popular religious experience of faith deconstruction is *not* what Derrida had in mind. There are parallels in the process—like challenging authoritarian positions, insisting on personal prerogatives, and the examining of presuppositions—just as there would be if using another descriptive term, like "disassemble" or "reverse engineer," but the overall scope of the process exceeds a literary study. It overflows the banks of text interpretation, even if that text is Holy Scripture, and cascades into the streets and alleys of a person's life. Faith deconstruction can be—often is—traumatic. It is so much more than an academic exercise.

Other words (like "disassemble") might work just as well, and avoid the possible confusion and conflation with Derrida's ideas.[69] And the characteristic *un*-systematic way in which most undergo this deeply personal experience belies the philosophical discipline of Derrida's process. As one detractor wrote, the popular use of the term "really seems to mean something akin to 'dismantle,' the (mis)use of the Derridean d-word gives the whole a specious veneer of intellectualism and a certain superannuated postmodern chic."[70] Obviously, he was not a fan of either the word or the practice.

What the typical religious deconstructor experiences more closely resembles the process of "critical distance" described by another French philosopher, Paul Ricoeur, in the late 1960s and early '70s. He famously described the process of faith development as a three-stage journey. It begins at a pre-critical "First Naïveté" characterized by an unquestioning, child-like acceptance of the sacred stories we inherited in their literal sense, as well as the religious doctrines derived from them. "Naïveté" here shouldn't be thought of in negative terms, as it is sometimes used in popular pejorative descriptions. Ricoeur intends the word's original sense of "innocence" or "simplicity." A religious person might spend his or her entire lifetime comfortably seated in this naïve state. Many do.

But for the person pursuing deeper meaning and greater spiritual growth, this first stage may be followed by a more reflective "critical" stage where that simplistic belief is challenged. This often leads to a period of doubt and abandoning those basic interpretations. This turbulent middle period, sometimes referred to as a "desert of criticism," more closely corresponds with the mental and emotional anguish that often accompanies what we popularly call "deconstruction." It can be long and seemingly dry. But hopefully, with time, maturity and faithful perseverance, the person arrives at a "post-critical" return to faith, a "Second Naïveté," where a deeper faith is realized. Here, the mystery and symbolic richness of the stories can be embraced without having to insist on their scientific or historic fact—that those stories need not be literally true to convey deeply meaningful Truth. A person arrives at this final stage of peace, able to re-embrace the texts and symbols of his or her faith, mindful of the insights gained from critical investigation, while discovering their deeper existential meanings.[71]

Ricoeur's model suggests that mature faith requires a journey of personal wrestling with doubts and questions to arrive at a deeper, more profound faith that acknowledges complexity. This was the ultimate goal of this experiment in launching a facilitated discussion group: to walk alongside those on that journey.

The D/R Journey: A Pathology of Deconstruction

This spiritual wrestling process is almost universally recognized by psychologists, philosophers and theologians, though given different labels.

The process can take an extended period of time in a person's life, and is often depicted in related literature as an emotionally- and psychically-charged "journey." Mark Karris, a pastor and family therapist, explains:

> This season of questioning one's faith and religious beliefs can be excruciatingly painful. ... It feels like walking on a wobbly waterbed rather than on solid ground. It feels unsafe and dangerous. It feels lonely and isolating. The fear of rejection from God and from others feels suffocating as emotions such as shame, guilt, fear, anger, and sadness take center stage. The consequences of such a prismatic array of emotions are sleepless nights, hiding, pretending, unhealthy addictions, isolating, ruminating, and engaging in a whole variety of other coping behaviors.[72]

It is a holistically disruptive and life-altering experience.

Deconstruction is not only an internal process. It impacts social relations—our families and church relationships. There is a significant amount of isolation and alienation experienced by the deconstructor, feeling a separation from the common bonds of shared belief. Rejection, shunning, or simple avoidance often results as former co-believers now see the questioner as a dangerous trouble-maker, on the verge of heresy or apostasy, and a possible risk of infecting others with their doubt. (As a real-life case in point, as I was working on finishing touches to the first draft of my thesis, one of the Gen Z group participants, just back from Christmas holiday with his family, reported overhearing his religious father speaking with his former youth pastor about how "deconstruction is the work of the devil" to destroy souls and the church.) And for many, the resulting loss of fellowship with their faith community is one of the most traumatizing parts of the process.

The whole "desert" experience can be so unsettling and confusing that Karris gave the collective pathological features its own label: "Religious Disorientation Growth Syndrome" (RDGS). This descriptive term encompasses the unique locus and object of the experience: it is situated specifically in religious belief, results in temporary psychological disorientation, triggered by, and with the anticipated outcome of, personal religious/spiritual growth. He identified some common symptoms encountered by those under his care:

1. Doubting or denying one's religious beliefs that were once held as true.
2. Subtle or intense anxiety about a person's relationship with God.
3. Increase of painful emotions, such as anger, loneliness, shame, guilt, sadness, and despair.

4. Isolation and criticism (feared or realized) from members within their own family and/or religious community.
5. Existential angst concerning a person's identity and future self.[73]

(During the course of the original Discussion Group, I could identify each one of these symptoms in some of the group participants. Some symptoms were short-lived, and noticeably diminished or disappeared over a few sessions. Some were conspicuous in varying degrees over the course of the year that the project continued.)

It needs to be emphasized here that this D/R journey, as traumatizing as it can be, is (hopefully) ultimately a healthy one, because regardless of the outcome, the person is engaging their faith on a personal level in a real way. The doubt and questioning can feel paralyzing at times, but it is a good thing. Peter Enns, the popular apostle of uncertainty, writes, "Doubt is only the enemy of faith when we equate faith with certainty in our thinking.... Doubt means spiritual relocation is happening. It's God's way of saying, 'Time to move on.'"[74]

It is the messiness of disorder on the way to new order; the middle stage in a healthy progression of spiritual growth and transformation which Richard Rohr ubiquitously describes as the "Order—Disorder—Reorder" sequence. "We grow by passing beyond some perfect order, through a usually painful and seemingly unnecessary disorder, to an enlightened reorder or 'resurrection.' ... We must be moved from *Order* to *Disorder* and then ultimately to *Reorder*."[75]

Tyler Huckabee, editor of the evangelical, youth-oriented *Relevant Magazine*, paraphrases Rohr's model this way: "Most Christians begin their faith journey with *construction* (deciding what they believe, usually by hearing it from others) and then later on, enter a phase of *deconstruction* (rethinking some of their original beliefs)." This middle phase can be scary, disorienting, and lonely, but when engaged deliberately and honestly, can lead to the healthy place of re-orientation, re-order, re-construction. "Deconstruction can be a very positive process, done alongside the Holy Spirit and with loving encouragement of trusted friends. In fact, *deconstruction* usually leads to *reconstruction,* in which you rebuild what you've torn down. ... No matter how it may look to observers, you're actually working very hard to hold onto your faith."[76] Far from being a spiritual sickness in need of a "gospel cure," as The Gospel Coalition had proposed, it is a sign of spiritual health and growth.

Different scholars describe it in different terms, but the general process of spiritual growth is not some modern phenomenon. Theologian and Old Testament scholar, Walter Brueggemann, views this process as the necessary spiritual journey that "each of God's children is in transit along with the flow of orientation, disorientation, and reorientation."[77] Or, using Brian McLaren's 4-stage paradigm of spiritual development, Simplicity, Complexity, Perplexity, and finally Harmony,[78] where Perplexity corresponds with the disorienting, questioning stage of faith. Likewise, Christian psychiatrist Morgan Peck, in the 1980s, proposed a model he found common among American Christians: Chaos, Fundamentalism, Skepticism, Mysticism[79]—where the deconstruction process would occur in his Skepticism stage. This is where people begin acknowledging their doubts and actively challenging their beliefs. What was once orthodox and unassailable in the Simplicity/Fundamentalism stage no longer seems so certain. It is the stepping back and making a critical examination, matching Ricoeur's "critical distance" between a place of "first naïveté" and the hoped-for outcome of a "second naïveté"—a richer personal spirituality.

A paradigm more specifically descriptive of deconstruction was derived by Kathy Escobar based on the numerous people undergoing faith crisis she counseled over many years. She identified six stages of what she called a "Faith Shift": Fusing, Shifting, optional Returning, Unraveling, optional Severing, and ultimate Rebuilding.[80] Acknowledging doubts begins in the Shifting stage; the questions surface, and cracks in the unshakable foundation of one's faith begin to destabilize the person. The shift may scare them, and they may Return for a time to the security of their former faith and community, but often the questions persist to the point one's faith begins Unraveling. This may or may not result in a Severing from the familiar faith community (voluntarily or involuntarily). But those who persisted in hope, who pursued freedom, mystery, diversity over the comforts of certainty, conformity and affiliation, typically landed in the Rebuilding stage where the work "requires excavating all of the rubble to find what remains, what is still part of our faith, no matter how big or small."[81]

At the risk of belaboring the point, Karris's own 8-positioned taxonomy is noteworthy for the insight he offers in referring to the various common states as "stations" rather than "stages." The word "stage," he says, implies a well-defined order, a progression, often with comparative or judgmental overtones (as in, "I'm at a higher stage of my spiritual development"). "Stations," on the other hand, suggests places where travelers gather together. They may or may not move on to another station together, or in the same sequence, and because nothing is ever perfectly neat and orderly where people are concerned, travelers can return to familiar stations as needed.[82] This distinction highlights the difference between "phases of spiritual growth" or "human development,"[83] which tend to portray a linear, one-way progression in overall personal development, and the nonlinear D/R process, where there is usually much circling back, cycling through the steps/stations again over multiple different issues. (One may, for example, deconstruct their position on the role of women in ministry, and then repeat the process, somewhat differently, for one's belief in penal substitutionary atonement.)

Through the process of deconstruction—by any other name—a person moves from a comfortable and certain place of Naïveté, Simplicity, Fundamentalism and Certainty, Order and Orientation in their faith through a state of Disorder and Disorientation, Perplexity, Skepticism, Shifting and Unraveling, and after much internal processing and with the help of trusted friends and the guidance of the Holy Spirit, arrives at a place of more profound maturity in a state of Reorder, Reorientation, Harmony, Mysticism—reconstruction. The process normally occurs over a period of years due to the deep internal work required to unshackle from long-held positions, but also often because of the repetitive process of breaking from one deeply rooted belief only to cycle through again with each genuinely held belief.

Deconstruction within the Social Context

Although the term "deconstruction" has been applied to this type of faith crisis since about the turn of the millennium, it has exploded in popular awareness—both as an experiential phenomenon and the word itself—since 2020. For example, at the time of the initial writing of my doctoral thesis (Nov 2022), there were over 81,000 posts on Facebook marked with the #Deconstruction hashtag, and 348,000+ entries on Instagram. The concept was trending, and the attention it was getting in religious circles had exploded, but it did not appear in a vacuum. As a spiritual phenomenon, it seems the natural product of the crisis evangelicalism has been undergoing for the past few decades. However, people did not just start re-evaluating their faith due to the politicking of the Religious Right or the sexual corruption within established churches. The church "gray hairs" mentioned earlier sounded the alarm over the mass exodus from parental religion by the younger generation back even in the 1960s and '70s.

Phyllis Tickle sees the early days of the "spiritual but not religious" movement in the popularization of Alcoholics Anonymous, with its embracing a nonreligious Higher Power, and with the penetration of Eastern religions, particularly Buddhism, into American popular culture in the 1960s. Buddhism captured the attention of spiritual seekers, with "its rich narrative of wisdom experience, with its centuries of comfortable conversation about the life of the human spirit, with its full vocabulary and lush rhetoric, with its sensible and sensate practices for incorporating the body into the spirit's world, ... and its teaching about the reality beyond the illusion ... with all the tools and appointments needed to enter the subjective experience ... fully, fearlessly, and unencumbered by theism."[84]

White Protestant Christianity paled in comparison. It had little to offer by way of subjective experience, religious practice or disciplines, transformative power, or even religious vocabulary. It seemed sterile and impotent.

The neo-pentecostal/charismatic tradition and the non-denominational mega-church movement since the mid-1980s to some extent offered a welcome alternative. Their emphasis on spiritual gifts and the sensate presence of God, experienced both in corporate praise and worship music and in one's personal devotional life, seemed like an oasis in the religious desert of the time. The charismatic movement, especially in streams influenced by Word of Faith teaching,[85] shifted religious focus on the sphere of God's presence and activity from the next life in the hereafter to this life in the here and now. Probably for this reason, even decades into the 21st century, the nondenominational church sector defies religious trends as the only strand of Protestant Christianity that is actually growing.[86]

But even among churches involved in charismatic renewal, doctrine and social outlook were predominantly conservative, and little was offered in the way of ritualized or practiced spiritual disciplines.

Father Thomas Keating's story about how he became involved in developing Centering Prayer as a form of Christian meditation in the mid-1960s at St. Joseph's Abbey, illuminates this point. When a Buddhist group converted a nearby Catholic retreat house to the Insight Meditation Center, the monks at St. Joseph's noticed an increase in the number of people stopping by the monastery to ask for directions to the Center, particularly young people. When Fr. Keating would inquire what they were seeking at the meditation center, he would invariably hear, in the jargon of the 1960s, "A path, man! We're seeking a path." And when he asked why these young people did not pursue a spiritual path within their own Christian traditions, they inevitably responded that they didn't know Christianity even offered one. "You mean Christianity has a *path*?"[87]

This story highlights the sad state of the Christian Church from the mid-20th century onward—Protestant and Catholic—with its lack of spiritual power or appeal to people seeking authentic spiritual experience and truth.

As an aside, while the focus here is on the evangelical and fundamentalist Christian world, one might ask what role mainline Protestant denominations played in the rise of the Nones and SBNRs and the more recent wave of deconstruction among the faithful. The turning point, as mentioned earlier, was clearly in the early 1990s. This was not only a time of undeniable conservative evangelical meddling in national politics, but also the early years of the nondenominational mega-church boom. These mega-churches were almost exclusively bastions of conservative evangelical theology. Thus, the major religious social influences of the time were conservative in nature. The point might be argued, but unfortunately, mainline, progressive churches did not have significant cultural presence at that time. Likewise, deconstruction is often a reaction against dogmatic certainty and right-leaning political positions, neither of which is generally associated with mainline, progressive churches.

Outside of the charismatic and nondenominational traditions, neither evangelical nor mainline churches were well-known for having much to offer in the way of practiced or experiential spirituality—something younger generations have been seeking since at least the 1960s. American Christianity as a whole was, in effect, perceived as religious but not spiritual. This pointed the spiritually-hungry away from the Church toward alternative spiritualities, and Buddhism and neo-paganism appeared luminous by comparison to an enchantment-starved worldview.

Then as now, why would spiritual-reality-starved people *not* challenge the status quo, *not* ask questions, *not* rethink everything they had been taught by the seemingly dead religious establishment? Why would they not seek answers of their own, even if it led them outside their inherited faith?

The contemporary Deconstruction/Reconstruction movement is the latest, but surely not last, effort within American Christianity to clean out the dusty attic of the faith, throw out the old, the broken, the ineffective, sort out what is to be retained and cherished, and return to what is at the core of the faith: a way of living based in love, authenticity, and spiritual reality.

It may well be the very revival evangelicals have been praying for for decades, but most have failed to recognize it.

3

A Biblical Theology of Deconstruction

"This is my beloved Son; with him I am well pleased. Listen to him!"

~ *Matthew 17:5*

One of the first efforts I made with the Discussion Group at the heart of this project was to reassure them that questioning the faith was not an affront to God, and that it was, in fact, a healthy, God-desired act of personal growth in one's relationship with God.

In this chapter, I will highlight some of the biblical passages I cited to promote that idea—beginning with a few examples from the Hebrew Bible, then looking at the early church in the Book of Acts, with special emphasis on the hermeneutic style of Jesus. I will then suggest a "deconstructing hermeneutic," an intentional way of reading Scripture that is true to the method used by Jesus and the apostles. The intent is to show that deconstruction is, in fact, a biblically-based act of faith.

The impression of God promoted by fundamentalism and evangelicalism is one of an uncompromising and wrathful deity. "God is Love"—yes, to be sure, unless you disagree with him. And only if you accept the singular and exclusive Way he designed, explained through Scripture and passed on by his approved messengers. Or, as Jon Bloom summarizes his view of faith deconstruction, "In the Christian world, this [deconstruction] translates to critically questioning traditional modes of Christian belief, and often refusing to recognize as authorities those perceived as occupying privileged Christian institutional positions who 'supposedly speak for God.'"[1] Disagreeing with established doctrine, questioning one's church leaders, was tantamount to disagreeing with God himself—and the consequences of that were severe. As a pastor, I believed this was the first hurdle that needed to be addressed.

I do not equate rethinking our doctrines and religious practices with disputing God, but I understood that some of our people did, at least initially. Our former Church of Christ people specifically did. As Eric and Mark both expressed to me, questioning church doctrine carried the emotional and mental weight (guilt) equivalent to committing apostasy, to virtually spitting in God's face. So, to demonstrate that "challenging God" was an activity in the spirit of the best biblical traditions, I intentionally wove into our early discussions instances from the bible of characters who questioned or argued with God, with special attention to God's response.

Wrestling with God

I began with the biblical story of Jacob wrestling with an angel at night (Gen 32) as my primary illustrating example, making a few homiletic comments to drive home the point. First, Jacob "wrestled" with God. (I explained that "angel" was often a Hebrew expression for the earthly manifestation of God—a theophany—so the question of whether it was actually God or a lower celestial being who wrestled with Jacob was more a modern distraction). Wrestling with God, arguing, debating, bargaining with the Divine was something that many of the biblical heroes of the faith did; it was not unusual or a sign of faithlessness. Jacob wrestled, just as we wrestle with our questions, with our theologies, with our understandings of God. Wrestling means that our faith is alive, it is dynamic, it is active and relevant to our on-going lives.

Second, Jacob was not reprimanded for the struggle. He was blessed; he got a name-change. This is no trivial detail; it is a permanent marker that he had entered a new stage of life. It was like a rebirth, a turning point, a sign that his identity and relationship with God had moved to a new place. Like the renaming of Abram to Abraham and Sarai to Sarah, it was a positive sign of God's favor. In the bible, names are "inextricably intertwined with personality and destiny," so by changing Jacob's name to Israel—meaning essentially, "wrestles with God"—God was signaling that contending with God would be a hallmark characteristic of God's people going forward.[2] We follow in that faith tradition of struggling with God—really, with our understanding of God—and far from being a sign of our abandoning the faith, it is actually evidence that we are truly living and engaged with that faith.

Third, Jacob/Israel walked away with a limp. He was forever changed by that encounter. His walk, the way he moved through life, was permanently changed. This is how it is supposed to be. As we encounter God, as we wrestle with the faith and our perception, God changes us, and it effects the rest of our lives. We no longer live or act or think or believe or see the world the same way. We are, in very real ways, a different person. The wrestling changes us. And it is a good thing, a God-blessed thing.

Deconstruction is that wrestling process. And just as Jacob's wrestling match occurred in the dark of night, it can feel like night while we're struggling. But, as in the story, the sun is coming up, and we are about to enter into a new phase, a new identity, with a new clarity in our walk with God.

From a personal stand-point, this insight had been intensely meaningful to me in my own D/R journey. Typical of the "Religious Disorientation Growth Syndrome" pathology, I wondered if I were, argument by argument, slowly walking my way away from the faith. Instead, I discovered that I was following in a great spiritual tradition, walking *toward* God.

James Kugel, Harvard University professor of Hebrew Literature, raises another insightful point in the Jacob story that can be marshalled in defense of deconstruction. Traditionally, Jacob's new name, Israel, has been understood to mean "struggled with God" *(isra-el),* as the text suggests: "Your name shall no longer be called Jacob, but Israel, for you have struggled with God and with men, and you have prevailed" (Gen 32:27-28). Citing a mix of Jewish and early Christian interpreters, Kugel offers another historical rendering: "man who saw God" *(ish-ra'a-el)* or perhaps, "he sees God" *(yashur-el).*[3] Philo of Alexandria, a Hellenistic Jewish philosopher and bible interpreter writing at the time of the first apostles, seems to read it that way: "For seeing is the lot of the freeborn and firstborn Israel, which translated is '[the one] seeing God'" (*On Flight and Finding* 208; also, *On Dreams* 172). And the later 10th century midrash attributed to the "school of Elijah the Prophet," *Seder Eliahu Rabba* 25, reads, "In place of 'Israel,' read '[each] man saw God' *('ish ra'a el)*, for all his deeds were straight before Him."[4]

This idea is not limited to Jewish texts. Kugel includes similar quotations from early Church thinkers, Hippolytus of Rome, Origen, Eusebius, John Chrysostom, Augustine, and even finds support in the Gnostic text *On the Origin of the World* 105:20-25, from the Nag Hammadi library: "Thereafter He created a congregation of angels ... and a firstborn called Israel, which is 'the man that sees God.'"[5]

This has profound exegetical and homiletical implications about the divinely intended destination of God-seekers.

> For if, in its underlying level of meaning, Israel meant "man seeing God" or (as Philo said) "the mind that contemplates God and the world," then the bible [becomes] not merely the saga of a particular people that had lived in a particular place and time, but the timeless, placeless account of *all* who seek to "see" God.[6]

Jacob's nighttime encounter, then, becomes the very case-in-point demonstrating that deconstruction/ reconstruction, the wrestling match with the divine, is a divinely-condoned prerogative of those "freeborn and firstborn" who seek to attain an expanded view of God.

Jacob, of course, was not the first in Scripture to contend with God. His grandfather, Abraham, famously dickered with God over the punishment of Sodom and Gomorrah (Gen 18). When the three angelic visitors appeared to Abraham (another textually-implied theophany) and announced that the cities were about to be destroyed, Abraham objected to the unjust killing of the righteous who also lived there. "Will you sweep away the righteous with the wicked? What if there are fifty righteous people in the city? ... Far be it from you to do such a thing. ... Far be it from you! Will not the Judge of all the earth do right?" (18:23-25). Abraham was bold in his challenge, and again, far from being rebuked, God relented. "If I find fifty righteous people in the city of Sodom, I will spare the whole place for their sake." Abraham does not stop there. The questions, the challenges, are not meant to be a one-time event. They are a lifestyle of the righteous. What if there are 45? What if there are 40? 30? 20? 10? Six different times Abraham challenges God, and each time God accedes to Abraham's challenge without rebuff.

Moses argues with God a number of times, from the very moment of his calling at the burning bush ("Who am I, that I should go?"; Ex 3:11) through his leading the people out of Egypt into the wilderness. At the foot of Sinai, when the emigrants cast a golden calf and worshipped it, and God announced his plan to destroy them, Moses again challenged God, and "then the LORD relented" (Ex 32:11-14).

One might cite episodes in the Hebrew prophets and wisdom literature where some back-and-forth occurred between God and the human, particularly the case of Job where he makes his plaintiff stance, "I would speak to the Almighty, to argue my case with God" (Job 13:3). God's notorious response to Job—"where were you when I laid the foundation of the earth? Tell me, if you have understanding ...." (Job 38:4)—so often understood as rebuke, can be read with a different tone and intent. Job, as the end of the story so clearly demonstrates, far from being crushed for his audacious challenge of God, is instead granted a new perspective on reality and is doubly blessed.

Bible and practical theology professor, Ellen Davis offers some beautiful insight into this complex story, suggesting that God, in his lengthy revelation to Job, unveils the "pizzazz" of creation, sharing with Job a "God's-eye view of the world."[7] It was not meant to "put Job in his place," to humiliate him in a bullying show of power, but instead to cause an eye-opening shift in his perspective. Job, by laying out his beliefs about God and the nature of the universe, open to correction and adjustment, is another paragon of deconstruction, and in the end, he is commended by God and richly favored. It is his friends who "had all the answers," who had such certainty and voiced the traditional "correct" views, who are ultimately rebuked and dismissed.

Davis makes a point that speaks to the evangelical fear of this D/R process: "Here is the acute paradox that lies at the heart of this book, and also the reason the church is afraid of it: Job rails against God, not as a skeptic, not as a stranger to God's justice, but precisely as a believer. It is the very depth of Job's commitment to God ... that makes his rage so fierce."[8] The act of deconstruction is born out of serious conviction, a genuine desire to get to the heart of truth. It is a courageous effort to experience (or not) the Divine in a new, unfettered way. Job, like the other biblical examples of those who dared to step out of a place of submissive acceptance and confront God, end up with an expanded view of reality, and walk away blessed, with a richer connection with the God they challenged. *This* is the heart and soul, the very purpose, of faith deconstruction.

The pastoral point I try to bring out from these passages is that God seems to enjoy, not simply indulge, engagement with his beloved creatures, those made in his image. It is through these sometimes-argumentative engagements that God reveals more of himself to us. And I frequently point back to our origin stories in Genesis which paint God walking with Adam and Eve in the Garden in the cool of the day. God, as portrayed in Scripture, is approachable, engageable, and even willing to argue and be persuaded by us.

This may be a surprising point for fundamentalists and evangelicals groomed for unquestioning obedience to the Almighty, but it is a familiar perspective in rabbinic literature as well. There is a well-known Talmudic story, recounted in Baba Metzia 59a-b, where the sages are debating a point of law over the ritual status of a new type of oven constructed at Akhnai. Rabbi Eliezer argued that it was pure, others that it was impure. Rabbi Eliezer invoked supernatural signs to convince his colleagues, including commanding a carob tree to be uprooted and moved 100 cubits away, causing a stream of water to flow backwards, the walls of the Beit Midrash (schoolhouse) to move, and finally calling upon a heavenly voice which agreed with him. When Rabbi Joshua disputed all these signs, stating that halachic decisions were not decided by miracles but by the rabbinic majority, it is said that God, who was watching and engaging—agreeing with Rabbi Eliezer—sat back and smiled. "What did the Holy One, blessed be He, do at that moment? [The prophet] Elijah replied: 'He laughed, saying, My children have defeated me, my children have defeated me.'"[9] Jewish tradition embraces the idea of dialogue and interchange—even disagreement—as a normal, even healthy, dynamic between God and humanity. The Holy One, the Creator and Master of the Universe, exalted as he is, delights in engaging his children.

The Apostles & the Early Church Deconstructed

This Talmudic story is engaging and illustrative, but for evangelicals would be unconvincing. To the point where deconstruction involves rethinking, reinterpreting Holy Scripture, even to contradicting its plain text meaning—ie, "arguing" with Scripture—more persuasive is the case of the early church recorded in Scripture itself.

The Acts of the Apostles recounts the debates, the struggle, involved in accepting non-Jewish believers into the early community of faith: were they obligated to embrace Torah observance, the Jewish Law, in order to be followers of Jesus, the Jewish Messiah? Hebrew Scripture clearly stated so. Circumcision, Sabbath observance, and a host of kashrut and purity laws were incumbent on any who would join the people of Israel. But imposing that requirement seemed to belittle the work accomplished by Christ. Was faith enough, or was the Law also needed for salvation and inclusion? The issue nearly split the nascent church, with heavy-weights like the Apostles Peter and Paul on one side, and the Apostle James and the "Judaizers" on the other. What decided the issue was *not* an appeal to Scripture. It was, in contrast with the rabbinic ruling over the oven of Akhnai, decided by a move of God himself.

The Book of Acts records a series of encounters where the Spirit's direct intervention testified definitively that Gentile inclusion—which the Apostle Paul would equate to "salvation"—was *not* dependent of Torah observance.[10] This point is particularly relevant to contemporary evangelicals, because salvation by faith in Christ alone is a cornerstone of evangelicalism,[11] and this fact is frequently used to justify ignoring "the Law" when it comes to lifestyle matters like dietary and clothing rules, and even the most sacrosanct commandments about circumcision and Sabbath observance. This can be a helpful defense for deconstructors when they are accused of "twisting" or "cherry-picking" Scripture to suit their liberal and "universalist" theology.

First, the Apostle Peter has a vision in Jaffa where a tablecloth bearing "unclean" meats was lowered from heaven and offered for him to eat (Acts 10). He refused three times, and each time, a heavenly voice commanded him, "Do not call anything impure that God has made clean." Peter understands this refers to Gentiles when servants from Cornelius, a Roman centurion, immediately appear at his door, inviting him to come preach the Good News to them in Caesarea. "God has shown me that I should not call any man impure or unclean. ... I now realize how true it is that God does not show favoritism but accepts men from every nation ..." (10:28,34-35). And while Peter shared the formerly exclusive Jewish gospel, the "gift of the Holy Spirit was poured out even on the Gentiles," to the surprise of the Jews present, and those Gentiles began "speaking in tongues and praising God" (10:43-46). Peter's revelation, and the miraculous experience that followed, directly contradicted the plain and accepted reading of the Hebrew Scriptures. When criticized by the other apostles for his fraternizing with Gentiles—"you went into the house of uncircumcised men and ate with them!" (11:2)—Peter used the divine initiative as his defense. "Who was I to think that I could oppose God?" (11:17). His argument was accepted.[12] The apostles and elders understood, typical of Jewish rules of exegesis, that Scripture was pliable, and interpretations and applications could legitimately stretch to accommodate real-life situations,[13] especially when God's hand was evident.

This is another turning-point moment, because it demonstrated that Scripture could be reinterpreted, even radically, and reapplied in a more gracious way if its traditional imposition seemed too burdensome or contrary to the manifest will of God. Peter's summation at the Council of Jerusalem: "Now then, why do you try to test God by putting on the necks of the disciples a yoke that neither we nor our fathers have been able to bear?" (15:10). Based on a new revelation, they could derive a new understanding of God's plan that had not before been considered—even seemingly contrary to what was plainly written in Scripture.[14]

Likewise, Saul/Paul had a visionary experience on the road to Damascus that overturned his strict understanding of Jewish purity, redefined his understanding of the coming of the Kingdom of God, the person and mission of Messiah and the community of faith, and even revolutionized his understanding of the nature of the Godhead. Protestants tend to view Paul's concern mostly over the role of Law versus Grace in the life of the believer, but this is far too narrow. Triggered by his new revelation, he was forced to rethink virtually *everything* he believed up to that point, and those new perspectives infused his spirituality and mysticism with fresh vitality and energy.[15]

Until that encounter on the road, he had been persecuting Jewish Christians, believing them to be corruptors of the pure faith. But when halted on his journey by a blinding light and heavenly voice, he was told "I am Jesus, whom you are persecuting" (Acts 9:1-6)—God was embodied in the people of this new, "heretical" movement. This encounter contradicted everything in his religious worldview. Then began a multi-year journey of re-evaluating everything he knew until then to be true. His deconstruction led him to challenge not only the traditions of his former faith but even the accepted religious leaders and authoritative voices of his new faith.[16] The result of that long and painful process, however, was that Saul/Paul became the "apostle to the Gentiles," and was responsible for writing about one-third of what would become the New Testament.

Paul's vision triggered new perspectives on his former beliefs, and reshaped how he understood God from that point onward.[17] "Christ crucified"—the absurd innovation of a Messiah who accomplishes cosmic and spiritual redemption of his people through his earthly failure and death[18]—became his new hermeneutical lens through which he would reinterpret and expound Scripture. And with that new perspective, he would be a principal force in the movement of reconciling Jewish and non-Jewish converts into the new faith. He could then write with deepest conviction the new and radical idea that "there is no longer Jew or Greek; there is no longer slave or free; there is no longer male and female, for all of you are one in Christ Jesus" (Gal 3:28).

As Peter and Paul's experiences reveal, fresh revelation trumps religious convention. It even overrides a plain reading of written Scripture, birthing new insights, new meaning, from the holy texts—meanings which challenged both tradition and the religious establishment, but which also generated new life for the Church and for the spiritual seekers of that time. Peter and Paul were among the first in the new faith to undergo the deconstruction/reconstruction process.*

Jesus Deconstructed

But even Jesus, before the apostles, provides examples of deconstructing and reconstructing the institutional faith, challenging accepted tradition and readings of Scripture, providing alternate—sometimes directly contradictory—interpretations. In fact, "deconstructing" the Judaism of his day was one of Jesus's primary activities; the Gospels are full of his revisionist teachings of basic tenets of the faith, stripped down to their core to expose the heart of God's message. Jesus is, for Christians, our most convincing argument and example of theological deconstruction and reconstruction. A few examples will help illuminate the point.

"Repent, for the kingdom of heaven is near." So begins Jesus's preaching ministry described in Mark and Matthew's gospels. It is tempting to jump immediately on the very first word proclaimed, "repent," and rush to its Greek meaning: *metanoia*, literally to change one's mind, change one's thinking.[19] This is certainly appropriate to theological deconstruction. But Jesus was a Palestinian rabbi. He almost certainly

---

* These points are all particularly relevant to the discussion of LGBTQ+ affirmation in the church. Evangelicals typically rely on a handful of "clobber passages" in the bible which seem to condemn same-sex sexual relations. There are legitimate arguments to be made in retranslating the passages and investigating their historical context to arrive at other conclusions, but Peter and Paul's revelatory experiences which show the love and inclusion of God overriding the "plain text" of Scripture can be more persuasive to evangelicals. "Call no one unclean whom I have called clean," is as powerful, revolutionary, and irresistible today as it was in the first century.

was not speaking Greek.[20] The Hebrew or Aramaic equivalent which he most likely would have used would have been *shuv*, meaning simply to "return." It has practical, lifestyle implications, emphasizing a change in one's behavior. This becomes clear when we notice that Jesus's words are anticipated by John the Baptist's use of exactly the same exhortation (Mt 3:2), where he elaborates the meaning of "repent": "Produce fruit in keeping with repentance ... every tree that does not produce good fruit will be cut down and thrown into the fire" (3:8-10). In Luke's account, John is asked to clarify, "What should we *do* then?," to which he instructs them to share tunics, not to collect more than the required taxes, not to extort money or wrongfully accuse people (Lk 3:10-14). The emphasis was on action, on doing what was right in God's sight.

But the word was understood to encompass a change in the orientation of one's heart as well. Thus, the call to repent would better be understood as a call to "return to God" or "return to the way of God" more than "change your mind" understood in a pensive way. Redirecting one's heart toward God, toward following the way of God, would naturally have outward repercussions: such repentance would lead to treating one's neighbor justly and with love. Jesus, in this matter, was following in the long line of Hebrew prophets calling the people back to Judaism's basic tenets of social justice—something the evangelical world, so tainted by its history of political machinations geared toward misogyny and patriarchy, racism and homophobia could well stand to give ear to. In this practical, "love your neighbor" sense, repentance is the first priority of faith deconstruction.

From that point on in his ministry, Jesus began systematically to dismantle and reassemble aspects of Judaism from within. The "kingdom of God" which he announced was a developing concept at the time, popularly understood in its apocalyptic sense when God would erupt into human history to establish a new world order based on justice, the security of the people of Israel, and God's manifest presence on earth. It was also understood by the more religiously sophisticated on a more personal level to refer to the "rule of God" in one's heart; that is, when one accepted the rule of God by declaring God's sovereignty (reciting the *Shema*) and accepting the "yoke of the commandments."[21] Jesus devoted much of his teaching to this second, "real-life" perspective of the kingdom. It was not something to passively wait for at the consummation of time; it was activated in one's life by repentance. As noted Jewish scholar Geza Vermes puts it, for Jesus, "the Kingdom of God is a mystery attainable only with human co-operation."[22] Put simply, the presence and power of God could be experienced in the here and now, for those who returned to God.

Jesus thus begins his ministry with addressing and correcting the basic perception of God's activity on earth, moving it from the apocalyptic future to the mundane present. He deconstructs the core concept of how God is perceived to work in the world, and for those who could accept it, it was indeed Good News (Mk 1:15).

In a similar fashion, Jesus challenged other accepted religious beliefs and practices, offering his own re-oriented alternatives. Sabbath observance, for example, was another area of religious life which had been misapplied, and instead of being a blessing and relief to people, had instead become a burden. In the synagogue and in personal homes, Jesus is criticized when he heals the sick on the Sabbath, since healing was considered work and therefore forbidden on the Sabbath. In one case, a man's right hand was shriveled, and Jesus restored his hand (Lk 6:6 ff); in another case, Jesus heals a man suffering from dropsy (Lk 14:1 ff). In both instances, his acts of compassion—despite clearly being displays of the benevolent power of God—arouse anger and criticism by Pharisees and teachers of the law because they violate religious convention. Jesus, in good pedagogic fashion, tries to get these religious leaders to see things differently by asking simple questions which get to the heart of the matter. "Which is lawful on the Sabbath: to do good or to do evil, to save life or to destroy it?" (Lk 6:9), or, "Is it lawful to heal on the Sabbath or not?" (Lk 14:3). If that were not fundamental enough, he points out that if their son, or their ox, had fallen into a well, surely they would be compelled by compassion to pull them out, even on a Sabbath. By drawing on specific, concrete examples, he is trying to lead them to make a broader conclusion.

On another occasion, his disciples are caught on the Sabbath plucking heads of grain in a field, rubbing them in their hands, and eating the kernels because they were hungry. This was considered threshing, clearly an act forbidden on the Sabbath. Jesus defends them by citing biblical precedent: didn't David and his companions eat consecrated bread reserved for the priests because they were hungry? And don't priests violate the Sabbath by performing their Temple duties—wasn't that work? These questions were meant to shift their point of view and return them to the original premise of the Sabbath as a gift to humanity: "Sabbath was made for man, not man for the Sabbath" (Mk 2:27). Their doctrinal rigidity missed the central principle and caused them to point accusing fingers at the guiltless: "If you had known what these words mean, 'I desire mercy, not sacrifice,' you would not have condemned the innocent" (Mt 12:7). Jesus rejects a heartless interpretation of a law, turning it back to a compassionate application.

This type of challenging accepted traditions and perspectives, often by referring to Scripture in a new way, is the basic premise of theological deconstruction. Six times, for example, in Matthew's lengthy Sermon on the Mount Jesus points to a common religious understanding, and refutes it, offering his own as a better interpretation: "You have heard that it was said ... But I tell you ..." (Mt 5:21-48). He compares murder with anger and insult. He compares adultery with lust and with sinful behavior ("if your right hand causes you to sin, cut it off ..."). Divorce is equated with adultery. Taking oaths is contrasted with simple integrity and clarity of letting "your 'yes' be 'yes' and your 'no,' 'no'; anything else comes from the evil one." The practice of hating one's enemy is countered with the command to love, just as the Father in heaven is good and gracious to both the evil and the good. In each case, Jesus turns a practice whose origin might be based in Scripture or found in conventional religious thinking, and commands a different approach, one more consonant with the gracious character of God.

It should be noted that Jesus is not (necessarily) making these rulings based solely on his authority as Messiah or Son of God. The formula "you have heard, but I say" was a recognized style of rabbinic argument. As historical-Jesus scholar, E.P. Sanders, notes, "in traditional Jewish debate, the verb 'say' means 'interpret.'" Similar language is frequently encountered, for example, in the Dead Sea Scrolls where the phrase "concerning this we say" means "this is our interpretation," and likewise in rabbinic literature, the expression "Rabbi X says ..." is used in the same way.[23] Jesus was thus engaging in public discourse using conventional rules. It was "a Rabbinic form expressing a contrast between the 'hearing', the 'literal understanding', of a rule and what we must 'say' it actually signifies";[24] that is, rendering a corrective opinion more in line with the heart of the initial narrowly-construed passage. In doing this, Jesus declares he is *not* abolishing or destroying the Law, he is fulfilling it—again, the heart of deconstruction and reconstruction: stripping away the malpractices and misapplications that have accumulated over time, and rediscovering and returning to the heart of the faith.[25]

When Jesus's disciples are criticized for not performing ritual fasts as expected (Lk 5:33-39), he responds with an intriguing parable about patches and wineskins. "No one tears a patch from a new garment and sews it on an old one. ... And no one pours new wine into old wineskins. ... No, new wine must be poured into new wineskins" (Lk 5:36-39). Perhaps he is inviting comparison of current practice against original intent; they are mismatched, inappropriate, and lead to disastrous results. And, in a way, this parable is another apt description of what happens in the D/R process: new understandings and perceptions can no longer be contained in old ways of thinking. New wine requires new wineskins.

This might also offer insight into Jesus's mysterious words to Nicodemus about being "born again" (John 3). This passage is particularly cherished by evangelicals, as this characterization of the conversion experience is one of the four central criteria for being identified as an evangelical.[26] In the passage, Nicodemus doesn't ask his question directly; it is subtly implied in a statement: "Rabbi, we know you are a teacher who has come from God." The unspoken request seems to be along the lines of, "The things you say and do don't line up with my understanding of the faith. Help me understand how to make sense of this." Jesus cuts straight to the heart of the matter: "I tell you the truth, no one can see the kingdom of God unless he is born again" (John 3:3).[27]

Evangelicals typically understand this in an ontological way: one's human spirit must be regenerated by the Holy Spirit in order to be saved, to enter into the Kingdom of God.

This is supported by Jesus's subsequent statement that "Spirit gives birth to spirit ...," and the explanation, "so it is with everyone born of the Spirit" (3:6,8). There are, of course, other possible understandings of Jesus's words. The expression, "born again," was not new with Jesus; it was an idiom current in the cultural milieu of the day, almost always understood figuratively. A convert to Judaism, for example, could be compared to a child newly born,[28] and in the Greek mystery religions, an initiate was thought to have been "born again" or entering a new life after undergoing secret rites of induction and being introduced to spiritual truths. Whether the experience Jesus refers to is an actual, ontological spiritual regeneration or the consequent state after an impartation by the Spirit (revelation, new insight), it was a well-accepted idea that a person could enter a new, awakened phase of life, almost as if starting again, after a profound experience. All this to suggest that Jesus calls us, like Nicodemus, to a radical shift in our perspectives, a reorientation so paradigm-altering that it could be called a "new birth." As Brian McLaren puts it, "The truth is, most of us who identify ourselves as born-again Christians could stand to be born again *again*. In fact, we need to be born again *again and again* ... born into a lifelong experiential learning adventure of discipleship."[29] In that sense, Jesus invited Nicodemus—and by extension, all of us—on a Spirit-initiated journey of deconstruction.

This becomes vitally important, not just in matters of theological or spiritual insight, but in how we treat others. Jesus again is our exemplar. Time and again we see Jesus in the gospels treating the religiously marginalized with special attention and respect. He spends time with them, socializes with them, to the point he himself is identified with them by the religious elites. Whether it is a Samaritan woman with a questionable sexual/marriage history, a woman caught in adultery, or hated tax collectors viewed as Roman collaborators and traitors, Jesus sees these "sinners" as the "meek," the "lowly of heart," the "poor [in spirit]"—prospective inheritors of the Kingdom of God. The label "sinner" in Jewish culture of the time was not simply someone who sinned. It was acknowledged that everyone occasionally sinned and could find reconciliation and restoration through repentance and atonement. The label is better associated with the biblical term "the wicked," a word reserved for those who habitually rejected God's law in their lives.[30] These were worthy of exclusion and repudiation. Yet it is these very people whom Jesus considered worthy of compassion, people still bearing the *imago dei*, still deserving of invitation to God's kingdom of grace, forgiveness, and love. In this, Jesus rejects heartless standards of judging a person's worth, and models for us what "loving our neighbor" looks like. He deconstructs social, religious rules of inclusion, and points us back to the rule of love.

Over and over, Jesus peeled away the accretion of unhealthy sediment accumulated over years of tradition and established practice, and cut to the heart of the faith. This is why, when tested by a teacher of the Law to name the greatest commandment, Jesus could without hesitation point to the foundation of it all: loving the Lord your God with all your being, and loving your neighbor as yourself. "All the Law and the Prophets hang on these two commandments" (Mt 22:35-39). A similar story is recounted in the Talmud about the rabbinic sage, Hillel the Elder, in the decades before Jesus. A Roman approached him, seeking to convert to Judaism, but only on condition that the rabbi would teach him the entire Torah while he stood on one foot. (Rabbi Shammai, whom he had approached first, was insulted by the request, and chased him away with a measuring stick.) Hillel gently responded, "What is hateful to you, do not do to your neighbor. This is the whole of Torah. All the rest is commentary. Now, go and learn!"[31] Both Hillel and Jesus point back to the essential foundation on which all Judeo-Christian religious values are built.[32]

Returning to the core of the faith, to the heart of God, on which all the secondary religious aspects depend, even at the expense of scrapping beloved traditions and favored biblical interpretations, is what the D/R journey is all about. All the rest is, indeed, commentary.

A Deconstructing Hermeneutic

When those rabbis were debating the ritual purity of that new oven at Akhnai, the final argument that made all of Rabbi Eliezer's supernatural signs irrelevant, even the divine voice, was Rabbi Joshua's simple declaration: "It is not in heaven,"[33] a reference to Dt 30:12. It was thus understood that since Torah had been given at Mt Sinai, the authority for interpreting it now rested exclusively in human hands: "no, the word is very near you; even in your mouth and in your heart so you may obey it" (Dt 30:14).

Arguing with Scripture, reinterpreting it, is an essential part of a living faith. A deconstructing hermeneutic is consistent with the methods used by Jesus, the apostles, and their rabbinic contemporaries. It means that Scripture is not locked in stone with unequivocal (or literal) meaning. It is alive. The Spirit still speaks through it, making it relevant to our current situations—if our hearts are sensitive enough to hear.

This is an important concept because one of the principal points of contention about deconstruction among evangelicals is that deconstructors "cherry-pick" Scripture. They accuse people who are disassembling their faith of taking great liberties with the bible, selecting verses that support their new stances while dismissing others that would refute those positions, or of ignoring the biblical context in which their new readings occur. (The irony often escapes them that so much of evangelical theology, especially the parts that undergird their socio-political agenda, is based on exactly this practice.)

Selective reading, in particular, was a method used by Jesus and the apostles (and rabbis), because the divine inspiration of Scripture was a given. Each line of text was holy, was inspired, and carried a layer of meaning waiting to be excavated. (In fact, Rabbi Akiva was known, and criticized, for reading meaning even into the decorative crowns on the Hebrew letters, the *kotz*, or thorns, reminiscent of Jesus's saying that "not one jot or tittle [the smallest letter (yod) or the least calligraphic stroke of a pen] will pass from the Law until everything is accomplished.") The rabbis could quote a few words lifted from a biblical passage and use it as the basis for an argument—even if the extracted words contradicted their plain meaning in context.[34] Every word was significant, standing in its own right. Similar to the "you have heard ... but I say" argument used by Jesus and rabbis of the time, the lesson derived could even be opposed to the literal reading. "What the text 'says', *'amar*, or what is 'written' in it, *kathubh*, is constantly opposed to what it 'tells' you, *higgidh*. ... Frequently the contrast is between what the text 'says' or what is 'written' in it and what it 'teaches', *limmedh*, or what you may 'learn', *lamadh*."[35] Thus, "cherry-picking" was a credible method of deriving deeper meaning and practical application from holy text.

Jesus's inaugural sermon in Nazareth, where he reads from the Jubilee passage in Isaiah 61, is a primary example. Here, Jesus highlights all the positive aspects of God's redemptive action,

> The Spirit of the Lord is on me,
> because he has anointed me
> to proclaim good news to the poor.
> He has sent me to proclaim freedom for the prisoners
> and recovery of sight for the blind,
> to set the oppressed free,
> to proclaim the year of the Lord's favor
> (Lk 4:18-19 | Is 61:1-2).

What shocks the congregation gathered in the synagogue as much as his claim to fulfill that prophesy in their presence, was, perhaps, his omission of a beloved part of it: God's wrath. They awaited God's vindication of them as a nation. They eagerly anticipated the eruption of God into their reality, executing justice—judgment—on their oppressors, expelling their Roman occupiers, and ushering in a new, idyllic age of restoration, peace, joy, and comfort—just as Isaiah prophesied. In short, they expected God to *finally* fulfil the promises of his everlasting covenant with them. But where was the promised "day of vengeance of our God"—the very next line after "the year of the Lord's favor" in Isaiah's prophesy? Instead, there stood this humble man who had barely begun his ministry. Jesus "selectively" omits the violence imagined with that anticipated Day of the LORD. He instead emphasized the healing, the proclamation of freedom, and the restoration of the poor. He reshapes the tradition, turning the "accepted" understanding on its head. In doing so, he defines who he is and what his purpose and mission are—characterized by grace—despite public expectation. The result: "all the people in the synagogue were furious," and they drove him out of town, to the top of a hill to throw him down the cliff (Lk 4:28-29). Tampering with beloved traditions is generally not received well—now as much as then.

Similarly, later when John the Baptist is languishing in Herod's prison, waiting in frustration for Jesus to usher in that vengeful day, he sends his disciples to Jesus to ask about it: "Are you the one who was to come, or should we look for another?" (Lk 7:19). Jesus responds, "Go tell John what you see and hear," and then recites a summary of his activities which align with the positive aspects of prophetic expectation: the blind receive sight (Is 29:18; 35:5; 61:1-2), the lame walk (Is 35:6), lepers are cured (2 Kgs 5:1-27), the deaf hear (Is 29:18; 35:5), the dead are raised (Is 26:19; 1 Kgs 17:17-34), and the good news is proclaimed to the poor (Is 29:19).[36]

What is telling is what Jesus *omits* from those same referenced texts. From Isaiah, he omits mention of eliminating the tyrant and scoffers, cutting off the evil doers (Is 29:20). He omits God coming with "vengeance and terrible recompense" (Is 35:4; Is 61:2).[37] In the judicious choice of Scripture, Jesus redefines his messianic role and the expectation of what divine deliverance looks like. Or, as New Testament scholar Joseph Fitzmyer puts it, "Yes, I have come, but not in the sense that you mean it, not as a fiery reformer."[38]

It would take another full length book to scan through the Book of Acts and demonstrate how the apostles selectively used Hebrew Scripture to "read" Jesus into them, and how the Apostle Paul in his epistles also picked and chose phrases from Scripture to defend his evangelistic claim of "Christ crucified" and Gentile inclusion while deliberately omitting complete sections in context that portray the wrathful side of God.[39] The point is not simply that Jesus and the apostles cherry-picked, but that they reshaped the message they proclaimed through the process. They redefined the message of the gospel, highlighting the love and mercy of God while simultaneously hiding the violent and vengeful aspects ascribed to God by the ancient writers. That is, they intentionally read—and deliberately reinterpreted—Scripture through the hermeneutical lens of divine love and grace.

In this sense, the rabbis, Jesus, the apostles, and we today, all read our sacred texts in ways that are meaningful and specific to our immediate context—meanings that may be quite foreign to the author's original intent (if that were even discernible). And, to belabor the point a little longer, it highlights the actual *dangers* of holding too tightly to a literal reading of Scripture, what Ricoeur called the "fallacy of the absolute text," as distinguished from the "semantic autonomy" utilized by Jesus, the rabbis and apostles. As Ricoeur puts it, the "author's intention and the meaning of the text cease to coincide ... [and] what the text means now matters more than what the author meant when he wrote it."[40] If Jesus and the apostles had been confined to a literal reading of existing Scripture, bound to the authors' "original intent," our gospel and theology would now be limited to the short-term, narrow vision and incomplete understanding of the ancient writers. Such a tight holding limits us and limits what God wants to reveal to us.

Thus, in cherry-picking a text, in reading it selectively, one *may* actually extract a meaning believed to be more consistent with an evolved or enlightened ("better," more desirable) view of both God and God's activity on earth, the Kingdom of God. And while the results could go in either direction (a gross misreading or a fresh, more loving understanding), this "hermeneutic of love," of nonviolence and non-vengeance, gets us closer to the character of God so carefully presented to us by Jesus. It is the portrait of the *Abba* of Jesus's "Prodigal Son" who longs for our return, who extends grace and forgiveness unilaterally, who sits with the "clean" and the "unclean" alike, and whose redemptive power is active in the here and now.

A Christian deconstructing hermeneutic follows this "cherry-picking" methodology with the specific goal of presenting God and the gospel in the light of these benevolent images. References to wrath and destruction are to be downplayed or selectively omitted—as Jesus, and to some degree Paul, did. Jesus presented himself as the fulfillment and embodiment of the blessings of the covenant with God. Why would Christians choose to bypass that preferred portrayal and focus instead on the blood-demanding, sin-hating, angry God needing appeasement before he can even be approached? If Jesus is the image of the invisible God, the exact imprint of God's nature, as is repeatedly asserted in the New Testament,[41] then God must look—be—more like Jesus than these other more negative images.[42] The deconstructing hermeneutic reads Scripture through the lens of Jesus, and sees in God only the welcoming, forgiving, reconciling, gracious, and loving Divine Parent. It is not an unfaithful witness to the full testimony of Scripture any more than Jesus's use was unfaithful, but rather chooses to read Scripture with eyes set on its fulfillment and ultimate blessing.[43]

This is the approach needed to heal generations scarred by centuries of doctrine focused centrally on sin, punishment, and a wrathful God. It is the message, the Good News, that can save the individual and redeem the Church.

This is what the faith deconstruction process attempts to do.

Conclusion

We spent much of this discussion focused on Jesus because he is, for Christians, the final and ultimate authority. "This is my beloved Son; with him I am well pleased. Listen to him," the heavenly voice declared at Jesus's transfiguration on the mountain. And Jesus repeatedly points us away from our entrenched beliefs, he challenges us to tear down the religious edifices we have constructed, and to rebuild, re-construct, afresh on the foundations of mercy and love.

The Hebrew patriarchs and prophets argued with God. The apostles and early church wrestled with themselves, their culture, and with Scripture. They all grappled with their accepted beliefs and comfortable perspectives, they struggled to understand real-life circumstances in a new way. And they inevitably came out of those dark, confusing moments of conflict with a clarity and an expanded vision of God and the world around them. And that new vision was always a re-affirmation of the core of the faith they held so dear, yet with a deeper and wider understanding of the gracious character of the God they thought they already knew.

This is the journey of faith deconstruction and reconstruction. It is essential not only for a renewal and reformation of the corporate faith, but is vital for the personal spiritual growth of the individual.

It is normative. It is healthy. And it is biblical.

4

The Act of Ministry: Launching the Evolving Faiths Discussion Group

"Most young adults I know aren't looking for a religion that answers all of their questions, but rather a community of faith in which they feel safe to ask them.

~ RACHEL HELD EVANS[1]

Chapter 2 discussed the somewhat "colorful" recent history of the evangelical church world in the U.S. The overt aggression of the Religious Right in civil rights social politics, in addition to the well-publicized scandals largely involving evangelical leaders, created an atmosphere of pessimism relating to the Church. People in general are still very spiritually-oriented, and those outside the Church looked elsewhere in statistically significant numbers. Those who stayed in, or were recently born into, the Church had good reason to question the doctrines and cultural values they were being fed. But fundamentalist and evangelical leaders are generally quick to stamp out questions, to resist challenges to tradition and to their authority, and to even instill fear of hell in those who seek a more compassionate and gracious God. This is why a bible-based defense of deconstruction, as laid out in Chapter 3, is so critical. Seekers who still cling to Scripture need a perspective that does justice to Scripture, at least to their minds' satisfaction. In effect, they need "biblical permission" to rethink what they'd been taught.

In my church, I began to plant the seeds of that theology before we launched the Discussion Group, but in reality, the people who quickly joined the project were already ripe and waiting.

In this chapter, I will retrace the steps and the questions that were addressed in launching and maintaining the Discussion Group: questions of intent, of self-definition, of format, duration, and even something as mundane as meeting frequency and preferred day of the week. (It is often those mundane, trivial details that will make or break a church-implemented program.) From the beginning, the pastoral staff adopted a "roll with it" attitude, somewhat in line with the dynamic nature of action research, recognizing that we would be largely improvising and making adjustments along the way as needed.

This chapter will also describe who showed up and who stayed, along with providing a sample of the wide-range of topics we explored. People have a voracious appetite for discussion on theology as it relates to all the aspects of their lives, and a sampling of some of the participants' comments will be included to offer a sense of what was going on at the time. Finally, I will offer a few take-away observations gleaned from the process. Fuller use of participant significant statements along with analysis and interpretation of the qualitative data will be presented in the next chapter.

Planning the Project: What Happened?

After the pastoral team agreed to implement the support group, one of my first hurdles was coming up with a name for it. The image of the biblical patriarch Jacob wrestling with God, and that becoming the naming characteristic of God's chosen people, prompted the idea of calling it the "Israel Group." How better to demonstrate that questioning God and one's faith is completely in line with God's will and desire for his people. As I'd been saying in sermons leading up the official announcement, God, I believe, is delighted with our questions; he is not challenged, nor angered by them. They are not a sign of doubt and skepticism, but rather the sign of a vibrant, living, and growing (dare I say, "evolving") faith. But maybe "Israel" was too problematic, too political: the Israeli/Palestinian conflict is never far from the news, and I did not want our name to suggest we were a Christian Zionist group nor that we were taking sides in a political and ethical struggle.

We considered the obvious choice of calling it "the Deconstruction Group." But by then, we'd all been inundated with the on-going heated diatribes of the evangelical press over the term "deconstruction," to the point we often wanted to dissociate from the word entirely. Like the word "evangelical" itself, or even "Christian," "deconstruction" was accumulating a heavy baggage of meanings and reactions we felt might smother the group even before it began.[2] After much back and forth between my co-pastor Neill and myself, we decided that officially it would be called "Evolving Faiths Discussion Group" and informally simply as "the Discussion Group."

• Logistics

Planning and organizing the support group consumed more time and mental energy than the actual group meetings would. Because we were renting an event center for our Sunday services and did not have access to the building during the rest of the week, we felt at a distinct disadvantage. The plans would begin to take shape slowly, and were a collaborative effort.

The church already had a Thursday fellowship group which had been going on for months, meeting weekly at various restaurants where we could gather, eat, and have some kind of casual conversation. It was from these weekly meetings that the pressure to launch the D/R Group grew. Eric and Lauren were the latest to add their voices. They were a straight, married couple who had first visited The Abbey one Sunday in October, and like Kevin and Analise months before, seemed to deliberately use the "D-word" as though it were a secret password. Then the following week, they showed up at our Thursday fellowship group dinner at The Garage. They had an agenda: they wanted to know more about the church, our beliefs and backgrounds, especially our views on women in ministry and whether they, as a straight couple, would "cramp our style" (Lauren's words).

Minutes later, as we'd resumed consuming our burgers and sweet potato fries, she casually turned to me. "Steve, didn't I hear that you're working on your doctoral degree?" That caught me off guard because I couldn't recall mentioning it anywhere she might have heard that in the two weeks since they'd first visited us, but I was happy to launch into a quick introduction to my D.Min. program at VTS. I must have mentioned the topic of deconstruction because she jumped on the term immediately: "yes, yes, Eric and I are both deconstructing ..." and she began describing their Church of Christ background and how they were no longer satisfied with their church's doctrines and positions. Their children, both in their teens, were so much more inclusive and progressive, and were challenging their parents to be as well. "So, when are you going to start the deconstruction group?" "Funny," I replied, "we were talking about it last week, and I was just about to bring it up again."

One of our initial logistical questions in planning the group had been about whether meeting on another night of the week, in addition to our Fellowship group, was practical. Eric and Lauren confirmed that adding another night for the group would not work with their already busy schedules. That cinched the Thursday night slot for me. But trying to have meaningful theological—and personal—conversations in a crowded restaurant over dinner presented genuine logistical problems. Not only were acoustics an issue—hearing each other over the din—but confidentiality and privacy issues were involved. Would people feel free to expose their doubts and questions in a place where they might be overheard by strangers or by people who might know them? Someone proposed using a meeting room at the public library down the street. My immediate sense was negative, but no other option presented itself.

I debated the idea over the next week, feeling particularly conflicted. My co-pastor loved the idea. It would open us up to the community and might be a legitimate outreach ministry to those outside our little church family. But I felt that meeting at one place for dinner, then leaving and all meeting up again at another venue 15 minutes later was inviting people to simply go home after they got in their cars. I was also uncomfortable with the idea of a public group. I thought the potential for constantly shifting attenders, along with the inherent lack of confidentiality, would limit the personal growth that could occur within a stable group.[3] It would, of necessity, keep us tied to isolated conversations;

there potentially would be no continuity or flow from week to week.

Michael solved the problem for us the following week. When the topic of proposed location for the group was mentioned, along with my concerns about privacy issues, he chimed in that he really loved the private room at Louie's Grill we'd met at months before. It was perfect. We could eat and then flow right into focused discussion without having to move from our seats. No disruptions. And we could stomach their menu one night a month. That settled the matter, and I announced it from the pulpit the next Sunday.

This incident demonstrates a principle I hoped to see proven repeatedly over the coming months: the voice of God conveyed through the voice of our people. It was a logical extension of the basic concept for the D/R group: that wisdom and revelation would come from God's people as they sat and talked together. "Where two or three are gathered in my name," as Jesus had said, we expected not just his presence but his voice. And, functionally, it conformed to the adaptability of the action research paradigm I modeled the project after.

The group also unanimously altered our schedule. I had announced that on the first Thursday of every month, our weekly eat-out meet-up would be split into two activities. From 7:00 to 8:00 pm, we would eat and hang out together as usual. But from 8:00 to 9:00 we would shift gears and focus on spiritual topics of conversation, especially those related to deconstruction. By the end of our first discussion, the group decided they wanted to do this more than once a month. Some suggested doing it every week, eating and then focused conversation, but I also heard from others that they didn't want to miss group meetings, but eating out every week was an expense they would be uncomfortable affording. Ultimately, I made the decision that we would (at least for the immediate future) meet twice a month, on the first and third Thursdays, for food and discussion. Out of this financial consideration, the venue also eventually changed, where we would meet at a local residential community clubhouse for Discussion Group instead of at a restaurant. This proved to be a more agreeable and affordable option.

That first meeting in a private room of Louie's Grill was such an unexpected success with all involved that I made this comment on social media the next morning:

> We had our first "Decon/Recon" Discussion/Support group meeting last night. And this morning all that is going thru my head is that Pauline prayer about "the glorious riches in the inheritance in the saints." Such beautiful, wonderful, and entertainingly neurotic, saints I get to hang out with. This morning, I feel incredibly blessed. And I thank God for bringing such a rich and diverse collection of people into my life. I am truly richer because of all you beautiful people.

By way of personal comment, as a "participant-researcher," I have to add that I was—and continue to be—amazed at the success of this experiment. Going in, I was not sure how many people would attend or how long it would last. I felt certain that the time was ripe, even if just for a short window of time, to launch this group, but as somewhat of a reluctant pastor and a bit of a pessimist, I half-expected it to die out after a few meetings. But, through winter storms, pandemic resurgence where we met twice virtually via Zoom, the holiday season, and summer vacations and lethargy, the group continued to meet twice monthly, and has proven to be the most spiritually enriching and personally gratifying ministry experience of this pastor. Our fourth group meeting fell on my 60th birthday. We met at Louie's Grill in the private room, just a handful of us (as half our group at the time were self-isolating due to COVID exposure). No one knew it was my birthday, let alone a milestone one, and I was feeling so happy to be there with that group, talking about serious and trivial matters of faith and our spiritual journeys. And I remember thinking I wouldn't want to be anywhere else.

The morning after another group meeting, still reeling from the mental and social stimulation of the wide-ranging topics we discussed, I posted on Facebook, and copied into my research notes as I had that first entry:

> You know those moments in life when you feel like you're in exactly the right spot doing exactly what you were born to do?
>
> That's how I felt last night at The Abbey deconstruction discussion group.
>
> So many different topics during the conversation (must have been about a dozen), so many insights from the group members, so many fresh perspectives—from people asking questions about their faith. Not in skepticism, not cynically, but genuine, heart-felt and open-minded.
>
> We hit on heaven and hell, the nature of God, the nature of the soul, Elie Weisel, process theology, advaita and Hinduism, free will and choices and mathematical models of probability (possibility and the multiverse), paradigm-breaking to get a bigger view of God, the power of ritual and symbols in expressing spirituality and the ability to interconnect us, living without regard to the afterlife or promise/threat of eternal reward or punishment (living to live, not living to die), the restoration (vs destruction) of the earth in the ultimate divine design,

> Judgment Day and how that might be more reflective of the Hebrew concept of justice (restoration and healing, not punishment-focused)...
>
> All in 2 hours over burgers and pizza.
>
> The famous rabbi and scholar Abraham Joshua Heschel once said that "We are closer to God when we are asking questions than when we think we have the answers." And I felt the presence of the Spirit in that group last night.
>
> You guys are awesome. You're rocking my faith and my world. And I love you all. You're in the right place.

I had never experienced anything like this.

• What kind of group is this?

Another question I wrestled with during the initial months of planning was, were we a "recovery" group or not? We were first and foremost a pastoral ministry. We would deal with the hurt and issues that caused people to deconstruct. Did we need to lay down ground rules for group behavior before we even began (as seemed wise), or would that stifle the natural flow and authenticity of the personality-dynamics already in play in the fellowship group? As a model for a Christian support group, I looked at Celebrate Recovery's five "Small Group Guidelines,"[4] but really only liked Number 3: "We are here to support one another, not 'fix' one another." This aligned with what I'd been saying from the pulpit about a core principle for the group: "We're not here to supply the 'right answers'; we're here to support and spur each other on our journey. Let's treat each other's evolving views with respect, even if we don't agree with them."

Reading further in Celebrate Recovery's literature settled the issue for me, as I wrote in my notes. I wanted to embrace some of the supportive aspects of a 12-Step program, but a quick look at Celebrate Recovery's devotional, for example, proved that this was the wrong approach. The very first devotional, "Day 1: The First Step," began with a quotation from Romans 7:18: "I know that nothing good lives in me, that is, in my sinful nature (flesh). For I have the desire to do good, but cannot carry it out."[5] This was exactly the *opposite* approach to what I intended. We *affirm* the human condition and the flesh; we believe the quest is God-inspired and not a fault of sinful minds resisting God or truth. We are not trying to break a bad or addictive habit. We are pursuing, exploring something good. Along the same lines, their 5th Guideline I particularly disagreed with: "Offensive language has no place in a Christ-centered recovery group."[6] They obviously did not have much experience with LGBTQ folk. Profanity and sexuality were part of the common vernacular, considered an essential part of one's humanity—even among LGBTQ Christians. To stifle that would be to stifle authenticity and impose a form of church oppression most of us were rebelling and "recovering" from! Celebrate Recovery's approach would definitely not work for us.

I continued researching support group formats and discovered the ten foundational principles of support/ recovery groups for the National Alliance on Mental Illness (NAMI). Obviously, I did not consider deconstruction any form of mental illness, but the underlying tone and framework for support group dynamics seemed much more in line with how I envisioned our D/R Discussion Group.

1. **Self-Direction**. Individuals determine their own path of recovery with autonomy, independence, and control of their resources.

2. **Individualized and Person-Centered**. There are multiple pathways to recovery based on an individual's unique strengths as well as his or her needs, preferences, experiences, and cultural background.
3. **Empowerment**. Consumers have the authority to participate in all decisions that will affect their lives, and they are educated and supported in this process.
4. **Holistic**. Recovery encompasses an individual's whole life, including mind, body, spirit, and community. Recovery embraces all aspects of life, including housing, social networks, employment, education, mental health and health care treatment, and family supports.
5. **Non-Linear**. Recovery is not a step-by step process but one based on continual growth, occasional setbacks, and learning from experience.
6. **Strengths-Based**. Recovery focuses on valuing and building on the multiple capacities, resiliencies, talents, coping abilities, and inherent worth of individuals. The process of recovery moves forward through interaction with others in supportive, trust-based relationships.
7. **Peer Support**. Mutual support plays an invaluable role in recovery. Consumers encourage and engage others in recovery and provide each other with a sense of belonging.
8. **Respect**. Eliminating discrimination and stigma are crucial in achieving recovery. Self-acceptance and regaining belief in oneself are particularly vital.
9. **Responsibility**. Consumers have a personal responsibility for their own self-care and journeys

of recovery. Consumers identify coping strategies and healing processes to promote their own wellness.

10. **Hope**. Hope is the catalyst of the recovery process and provides the essential and motivating message of a positive future. Peers, families, friends, providers, and others can help foster hope.[7]

Individualized, empowerment, holistic, non-linear, peer support, respect, hope—these were values that resonated with my vision for this group.

My initial desire had been primarily to create a "safe space," and as discussed in Chapter 2, sociological research for the past 20 years confirmed that "authenticity"—the freedom to be one's true self, unfiltered by religious pretension—was a critical concern of Millennials and Gen Zs in selecting (or declining) religious affiliation. Echoing that concern, Mary Clark Moschella, professor of pastoral care and counseling at Yale Divinity School, wrote about the qualities that differentiated a "real" community from a "pseudo-community." A real community, she writes, is "a place where people are free to be themselves and know that they will be accepted, a space where conflict can be expressed and resolved, and a place where diversity of opinion is honored. A pseudo-community, by contrast, may seem friendly at first, but it is really not a safe place in which to express an opinion that diverges from the group's stated values. If you are different in a pseudo-community, you feel it immediately; you feel pressured, not safe. You sense that you don't fit in, that there is no room for difference of opinion, and you may 'go into hiding.'"[8] This is exactly what the younger generations, particularly in the LGBTQ community, sense intuitively, and I wanted to address.

Adopting these group principles defined by NAMI, with special attention paid to the importance of authenticity, would help create the kind of environment that would meet those "safe" and "real" community criteria.

• Who's in charge here?

I wrestled, too, with the organization and leadership-style of the group. I had seen 12-Step programs where each person had the opportunity to speak, with defined time constraints, and moderated by one member of the group. Should we do this "go around the room" approach? Renowned communications and management consultant, Margaret Wheatley, seemed to affirm my reluctance, highlighting the need to let things get "messy." She encourages a more organic flow of natural conversation—otherwise, no one listens. In thinking about an organization, she writes, "Self-organizing systems have the capacity to create for themselves the aspects of organization that we thought leaders had to provide. ... Rather than thinking of organization as an imposed structure, plan, design or role, it is clear that in life, organization arises from interaction and the needs of individuals who have decided to come together."[9] In other words, the group should have its own organic flow. A conversation at that time with my friend and spiritual director (and professor of communications), David Gormong, reinforced this idea—especially as appropriate for Millennials and Gen Z. He suggested that this current generation is more *ad hoc* about socializing, less concerned about formalized structures and institutions. The need for community is still felt, still very real, but it is addressed in more free-flowing, dynamic, less-committed structures.[10] If I wanted this group to be comfortable and organic, I might need to let go of my impulse to impose order on the conversations.

Along the same lines of order, I debated whether there should be a planned discussion topic, or allow the conversations to flow more along the lines of an open forum? The first would require more preparation work for me as group leader/facilitator, while the latter might better suit a group dedicated to responding to people's immediate need: "What is on your heart recently?" I could imagine all kinds of chaos if *some* sort of leadership control were not imposed on the group, so the first several sessions I came prepared with topics to discuss, along with some background research and study, to supply fodder for discussion should the need arise. I hoped this would set the pattern of focused discussion on serious topics.

Over the months that followed, I abandoned the planned-topic approach, primarily for three reasons. First, from the outset, people introduced serious topics that were major faith issues in their life. Our very first discussion was on the nature of prayer, and why should we pray if our prayers are seemingly ignored by God more often than they are answered? Was it just a hollow exercise in "confirmation bias," as Kevin posed for debate? The discussion was for me personally one of the most profound and perspective-shifting discussions we've ever had, and based on several subsequent mentions by group participants, many felt the same.

The second reason was the free-flowing dynamic of the conversation allowed people to interject when it was relevant to them, when the conversation struck a nerve or ignited a fresh idea. Compelling them to sit silently until it was their turn to speak would have killed this fresh, living flow to the conversation. As is often the case, by the time their turn rolled around, they would have forgotten what they wanted to respond to. Allowing them to share their thoughts and stories, allowing "cross-talk"—whether spontaneous and brief or somewhat lengthy—seemed to align better with the authentic dynamic we were trying to create.

The third, last, reason arose after several rather unstructured, "popcorn" conversations that were a bit unsettling to me but seemed to ignite lively conversation among our younger participants. Gen Z individuals think differently than Millennials or Gen X'ers. While we older participants were accustomed to more formalized structures in meetings and discussions, many of our Zoomers had been homeschooled, and all of them had grown up "wired"—they never knew a time when they were not connected the vast hivemind of humanity on the internet. They had shorter attention spans and were much more at home in stream-of-consciousness conversations, bouncing from one topic to another. It was more organic and interconnected. One of the Gen X members in the group aptly described it as "popcorn" conversation: how one idea sparked another idea in a different person, who then "popped" it back to the group, where another fed off it and burst into another related idea it had sparked in him or her. This seemed chaotic to me as purported facilitator, but the Gen Z'ers enlightened me afterwards that that is how they thought, how they learned, and what they preferred.[11] It could be—would be—messy. And that was perfectly okay.

I had already determined that this was not a "teaching" session; I would not be delivering lectures on selected topics. I would be a listener, a facilitator, asking leading questions when necessary, but my job was primarily to listen and allow the conversation to go where it would. I would be a "navigator of discussion," not a "teacher of curriculum."[12] As the most theologically trained and (presumably) the most spiritually practiced and mature person in the room (I was also usually the oldest), I would act as a resource, offering bits of my expertise in Church history, bible knowledge, biblical languages, and ideas gleaned from other religions. It was often very gratifying and ego-affirming to be able to drop a relevant, if esoteric, bit of knowledge that helped further or guide the discussion, or offer some new perspective. But I frequently reminded myself that my primary job was to encourage open dialogue, to make room for other insights and experiences, not simply give them "my" answers.

Admittedly, this is not the easiest thing for pastors to do. Mary Moschella explains that "listening is difficult because it requires us to give up the role of expert"—a role I tend to enjoy—"and become a learner again." But this kind of listening "honors the speaker and invites him or her to enter into theological conversation, free to express his or her own thoughts about God, rather than merely receiving the ideas of experts."[13]

The popcorn nature of the discussions, however, often left my Gen X brain wondering "what just happened?" I would continue having a topic ready in the back of my thoughts as a conversation starter in case no one else introduced anything fresh, but there was never a time when the group sat there in silence with nothing to say.

The hottest topics triggering our deconstruction seemed to be exhausted within the first handful of meetings. Our 14th meeting, for example, was particularly disconcerting to me with my embedded agenda of spirituality-based discussions. One of our participants introduced the topic of whether AI (artificial intelligence) could have or become a soul. He is a Gen Z engineer, inclined toward analytical thinking and fantasy role-play games, so this was not just a passing whim. The conversation bounced around the room with all of us contributing our related thoughts, ranging from mechanical to spiritual and biblical considerations, but it was largely directed between him and another engineer in our group. To be fair, the U.S. Supreme Court was about to release its ruling in *Dobbs v. Jackson*—either affirming or overturning *Roe v. Wade*—so the topic of abortion was on the collective minds of most of America, and central to many Christians' opinion on the matter revolved around whether fetuses had souls, or at what point a ganglia of cells become a living soul. When, if, how something received a soul was central to this question about AI and the possibility that the scientific community was on the verge of creating a machine that could become self-aware.

That particular conversation left me a bit dry, but was actively engaged by most in the group. It was a healthy reminder that not every topic would be of faith-shaking relevance to every member of the group every time. And it highlighted to me as facilitator that our Deconstruction group was slowly evolving into a more general spiritual topics group less focused on the core theme of deconstruction/reconstruction. If the initial idea for this group was in response to a specific stated crisis experience, it perhaps should have been anticipated that once the "crisis" was processed, the participants would move on in a healthy way. This seemed to be occurring. Questions were becoming normalized, "crisis" was dulled. No one was losing faith over issues and conflicts. Many were progressing into simply enjoying the group based on curiosity and stimulating conversation. The group was morphing from spiritual Emergency Room to a Health Maintenance activity. As Jordan, one of our Gen Z participants, told me months later at our final "review" session, "I felt like we tackled the most significant topics the first couple of weeks of our group sessions. Now, I'm kinda 'post-deconstruction.'"

(Demonstrating the responsive nature fundamental to action research, this group evolution would, in turn, prompt the creation of a new ministry activity: a "Book and Brew" group that would meet monthly at a local brewery, devoted to the dual objectives of fellowship and reading/discussing books which delved deeper into spiritual topics. There, the conversation could be generally more contained, staying more or less within the scope of the book we were reading.)

The shift in group focus also demonstrated an observation that arose during my first "touching bases" interview. While many of us—particularly older Millennials, Gen X'ers and Boomers—had initial "crisis" events or theological conflicts which triggered our D/R process, this was not always the case, especially with our younger participants. For them, questions and challenging conventional thinking was intrinsic to who they were; it was part of their generational identity. As Kevin explained to me in our lengthy private conversation, "For me, 'deconstruction' was part of my identity formation. There's been no real 'crisis' in my life, just a constant evolution." Whether the participants were LGBTQ or simply dissociating from socially conservative church beliefs, the younger ones were already comfortable with questions, uncertainty,[14] and acceptance of a spiritual journey as "normal."[15]

However, by the 20th or so meeting, this unfocused stream-of-consciousness conversation style, to my mind, was having a negative effect on the group's motivation. (More on this in Chapter 5 where I examine "The Group Experience.") Perhaps we should have put the group on summer hiatus, but apathy was becoming apparent in July and August. Whether due to other commitments (like sending children off to college) or summer *ennui*, attendance began to dwindle, and in our first meeting in September, there was only one other participant besides myself. We had an engaging and enlightening conversation where I felt I gained better insight into his life; however, I have to admit that I felt discouraged and had wondered if the project had run its course.[16]

One of the insights that arose from that solo conversation, however, was about the group's direction. Eric confirmed that as far as he was concerned, the group was a success. He affirmed his sense of comfort with uncertainty, and his on-going curiosity and determination to continue a life-long journey of questions. More importantly to me as pastor, he declared that he felt closer to God now, in the midst of all his questions, than he had in years past with his doctrinal certainty. This would become one of my key questions during participant interviews and private conversations. Deconstruction most often led in one of two directions: either de-conversion and walking away from organized Christianity; or to *re*construction, with a new, enhanced experience of connection with God. As a pastor, this was my greatest concern, and Eric's comment reassured me that in this regard the project was fulfilling its primary objectives.

Eric admitted, though, that many of the foundational questions of his faith were still unanswered. So, I learned, we had *not* exhausted our D/R core issues. We had simply veered into areas of spiritual curiosity. Perhaps I had become too passive and permissive in my leadership role in the group. He suggested he'd be in favor of returning to a more guided approach, where we could focus on those fundamental (theological) questions. Just because we could be comfortable with questions did not mean we would abandon pursuing or exploring possible answers.

When I mentioned my intent to return to more guided conversation on selected topics to a few of the group's participants the following Sunday, they were all in favor of the idea. (There would still be some *ad lib* topic-hopping, given the proclivity of the younger participants, but we managed to stay "mostly relevant" for the few remaining sessions.) Jennifer suggested I ask the group members to propose themes that are still major issues for them. I did exactly that.

In the next group text that went out to remind people of upcoming sessions, I repeated Jennifer's idea that they forward any topic suggestions for consideration. No one responded. Heaving a well-practiced pastoral sigh (people have real lives to live and don't just sit around thinking about church all day—I understand that), I made a mental note to come up with a potential topic myself.

Interestingly, the topic I chose—Penal Substitutionary Atonement theory, so prevalent in evangelical churches—was confirmed when the day before our group meeting, Lauren texted me to ask if this very topic was out of bounds (she used the word "taboo"). She explained,

> God creates people with sin. Even if we don't believe in original sin, there's no doubt that there's inevitable sin. Perfection was never on the table. Then he has to sacrifice himself to himself to save us from the sin we were doomed to have from creation ... which he created. I just don't understand it ... The idea of having to sacrifice myself to myself to save the people, sounds almost mythical. If I weren't born into this, I would think it sounds like BS.

She had serious doubts about this doctrine and what it said about God, but thought it might be too volatile for our group. I reassured her it was not. And the following session was one of our most focused—even if it raised more foundational questions (like how literally should we interpret the bible) than it answered. For the remaining sessions before we broke for the holidays in mid-November through December, we'd stick with this focused-topic approach, addressing the "Big Questions."

• Data Collection & Recording

From the outset, I knew I'd be taking notes. I debated whether to make audio recordings of each session, but decided that would become a distraction. People would initially be hesitant to voice potentially controversial opinions if they knew there would be a permanent audio record of it. Plus, I did not want the sessions to feel too "clinical." I wanted them to be fellowship-based, free-flowing, spontaneous, and creative. At the first few sessions, Eric brought a small notebook and jotted notes. I followed his example, and for the next few meetings brought a steno pad to subtly, as inconspicuously as possible, track the topics of conversation. (The mental image of me typing on a laptop during discussion seemed immediately out of the question.) Some sessions, this was particularly helpful as the conversations proliferated. But again, to me it began to feel clinical, like a therapist taking notes as his patient unburdens his soul. In one session where I was jotting notes, one participant off-handedly remarked, "oh, he's just taking notes for his thesis," and I became self-conscious that the others would feel their comments were inconsequential unless I wrote them down. After that, I began leaving the notebook at home (as did Eric).

I had been keeping "Contemporaneous Notes" of conversations all along during the planning process, tracking outlines of dates, topics, persons involved, and highlights of the conversations—all, immediately after the fact. This became my default method of recording significant statements made during group sessions, impressions of the mood and people's demeanor, along with any other observations and notes for future consideration. Some evenings, I made notes immediately after returning home from the group, and other times I would write them the following morning. I discovered that, unless there was a particular or unusual thought I might lose track of, by recording my impressions the next day, the most salient points would stand out, not lost in the fog of detail of our "popcorn" discussions. For example, in one session in November 2021, one of the participants used a psychological term I'd never encountered before, and I started out my project notes with this bullet-point entry that night when I got home:

> Jordan commented on his faith development, that he had **"identity foreclosure"** when he was a kid, 100% homeschooled with fundamentalist curriculum, and only later (in college) began sorting through that. He said if he were not gay, he probably wouldn't be a Christian any longer, that being gay has made God more real to him. ... Echoing my texts with Sebastian earlier.

In a different conversation months later, another participant used the term "dramaturgical effect" in a discussion on spiritual identity, and I had to quickly make a note to look it up later. This, I found, would become fairly routine, as a number of the participants had backgrounds in psychology or counseling.

I also included pastoral observations and "identity memos" in my project notes. Sometimes the responses of the participants would trigger a degree of pastoral alarm, something I needed to be aware of or address in future conversations, sermons, teaching, or prayer. These were all of a spiritual or theological nature, nothing that would need to involve secular authorities. The "identity memos," a key tool of heuristic phenomenology, were snapshots of my own theological evolution, changes in perspective, or something that was said that would cause me to rethink some of my beliefs and positions. These memos are typically used for recording the researcher's own self-reflection,[17] and I wanted to track how *I* was being affected through the process. It was actually an encouraging sign to me to see that I was being stretched, challenged, and growing as much as the other participants.

In addition, I culled relevant text and Facebook messages from participants (and others outside the group who commented on their D/R process), pasting them into my notes so they would be preserved in one file. Salient points from personal conversations with friends and colleagues on topics relating to their own D/R experiences would also end up in my notes; sometimes with their explicit knowledge ("I'm gonna use that in my thesis…"), or otherwise recorded for anonymous citation.

On one occasion, after about the 12th session, I emailed a questionnaire to each participant with some specific and some open-ended questions as a form of in-progress survey.[18] The idea was then to follow-up with personal interviews for more detailed descriptions, but we were entering into the Summer season, and appointments were postponed as people made plans for vacations and other family obligations. Consistent with the dynamic nature of action research—and everything related to this group—my interview strategy adapted to accommodate the circumstances, and in most cases, I was able to have multiple shorter, less formal, conversations one-on-one, in which I asked the same basic questions in place of a lengthier interview. I extracted a number of "significant statements" from the conversations and from the handful of email responses—many which affirmed the relevance and importance of the project in their lives, and, I must admit as an unobjective project facilitator, validated the energy and effort that went into maintaining the group. This I mention in contrast to my disappointment at the scarcity of responses to the email survey. A number of the participants had warned me in advance they were unlikely to write out responses, citing busyness and time-constraints as well as personal preference to "talk it out" instead of writing it out.

Our final "Wrap Up and Evaluation" session before putting the group on holiday hiatus at the end of our 12-months, yielded further material for my project notes. These helped summarize, and put into perspective, the significant statements I had been collecting from the participant discussions all year, as well as provided feedback on the style and format of our previous sessions.

Composition of Group

From the beginning, the group was open to any who wished to attend, whether a congregant of The Abbey or not. I had no expectation as to who would show up and what the regular composition of the group would look like, except that I *hoped* those who had explicitly indicated an interest would actually follow through and show up—something past church experience had disabused me of. Often, I found, people will vocalize a need they see or feel, and I believe it is a genuine concern and of some degree of urgency to them at the moment. However, just as frequently, that concern will dissipate for whatever reason, and their actual participation in the program they specifically requested will evaporate as quickly. To some extent, this also happened with our Discussion Group. A few of the primary password-holders—those who had uttered the magic "D-word"—attended one or two sessions, but then disappeared.

For example, of the people who initially personified the problem which underlines this project, Aaron, the trans-male Jewish convert, never became a part of the group. He relocated out of state for a job weeks before the group was launched. Matthew was a "charter member" of the group and attended when he could, but had frequent schedule conflicts with work. Kevin and Analise attended the first few sessions and volunteered their frustration with prayer as our first intensive and focused discussion topic, but stopped coming, and shortly after discontinued attending the church.

However, overall, I was delighted and excited that a core group of regulars consistently showed up. Ideally, phenomenological research involves a small number of participant "co-researchers." That number can be as low as *one* participant (particularly in heuristic phenomenology where the researcher him- or herself is the primary subject), but works best with a larger group up to as many as 10-15.[19] Our group fairly consistently met with 7 or 8 participants at a time, with a one-time high of 14, and twice with a low of 2.

The group was also mixed orientation, multi-denominational, and multi-generational, to my delight and surprise. As mentioned in Chapter 1, I had suspected that sexual orientation and denominational background would be the primary considerations in describing the D/R process, but quickly learned that different generations responded in surprisingly different manners. I would then begin taking note of the participants' age-group when recording significant statements made by them. This would lead me to draw a specific conclusion, listed among "What I Learned" later in this chapter, which I had not anticipated.

Of the 19 individuals who attended at least once, 11 were LGBTQ+ and 8 were straight. Two represented the Boomer generation, 6 were Gen X, 5 were Millennials, and 6 were Gen Z. In total, there were 14 males, 5 females; 11 were single/unmarried, 8 were married. Three of the married couples had children. Race/ethnicity was not tracked specifically, but a superficial glance of the group would suggest that most were White, with a few of each Native American and Hispanic/Latinx origins. The group also reflected the denominational diversity of our church. The 10 participants who made up the stable core attending the majority of our sessions came from the spectrum of fundamentalist, evangelical, Pentecostal/charismatic, and Catholic/Episcopal traditions. These diversified demographics would offer a well-balanced sampling of perspectives and provide for some lively conversations.

Topics Discussed

The conversations of our Discussion Group ranged widely and wildly. Some issues we might dedicate an entire session to (discounting the natural veering off into related tangents), such as prayer; ritual, symbols and religion; how we view the bible; or the nature of God. Other times, we might hit as many as a dozen or more themes in one sitting—obviously not reaching much depth in any of them, but I justified this laxity of discipline and control, believing that the experience of simply mentioning them, bouncing a few spontaneous thoughts back and forth between the participants for even just a few minutes, could potentially provide therapeutic relief. Culling from my Notes, here is list of topics (in relative chronological order) we touched on in our group. I list them here at length to convey the sheer magnitude of breadth covered.

- Denominational backgrounds and perspectives
- Prayer (multiple times)
- World religions; specifically, Hinduism and Buddhism
- The value of questioning to a healthy spirituality (multiple times)
- The "sin of certainty" and dogmatism
- Homosexuality, in real life and in the bible
- Sexual ethics and morality: what's "allowable"; what's healthy; "what I don't want my kids doing"

- "Coming out" experiences; gay stereotyping, and the "Gay Body Type Triangle: Twinks, Hunks, and Bears (Oh my!)"
- Forms of church government / polity
- Homeschooling vs public schooling in our religious identity formation
- Omniscience of God: traditional views vs Process and Open theologies
- Afterlife: Heaven, hell, soul-sleep, remaining present (communion of the saints), "heaven" as a space-time dimension; ghosts, ancestors, and "the witch at Endor"
- Judgment Day: judgment as reward/punishment vs justice and restoration/healing
- Angels, aliens, overlapping dimensions, the multiverse, free will and mathematical models of probability
- Rhythms, rituals, and symbol in worship and in daily life; ritual as "embodied spirituality," symbol as "the language of spirituality" (multiple times)
- Spiderman
- Crisis levels of faith
- Movements in Church history (from early church and Catholicism to Reformation, to Great Awakenings, to Pentecostal and charismatic movements) as God, like an "Italian grandmother," offering more on the plate. "You like that? Now try this. Take some more of this."
- The Gospel Coalition's list of 4 reasons people deconstruct (church hurt, poor teaching, desire to sin, street cred), and where we fit on that list
- Role of architecture in churches vs plain white walls or converted gyms, and its relation to worship

- A Cross versus a Crucifix: what they mean. Should we use both?
- Use of a rosary. Repetition and meditation, praying to the saints. Lighting prayer candles. Evangelicals curious about Catholicism.
- Use of "the D-word": whether we like the word "deconstruction"; how it is used and misused
- "Jesus & John Wayne": Christian nationalism, militant/toxic masculinity, and white supremacy in the Church
- Nature of Grace, "Depravity", the [supposed] Fall of Humanity, John Calvin and Timothy Keller
- Being allowed to serve in the church: as a woman, or as LGBTQ+
- Incarnational worldviews: monism, dualism, non-duality/advaita; deism vs theism; and their influence on how we view spirituality
- Communion/Eucharist: memorial, spiritual communion, "open table," the "spirituality of all things" (and Rob Bell)
- Tarot, Ouija boards, and horror movies: safe or a "gateway for demons"?
- Scripture: what does "inspiration," "inerrant," "infallible" and "authority" mean? Hermeneutics: How to interpret and make meaningful/relevant (multiple times)
- Abortion, and when a person gets/becomes a Soul
- Free will, predestination, the sovereignty of God
- God as Supreme Being, Ground of Being, or Abba?
- How does God speak to us?
- Atonement theories, and the offensiveness of "Penal Substitutionary Atonement" theory

That list takes us through the first 15 group sessions. As the reader can see, the topics were not exclusively about Christian theology and practice. Whatever was relevant to the participants at the moment, we addressed, even if simply in passing. But a handful of themes were revisited multiple times, indicating to me that they were pressing and on-going concerns.

When Catholic Bishop Robert Barron was asked at a convocation of younger Jesuits about the rise of the "Nones" and disaffiliation with the Church, Bishop Barron advised them, "I think you need to get back into your high schools, get back into your churches and universities, and address these apologetic issues that are really bugging young people. ... I think you're on the front lines of the most important struggle right now."[20] He was speaking about the "dumbing down" of the Church since Vatican II—an anti-intellectual movement that was incapable of responding to people's heart-felt questions. We need to address whatever issues are on the minds of our people; the Church cannot afford to abandon its role as teacher. Where else can people ask these questions? With whom else can they discuss these wide range of topics in a spiritual context? Discussion groups such as this Evolving Faiths group at The Abbey are indeed, I believe, on the front lines of "the most important struggle right now."

How did this hodge-podge field of topics play out with the group participants? Allow me to excerpt part of a lengthy text my co-pastor and I received from one of the regular attenders after our 10th session:

> ... I just wanted to make sure you knew that you have changed my life. You probably didn't create this church [and the discussion group] thinking that the straight people would have big transformations, but we really have. Our marriage is stronger, we are

> better parents, and our faith has grown exponentially since we joined The Abbey. I love you both and I'm so grateful for all you've done in this year—and all you'll do going forward.[21]

We were apparently doing something right.

What I Learned

Some of the following observations will be explored in greater detail in Chapters 5 and 6, "Deconstructing Theologies & the Group Experience" and "Closing Thoughts," but this seems an appropriate place to introduce some general learnings from the year-long project.

• THE POWER OF NORMALIZATION. In some cases, I saw noticeable changes in attitude and comfort-level among our participants simply by having the support group, even if they did not regularly attend. At first, I had to contend with my own sense of disappointment at their irregular participation. There were, at least in some cases, legitimate reasons they could not make the biweekly meetings consistently. That is the nature of church life. But noticing the change in their outlook, the acceptance of uncertainty in their beliefs, the flexibility with which they explored alternative spiritualities,[22] convinced me of the power of normalization. The mere existence of the D/R Discussion Group, the fact that the church supported it, seemed to have some power to convince them they were not alone, that this was, in fact, a normal, even healthy, phenomenon.

This realization was unexpected, but understandable. Wasn't this the same phenomenon we had experienced with LGBTQ affirmation? Knowing that the people in your environment not only accept or tolerate your differences but actually celebrate them as natural and healthy, causes a remarkable (if gradual) shift in self-confidence and decrease in shame. Shame is replaced by confidence. I concluded this was also the case with faith deconstruction. Once it was brought out of the closet of hidden doubt into the light of public "church normalcy," the participants were freer to engage more fully and enthusiastically.

• ACTIVE CURIOSITY OF THE FACILITATOR. With that long list of topics discussed, one take-away was the necessity for the facilitator to have an active curiosity, especially as relating to Christian theology and practice, but definitely not limited to those areas. As a post-evangelical pastor, I had to engage (or at least moderate) conversations that addressed science, science fiction, sociology and psychology, world religions, spiritual practices, Catholicism and Eastern Orthodoxy, politics and current events, sex/gender/orientation/identity, Queer theory, Marvel comics and movies. Obviously, one cannot be an expert in all areas of life, but a keen mind and cultural awareness proved essential. At times, my age and generational bias and blindness came thru clearly. At one point, Gen Z Jordan even commented, "Boy, you really *are* old." A healthy sense of self (and a sense of humor!) is also requisite.

And as surprising as it might be, I had to realize I wasn't the smartest guy in the room. Every one of the "regular" core group of 10 who showed up most frequently possessed a college degree, and a few had or were working on advanced degrees. Technical and psychological terms were sometimes bandied about, and I frequently had to play catch-up, either on the spot or afterwards. I was comfortable having the most expansive exposure and depth in areas of theology and religion (one would hope for their pastor/teacher), but in other areas, that was clearly not the case.

• DISCUSSION STYLE: STREAM OF CONSCIOUSNESS VS. GUIDED QUESTIONS. There is a place for each, but one lesson I learned: if I let the conversation go entirely free-style, the bigger questions would only get touched in passing. Sometimes this was fine; but other times this requires a more direct handling, a more guided, deliberate approach. People want to feel that they're accomplishing something, making progress. So, as far as that ongoing, initially-unanswered question about "What kind of group is this?", a support/recovery group approach only took us so far, where people were free to express whatever was on their minds. There also needed to be an actively facilitated discussion on real issues relevant to their D/R journeys.

And, while I could invite participant ideas in selecting topics, I could not rely exclusively on their input. Sometimes they just couldn't define or articulate what their main issues were, and I, as pastor, facilitator, and co-participant-researcher, would have to draw from my own D/R experience to fill in the gaps. This was where Moustaskas's insistence that the researcher *already have* experience of the phenomenon became evident.

• ONCE IS NOT ENOUGH. This should be obvious, but it took a few times of repeated conversations to realize that one dedicated session was not sufficient to change someone's long-held beliefs. We would, as a result, frequently hit on the same topic over several dispersed discussions. Even sessions which were dedicated to single-topics (rare as they were) only served to introduce new thinking, new perspectives; they did not "seal" the issue. It would take more than a few discussions before foundational thinking could be changed.

• NOT FOR EVERYONE. This type of group isn't for everyone. Some participants came mainly for the joy of socializing with a group of familiar people, but weren't that invested in the conversations or topics. Those most active in the group tended to be those with an introspective, philosophical bent. So, my co-pastor, for example, came out of a desire to support the group and loved the social aspect, but wasn't particularly interested in exploring many of the topics that deeply. His own D/R journey was more an emotional one than an intellectual one. And the Gen Zs who had not experienced a crisis event, tended to prefer the stream-of-consciousness chatter over focused, in-depth discussion (except when it came to sexuality and sexual ethics!).

• GENERATIONAL CONSIDERATIONS. Based on my own experience, and those highlighted in virtually all the literature I had read in my research, the D/R journey is marked by some degree of crisis.[23] It was startling and disorienting during my very first "touch bases" interview with one of the Millennials (Kevin) that he denied any real moment of crisis of faith. Like several of the Millennial and Gen Z participants, he maintained that questioning and doubt had been integral to his religious experience since his youth. Questioning began in childhood Sunday School, or at least definitely by high school age when challenging authority and tradition is a normal aspect of mental development. At least six others in the group, almost exclusively Millennial or Gen Z, specifically denied any sense of crisis.[24] They might have even considered leaving the faith altogether, but not due to any isolated event, any single doctrine, or any particular church behavior. But about half of the Millennials and virtually all of the Gen X and Boomer participants *did* in fact experience distinct and identifiable moments of crisis where their faith was directly challenged to a point of cognitive dissonance and mental trauma.

I drew two general conclusions about this. First, this difference in response was partially due to generational sensibilities. The younger generations were more accustomed to discrepancies, skepticism, not embracing wholesale whatever was fed to them. Perhaps it was attributable to the 24-

hour news cycle, the polarized bias of news media, and immediate access to often conflicting information on the internet available on the phone in their hands.

My second conclusion is that the degree of crisis was also related to the length of time the participants had spent invested in those religious systems. For the older generations, most of whom had grown up in church (regardless of denomination), challenge and change, questions and doubts, came at much greater personal cost. These were the ones the books and blogs were typically written about. Much material had been published in the first two decades of the 21st century on "the rise of the Nones" and the accelerated decline in church membership, but my own experience (albeit limited to my encounters in my own church setting) suggested that Gen Z experienced D/R in a significantly less traumatic way—and in fact, "deconstruction" might not even be an appropriate label for their experience. There was more of an ease and fluidity to their exploring, and less psychological or emotional commitment to any single religious view.

Put another way, the intensity of crisis seemed inversely relational to generational cohort. Boomers and Gen X seemed to have the highest degree of religious disorientation, while Millennials and Gen Z generally the least. This wasn't exclusively the case: some Gen Xers had an initial crisis but recovered quickly, and one of our Gen Z participants (Matthew) experienced significant RDGS initially (and was, in fact, one of principal reasons for this project), but has since experienced a great degree of spiritual freedom and comfort with uncertainty. It seems, reasonably, that the longer one spent entrenched in a fundamentalist/evangelical environment, the more traumatic stress and emotional/intellectual turmoil one would experience.

• NO SINGLE DESCRIPTION OF DECONSTRUCTION. Thus, from these primary learnings, I conclude that there is no single phenomenon of faith deconstruction/reconstruction to describe. There are distinct experiences, some of which may be grouped together and described, but personal religious background was more an indicator of the intensity of the questioning experience. (I will, none the less, attempt a composite/synthesis description of the lived D/R experience in our group in the Moustakas's next chapter.)

• GROUP LIFE-CYCLE: IT'S OKAY TO EVOLVE OR SHUT DOWN. This is a hard one for professional ministers to wrap their minds around. So often in seminary or in the churchworld, we're conditioned to think long-term, to build "permanent" or "life-long" ministries for the church. We're trained to think of "establishing" institutions, and committing to their long term existence. But as David Gormong pointed out, the post-millennial generations, with their noted shorter attention spans and their "casual wanderer" approach to spirituality, won't settle into long-term, permanent situations like former generations did. Attending the "family church"—the church my parents attend and I grew up in—may be a thing of the past. And we need to build our groups, our ministry activities, with that in mind. Don't think in terms of 10 or 20 years, he advises. Plan instead for 3–6 months. (Yes, 3–6 months!) Focus on short-term goals and projects, things that are easily let-go of. Activities that people can come, benefit from, and then move on. Plan with the spiritual wanderer and shifting needs of the people in mind.

I experienced this first hand that first summer when attendance began to wane and I wondered if we were "done." By our final session a few months later, after meeting for a year, it seemed everyone in the group felt ready to move on. As Jordan put it, he felt he was now "post-deconstruction."

The Evolving Faiths Discussion Group had served its purpose and officially shut down. But instead of ending permanently, it morphed into a book discussion group, allowing our interests and areas of exploration to expand. The topics of discussion changed, based on the books we chose, to suit contemporary (and temporary) topics. And even the format flexed over time, beginning as a once monthly "Book & Brew" meet-up eventually shifting to twice-a-month coffeeshop discussion group. Change is at the core of life; things need to be allowed to evolve or to die. And, if they've served their purpose, either is okay.

• Lastly, THESE TALKS ARE IMPORTANT. Probably more important than many ministry professionals recognize. One of the initial reasons for launching this project had been that Matthew was wrestling with critical issues and questions alone. Reiterating what Bishop Barron said, pastors and youth leaders and ministers *need* to get back into our churches and address these wide-ranging issues that are on people's minds. Yes, they can do a Google search or read some blogs. But they need a real person, with real-life experience and trained theological backgrounds to actually have conversations with.

And note, I'm not just talking about fellowship groups, bible studies, or teacher-led sessions. I'm specifically referring to discussion-style groups where there is free interchange of ideas, even "wrong" ideas. Where questions and doubts can be vocalized, a sense of uncertainty and openness can be normalized, and a diverse, even eclectic spirituality can be explored without shame. People, especially younger generations, are less willing than generations past simply to embrace doctrines handed to them or passed on by church elders. They have real questions, real concerns. And a real hunger to experience the transcendent. They are curious, spiritual explorers—as I think we *all* should be. If we cannot provide a safe space to have these conversations, they will look elsewhere. And that does not bode well for the future of the Church.

Along these lines, it is crucial to recognize from the beginning that, consistent with the "action research" approach, the process may be as important as the outcomes—and those outcomes need to be held loosely. The goal is individual spiritual growth, not doctrinal conformity. The conversations, discussions, are more important than theological "correctness." As pastoral leaders, our concern needs to be that our efforts lead the participants into a closer communion with God, and this can only happen when hearts and minds are open to the subjective move of the Spirit, not locked in to predefined answers.

This is the "front line" of spiritual seekers still within the Church's reach. These conversations can be life-changing, and they are indeed "the most important struggle right now."

5

Deconstructing Theologies & the Group Experience

"People believe, but they believe differently than they once did. The theological ground is moving: a spiritual revolution is afoot. And there is a gap between that revolution and the institutions of religious faith."
~ Diana Butler Bass[1]

Over the 12-month period the Discussion Group met, I kept contemporaneous notes, capturing the stories, the random, often quirky, comments, and the insightful observations of the group participants, as well as my own mood and sense of the room. My own interests revolved primarily around the topics of faith crisis and theological reformation, but as I would learn, they were not the central concerns of many in the group. The previous chapter related my surprise at discovering the relationship between generational cohort and the level of spiritual, psychic trauma experienced by group members. This new knowledge came about only through the dialogical act of listening and interacting with the spoken—and often, unarticulated—feelings of the people. Glimpses into their souls, descriptions of their experiences, came as often through the random comments as through lengthier conversations and interviews. The experience of simply being together, sharing presence, was as informative as it was healing and restorative.

In this chapter, I will review the key processes in heuristic phenomenology as they related to our group's interaction. I've chosen key themes that speak to the core of evangelical identity, and then offer an interpretation of the group experience itself—what it was like being together, whether it was helpful or transformative. Finally, consistent with phenomenological methodologies, I will present a composite description of the faith deconstruction experience among fundamentalist and evangelical Christians as represented by members of the group. In the next chapter, I'll offer some closing thoughts, summarizing this year-long project.

The Heuristic Process

Heuristic research allows a great deal of personal latitude in addressing a phenomenon and in presenting the data. Moustakas outlines six basic phases of the research process that reflect the sequence of his own experience using this methodology, which I have adapted to the specific situation of this act of ministry, the Evolving Faiths Discussion Group. They include, initial engagement, immersion, incubation, illumination, explication, and culminate in a creative synthesis.[2]

This methodology was appealing to me because, while the project was initiated as a pastoral response to the voiced experiences of Matthew, Aaron, Lauren and Eric, and others, it deeply resonated with me, and their voices echoed my own experiences in my faith journey. Personal involvement of the researcher is the cornerstone of heuristic research. It would, thus, allow me the medium of offering an environment of support to the group participants—creating a safe space—

while simultaneously providing a venue to explore spiritual and theological questions that occupy me. In addition, the phases of heuristic research overlap conveniently with some of the well-identified "stations" in the D/R process. For example, the research phases of incubation, illumination and explication were also times when I could be processing my own "Shifting, Unraveling, and Rebuilding" (using Escobar's model), and describing the similar experiences of those in the group. The umbrella topic of deconstruction/reconstruction would allow deeper exploration into aspects of the life of faith, including deep dives into theology which, for evangelicals in particular, is at the heart of so much of the characteristic psychological conflict.

That fateful conversation with Matthew served as the "initial engagement" for the project. I had been processing questions of my own theology at a leisurely pace for over a decade, spurred at random times by encounters with friends whose views differed from my own, or reading something that quietly stirred a vague notion of unrest in my portfolio of beliefs. Sometimes, as I explained in the hermeneutical autobiography in Chapter 1, those moments were prompted or illuminated by moments of new insight or epiphany. Sometimes, it was sheer trudge-work through rocky ground. But, little by little, my own theology was being reformed—deconstructed, even before I knew the word. Matthew and the others prompted this research project and provided a permission to engage this experience on a communal level.

Immersion, the second stage in heuristic research, is the period where the question becomes the focal point of the researcher's life. Moustakas writes, "the researcher lives the question in waking, sleeping, and even dream states. Everything in his or her life becomes crystalized around the question ... to live it and grow in knowledge and understanding of it."[3] I can attest that the discussions and follow-up conversations with this group of seekers, and the additional reading and research brought on by them, did in fact become my central focus for the 12-months the group met. Again, this likely would not have been the case had I not already had such personal investment in the topic.

I benefitted both from my own firsthand evangelical background, and from being pastor to this group and a fellow participant in the project. We were locating key issues and themes, and exploring them together. Many of us shared similar crisis moments, though some did not. This shared experience was the foundation for the heuristic phenomenological approach.

During heuristic's "incubation" phase, the researcher takes a step back, allowing him- or herself some distance from the intensity of the issue, which "enables the inner tacit dimension to reach its full possibilities,"[4] giving time and space for the ideas to settle, take root, germinate. It provides the opportunities for the ideas to mature. Without deliberately planning for this phase, I believe that the group sessions where there were fewer participants or where instead of a focused discussion, the conversation "popcorned" around the room, were effectively a "break" from the rigors and seriousness of our more organized talks. There were weeks when, it seemed, some of the participants just needed some time to let the dust settle. (Also, as a newsflash to the pastor, congregants did not have the luxury of devoting huge blocks of time to processing their questions or doing deep-dive theological investigations. They had jobs, kids, extracurricular activities—other real-life stuff—to consume their time and energy. Sometimes they just needed a break from all the thinking and wrestling with ideas.)

Out of that settling time, often fresh insights appear. Connections are made with other related, and sometimes seemingly unrelated, questions or aspects of faith. New perspectives, angles, broader implications, arise out of the former chaos, lending greater clarity. This is the fourth, "illumination," phase of heuristic research. "Illumination opens the door to a new awareness, a modification of an old understanding, a synthesis of fragmented knowledge, or an altogether new discovery of something that has been present for some time yet beyond immediate awareness."[5] In my experience, this corresponds with a time in the D/R process where a sense of "ownership" in the new perspective begins to take root. The red flags have been replaced with yellow, or even green, flags, signaling "it's okay; this is not as dangerous as I thought. It kind of makes sense to me now. It's safe to continue."

Moustakas's fifth phase is "explication," where a fuller comprehension of the experience takes place. Moustakas sees this more as an internal, psychological, moment for the researcher, where she engages in "focusing, indwelling, self-searching, and self-disclosure, and recognizes that meanings are unique and distinctive to an experience and depend upon internal frames of reference."[6] I chose to adapt this phase by adding an external component; it would be a time of additional reading or theological research, suited to my own driving questions.[7] "What do the evangelical theologians say about this? And do I agree? What are some other perspectives on this, and do they sit well with me?" For me, explication would be a time of dialoging with evangelical voices, listing the pros and cons, listening for trigger words in traditional doctrine, and rooting out underlying assumptions that no longer seem as sure or solid as they once did.

Consistent with Moustakas's paradigm, though, it is also a time of "self-verification," of becoming more convinced: "yes, this new way *feels* right to me." Ownership deepens, solidifies. And I must point out that this *feeling* is an essential part of both heuristic research *and* the D/R process. Deconstruction and reconstruction are as much intuitive, emotional, even physical, as they are intellectual. "How does this new perspective feel in my body? Is it causing me more stress, or to tense up? Or do I feel more calm, more relaxed; do I feel like my insides are untangling? Am I more at peace with this?" And importantly, "does this make me feel closer to God or farther away from God?" These questions relate back to specific key goals for this project: to become comfortable with uncertainty, with questions of faith, with the result of feeling a closer connection with God.[8]

This fifth phase of explication and self-confirmation doesn't always occur, though. Sometimes the questions defy easy answers or quick alternatives. Sometimes the questions remain, and we must simply become comfortable living with the uncertainty. This is particularly hard for me. As someone whose identity is rooted in the teacher's calling, I like to know answers. Questions may drive me deeper, may bring me closer to God, but they also drive me crazy. I have become more comfortable *saying* "I don't know," of admitting that I do not have all the answers, but I'm not more comfortable *accepting* that I don't know. The uncertainty still nags at me.

Among the group participants, about half fell on each side of this emotional line. The younger ones, the Gen Zs and younger Millennials, were more comfortable with a "meh" and a shrug of the shoulders, lightly dismissing the topic as not crucial to their faith identity. They were well acclimated to doubt and distrusting "pat answers" handed to them by their elders; a little uncertainty did not impact them significantly. The older participants, myself included, Gen Xers, Boomers, and older Millennials, those of us who have steeped longer in the evangelical ethos, tended to be more disturbed by lack of clarity. Although we were growing out of it, we still liked the simplicity of our black-and-white positions. It is also likely that it was the discomfort which drove many of us to buy a new book or do a more probing search on the internet, to explore the topic further.

The final phase in Moustakas's heuristic research paradigm is the "creative synthesis." While all participants in the project are considered "co-researchers" (in both heuristic inquiry and action research), this last phase is more concerned with the primary researcher summarizing the experience. "This usually takes the form of a narrative depiction utilizing verbatim material and examples, but [interestingly] it may be expressed as a poem, story, drawing, painting, or by some other creative form"[9] that suits the self-expression of the primary researcher. In fact, of the four examples of heuristic research Moustakas excerpts, each of the closing "syntheses" were expressions of creative writing, full of imagery and even poetry. Later in this chapter I will modify this approach somewhat to more closely resemble the composite or exhaustive description associated with phenomenological methodology.[10] It is an attempt to tell the story of your group, a composite drawn from the combined experiences of all the participants into a single story.[11]

I also adapted the phenomenological analysis procedure of grouping the over-150 significant statements raised in the discussions and related conversations (listed in Appendix C: Significant Statements). Moustakas's projects tended to focus on a single theme; like, the experience of feeling connected with nature, or the sense of touch in blindness, etc. There was a central experience-type to focus on. In this project, however, I employed a multiple-theme approach by taking aim at a selected few hot topics within the faith deconstruction experience. This was not intended to be a study of a single overarching topic, "what does it feel like to deconstruct?" Rather, I wanted to look at some specific components of that deconstruction relevant to evangelicals—How do you understand God now? What does it mean to pray? How do you understand the work of the cross now?—and to walk together through the wrestling process to arrive at personally satisfying solutions. These themes, presented below, so pivotal in our mostly-conservative shared-culture group, became the "meaning units" (themes) in my project notes and in planning topics for discussion.

Deconstructed Theologies

A full list of topics discussed by the group would take up pages, as we saw in Chapter 4. However, there were a handful of recurring themes, topics not easily dispensed with in one short conversation, topics that would pop up during other sessions ostensibly devoted to other things. These, as just mentioned, became the "meaning units" or themes into which I collated quotations from the group participants reflecting their various comments and positions during the various discussions. In keeping with common phenomenological practices, I will introduce each unit/theme with "textual descriptions" summarizing the "what" the participants experienced with the topic.[12] It is in a way, as I've chosen to label them, a "reading of the room."

In phenomenological studies, sometimes "structural descriptions" are included in the analysis, describing the "how" the experience occurred. Usually, these are descriptive of the physical context or setting in which the phenomenon was experienced.[13] Faith deconstruction, however, is not limited to a single time and place. So, for the purpose of rendering context, I will interject some relevant quotations and summary statements from known and respected voices in evangelical theology as representations of the doctrines discussed. These will serve to encapsulate a negative or offending position that is a point of deconstruction, and epitomize the unspoken argument to which the group participants may be reacting. These theologies are, in effect, a persistent "psychic space" in which deconstructors live, so I have chosen to identify them as "Trigger Points." They are the ever-present "background voices" most of us were deconstructing from.

After identifying the offending position will follow a summary of the discussions we had on the topic, including some "significant statements" made by the group participants reflecting their thoughts and reactions and experiences related to the theme, along with some of my own observations. I also include any proposed alternative positions reached by the group that seemed more palatable. Sometimes the "alternative position" will be my own take-away from the group or thoughts after further "immersion" and "explication." Because most of the participants came from fundamentalist or evangelical backgrounds, the alternative views would typically not stray too far from the former position if they were to be readily accepted. Sometimes individuals took radical positions in reaction to the hardline they had been formerly asked to tow, but in general, we tried to keep our alternative perspectives within sight of our evangelical roots, more in line with a post-evangelical (but not necessarily exvangelical) worldview.[14]

For the purpose of the dialogue with evangelical theology (in reality, more "reaction against"), I have chosen to interact with the systematic theologies of Wayne Grudem[15] and Millard Erickson.[16] Both of these texts are common in evangelical seminaries and popular among evangelical pastors and informed laity, and will serve well as representative, if silent, voices in our discussions.

It should be noted, naturally, that what follows is not intended to be thorough-going discussions of the various theologies. Rather, it is a record of our interaction with the theme and what it meant for us. These could well serve as introductory thoughts, points of entry into the topics, laying the groundwork for future further exploration.

Using this adapted phenomenological analysis rubric, I have chosen five major "meaning units," what I've chosen to call "rethinking topics," representing recurring themes in our conversations that seem to be at the core of deconstructing an evangelical identity. The sixth topic will focus on the lived experience of the group encounters themselves. Each unit will be introduced by a "Reading the Room" which summarizes in bullet-points the main ideas expressed by the group relating to that topic. After which I list some "Trigger Points" representing theological counter-points, the silent and opposing "other voices in the room" which are the subject of deconstruction in that unit. Then follows a narrative "Discussion," embedding some significant statements made by the group on that topic, interwoven with descriptive commentary, along with proposed alternative positions more amenable to post-evangelicals.

We begin, as Rethinking Topic #1, with a discussion of the nature of the bible—even before discussing what might seem like more important views of God or the Cross—because the bible is the starting point, the very cornerstone, of evangelical theology. It is not for no reason that Item #1 in the Statements of Faith of the Assemblies of God and Southern Baptist Convention (as representative denominations), as well as the National Association of Evangelicals, asserts their position on the nature of Scripture.[17] Against this belief in the supremacy of the bible's role in faith, all other topics of theology are usually measured. To whatever degree a view aligns with or departs from the bible (as we understand it) will likely indicate the degree of struggle a deconstructor may have when rethinking the theme. So the issue of how one understands the nature of the bible is paramount. Over the course of our year's Discussion Group sessions, the bible was referred to, if not quoted directly, in virtually every session.

Rethinking the Bible

Reading the Room

- There was a great deal of uncertainty about current beliefs about the bible
- Some felt lingering belief that Scripture is definitive, authoritative. Others were dismissive of its relevance, almost belligerently rejecting any absolute claim of authority or inerrancy
- "Inerrant" and "infallible" are hugely problematic terms for group participants
- There was consensus that the bible was inspired, but what that meant varied by participant
- The emotional level attached to this topic was high. Whatever conclusion we might arrive at, there was a unanimous agreement that it was a central issue.

Trigger Points

- "All Scripture is totally true and trustworthy."—Southern Baptist Convention[18]
- "If we deny inerrancy, we essentially make our own human minds a higher standard of truth than God's Word itself. ... If we deny inerrancy, then we must also say that the Bible is wrong not only in minor details but in some of its doctrines as well."[19]

Discussion

There were only two things most in the group agreed upon: that Scripture was "inspired" in some way and therefore—somehow—could be used by God to communicate with us; and, none of us was content with our current view.

Some of us were still painfully close to our former dogmatic positions, stuck in Ricoeur's "precritical" stage. We were told this is "God's Word." As Matthew put it in one of our first group meetings, "I was taught every word in the bible is carved in stone. You don't think the Holy Spirit dictated that specifically?" This was often the argument used by voices of authority to stifle any argument or question of tradition. So, for example, the participants in the group who came from a Church of Christ background had had the words of the Apostle Paul used to silence women in church and keep them out of pulpits. After years of submission to that idea, there was palpable anger beneath the surface about this topic and how it impacted their view of the bible. When the words of Paul were brought up in another context, Mark dismissed the biblical quotation: "At the end of that very same chapter Paul forbids women from speaking. I not sure I care what he has to say about the matter."

Neill countered, responding spontaneously without weighing his words as he normally does: "That was Paul's opinion, his own judgment. He was talking about a situation. But not every single word is inspired by the Holy Spirit; some were written just by man." Eric agreed. "The bible is full of contradictions. You can't use it to prove anything. Peter Enns [*Bible Tells Me So*] gave an example of two verses in Proverbs that directly contradict each other, and there they are, side by side." The books of Peter Enns would debut in many of our conversations.

In another conversation, Mark recounted a turning point in his view. "It took me a long time to be able to let myself say 'the bible is not inerrant; it is not infallible.' Once I did, I fell in love with the bible, and things started making more sense for me." Jennifer, in another venue, voiced a broader view she had recently embraced: "I think we have to hold the bible loosely in our hands, and not try to force it to be all consistent, all one point of view. If we hold it too tightly or too literally, we can prevent it from speaking to us and it loses its power." Mark chimed in again (apparently, they had had this conversation before): "The bible is not one book, even though we tend to think so. It's a library. It's got sections of law, poetry, history, mythology ... written across a few thousand years. 'The bible' doesn't *'say'* any one thing."

At least 6 participants in our group had read, and were convinced by, the works of Peter Enns, notably his *The Bible Tells Me So* and *How the Bible Actually Works*. Four of us had read his *The Sin of Certainty*. Mark had read each of these and seemed more informed—and settled—on the issue. He said something particularly intriguing one evening that caught my attention: "The bible is a history of man getting it wrong about God." The conversation continued on without much notice, but I texted him later and asked him to explain. He replied by text,

> The bible is a story of people's perceptions and interactions with God. It's a history of them continually saying 'this is who God is' and him correcting their thinking. It's adventures in missing the point. 'God wants us to conquer and kill our neighbors!' Not really. 'God favors us and dislikes others!' Nope, try again. Part of the miracle of Christ is God taking human form to show us who God really is—and people killed him because they couldn't take it. We see today that people continue to misunderstand who God is.

"Adventures in missing the point," I thought, was an astute observation, one that has stayed with me since. The bible is a record of God's communication with humanity at our current level of understanding. Humans wrote it, even under inspiration, and therefore, it cannot be "inerrant" or unquestioningly "authoritative."

We tossed around ideas about what that passage we had all be taught could mean: "All scripture is God-breathed and is useful for teaching, rebuking, correcting and training in righteousness" (2 Tim 3:16). "God-breathed" doesn't mean "dictated," and "profitable/useful for teaching" did *not* mean 100% accurate on all accounts. And didn't Jesus himself say that "scripture cannot be broken" (John 10:25)? Yet he then turned around and "broke" it—"you have heard it said, but I say to you ..." And the apostles clearly defied written scripture in making allowances for non-Jews to enter the faith (as discussed in Chapter 3). Clearly there was wiggle room in how that "unbreakableness" could be understood.

I am still comfortably ambiguous on my own stance on Scripture. I no longer believe our holy texts are inviolable as "The Word of God" in any absolute sense, but I *do* believe Scripture *contains* the Word (message) of God. The bible is the product of divine-human interaction; God impressing ideas upon humans, and humans preserving those spiritual insights through all their human frailty. The "truth" of God's message to a person and to the world is only grasped by illumination of the Holy Spirit. When the Spirit shines a light on a Scriptural text, it "comes alive" and energizes the reader or hearer—then it *becomes* the words of the Living God.

This "isn't but contains; isn't but becomes" perspective leaves room for (what evangelicals would consider) "dismissing" parts of Scripture that are offensive to rational people, like genocide, infanticide, misogyny, slavery, supposed anti-homosexual passages, and lesser issues like whether eating bacon or shrimp is an issue of concern to the Almighty. It allows us to continue associating "the Word of God" with the bible but without equating the two. It is a palatable pathway for evangelicals escaping the absolutes of doctrine.

Also, importantly, post-evangelicals generally will not embrace an approach that belittles the Gospels or the teachings or miracles of Jesus; they still hold Jesus as the ideal reflection of God's will. Our task is to find a view that is amenable, subtle, not extreme, that maintains respect for our holy texts without making idols out of them.

Rethinking God

Reading the Room

- God is bigger than we were taught
- Love is God's primary characteristic, overriding any demands of "holiness" or "justice"
- God looks like Jesus

Trigger Points

- God is jealous, wrathful, and vengeful—and he is angry at sinners.
- God is just and holy. "God's holiness means that he is separated from sin and devoted to seeking his own honor. ... God's wrath means that he intensely hates all sin."[20]
- "The primary reason [God punishes sin] is that *God's righteousness demands it*, so that he might be glorified... God's jealousy means that God continually seeks to protect his own honor."[21]

Discussion

Matthew neatly summarized the former experience of most in the group. In his former church, "God was put in a restrictive box, too narrow, too judgmental, too exclusive. So I essentially walked away from God, and became an ethical humanist." Too narrow an understanding of God will necessarily exclude any whose views or experiences of the divine don't fit within those defining lines. Whatever other issues we would discuss, a "too small" view of God seemed at the root of them. Kayla explained, "God is bigger than any one religion or perception. It's like standing in an estuary or stream, enjoying the water, and thinking that is God, and then seeing the ocean, and seeing now that that is God. Both are true." It was a position most of us had arrived at. As our view of God expanded, the limits of other doctrines loosened, although often slowly and with much pain, as well. As seekers and questioners, we all agreed with the words of Neill, "God is love, everything else is up to question."

This includes doctrines about divine judgment and wrath, including implications for the afterlife. We were all told from childhood that "God is love," but the existence of a literal hell seemed grossly incompatible with that premise. (The existence of hell is commonly the first major issue which leads evangelicals to deconstruct.) Lauren put it this way, "If *we* can have compassion on the worst criminals or pedophiles by getting to know them, how much more would God, who knows us so intimately, be compassionate, not punishment-oriented." Kayla had spent some time studying the concepts of wrath and judgment, and concluded, "I see judgment more in terms of justice, like how the Old Testament prophets saw it, as restoration. Returning things back to how they should have been. I don't see it being so much about punishment."

This restorative view of God was more consistent with the image we all held of Jesus. Jesus was inclusive, compassionate, forgiving, restoring. He embraced sinners, not reject them. Jesus taught turning the other cheek and loving one's enemies. Even on the cross, as his enemies were killing him, instead of responding with divine force or angelic armies, he forgave them: "Father, forgive them." If Jesus is, as Scripture says, the image of the invisible God, then God must therefore look and act more like Jesus. It was a crucial change in understanding that brought Matthew back from agnosticism into the faith: "I kept feeling the pull of love, wrapping around me. I couldn't escape it. And I threw out everything I used to believe and rebuilt everything from that. What didn't fit, I let go of."

I related my own moment of insight when talking with my friend about his Om mantra, and my sudden revelation that God have been leaving bread-crumb trails to himself for all humanity throughout all of history. And how the God who spoke the universe into existence, billions of light-years wide, full of such diversity and richness, could then turn around and make it impossible for all by a small fraction of humanity to spend eternity with him by believing the one, correct faith formula—it just seemed so absurd. The God many of us were coming to know was not a petty tyrant, not that narrow or exclusivist. Surely that God was perpetually standing with arms outstretched for his prodigal children to "come home." This was not what we were taught in Sunday School.

One good thing evangelicalism had done was raise recent generations on John 3:16. Everyone knows it. Deconstructors cannot help but compare everything else they read in Scripture and hear from pulpits with the God who "so loved the world." This is a good thing, and can be the compass for finding alternative pathways out of the desert of evangelical doctrine into a wider, freer faith.

Rethinking Prayer

Reading the Room

- Prayer is supposed to be important, but we do not fully know *why* or *how*
- Prayer somehow involves God in our lives and us in God's activity
- Prayer has personal and communal benefits

Trigger Points

- Prayer is a human attempt to convince God to do what we want[22]
- God already knows the future and what he will do, so prayer is pointless[23]
- Prayer is mostly an exercise in confirmation bias or self-pacification
- Prayer is the expected activity of "good Christians"[24]

Discussion

"I don't know if I really believe in prayer anymore. Isn't it just 'confirmation bias'? If a prayer gets answered, God gets glory, but if it's not answered, it must not have been God's will? Isn't that intellectually dishonest; aren't we just kidding ourselves?" That was Kevin, launching the group into one of our most productive and profound sessions. Many related their frustration with the seeming ineffectiveness of prayer. Sometimes prayers were answered, sometimes not. Jack interjected, "We can't treat prayer, God, like a genie in a bottle." I threw in my own personal observation about prayer, and the caution to not be too specific: "We have to watch our attitude. Expectation can lead to frustration. Anticipation that God will do something is different than expectation of specific outcomes. With prayer, we invite God into our situations, but we don't tell him what to do or how to do it." Clearly, we had a lot to talk about.

Jordan changed the direction of the conversation. "Does prayer change things or the situation, or does it change us? We can be so outcomes-focused!" Eric followed up on this line of thinking with the remark that "Prayer is more about us than about God. It's cathartic." "So," Kevin jumped in, "is prayer more a placebo effect?" None of us really liked that idea, but agreed that it *did* play a part. We talked about the role of faith, and "moving mountains," and what action that required of us to "cooperate with God" in answering the prayer. Kevin pulled some thoughts together, "Our faith is what sustains us to move the mountain, one stone at a time. I heard someone say, 'Faith doesn't mean the mountain will move all at once. Maybe it's that faith that sustains *us* to move the mountain one stone at a time.'"

Jack added another consideration: "Prayer can be a tool for empathy with other people, and for consolation for us. Isn't it more about communing with God, and maybe a way to relate to people, forming bonds with people?" So there were communal aspects to prayer that we hadn't yet weighed. His comment tied together both the personal effect—a tool for empathy, that prayer changes us—and a social aspect, of generating compassion and solidarity with others.

We did not come to any single conclusion, but most of us walked away with a wider view of what prayer is, how it works—and a relief that we were not the only ones who had such frustrations in our prayer life. As Kayla later wrote, "I felt reassured. When we don't talk about our questions on matters like prayer, it's easy to think everyone else has perfect faith or thinks the same way except me, but being honest about the struggle helps build authenticity and deeper community." And for Lauren, touching such a sacred topic gave her freedom to explore other topics: "We talked about prayer and I remember leaving feeling awestruck. I had imagined we would deconstruct controversial topics (homosexuality, abortion, etc), but I never dreamed we could touch something as sacred and universal as prayer. When we did that, it opened everything up. It gave me room to start questioning all of the basics and understanding them better for myself, in ways I had never even thought to question."

Rethinking Atonement theories

This topic can sound rather esoteric and academic, but it is a bread-and-butter basic for most evangelicals, even if they can't remember the jargon. Predominant in our backgrounds is the belief in Penal Substitutionary Atonement theory. Most in the group had been taught this view exclusively, so some were unaware that any other positions existed. But next to the topic of hell, this may be the most common troublesome belief that either triggers deconstruction or must be addressed during deconstruction. Why is it important? Because what Jesus accomplished on the cross reflects on the very nature of God and on our value as human beings.

Reading the Room

- The only interpretation of what happened on the cross that most had been taught is the Penal Substitutionary Atonement theory
- The underlying "primitive/pagan" assumptions about appeasing an offended god through blood sacrifice are unacceptable
- The death of Christ must mean something else entirely; especially when seen through the lens of God's love
- There are practical, ethical implications of our position

Trigger Points

- "In the cross we have a clear demonstration of the reason God punishes sin: if he did not punish sin he would not be a righteous God, and there would be no ultimate justice in the universe."[25]
- "Christ's death was 'penal' in that he bore a penalty when he died. His death was also a 'substitution' in that he was a substitute for us when he died."[26]

- "We deserve to *die* as the penalty for sin. We deserve to *bear God's wrath* against sin. We are *separated* from God by our sins. We are in *bondage to sin* and to the kingdom of Satan. These four needs are met by Christ's death..."[27]

Discussion

We all knew that the New Testament declared that Christ "died for us" or "for our sins." But what that meant—the range of meaning "for" could have, in English or in Koine Greek—was at the heart of this topic. Also, there was no getting around that what we decided here reflected on how we perceived the character of God.

Kayla is often quiet during our discussions, stepping in at strategic points to interject her well-thought-out views. Her words bear on why this topic is so important. "Love, compassion, is triumphant. If we see the cross as justice, then we will model 'justice' in our lives—it's all about paying our dues. But if we see the cross as love and compassion, then the practical implications for our real lives is that we will model love and compassion, undeserved. There are real, practical ethical implications to our theology."

Was Jesus's blood really necessary to appease God? It raises such unseemly paradoxes, as Lauren expressed: "God has to sacrifice himself to himself to save us from the sin we were doomed to have from creation ... which he created? I just don't understand it. ... If I weren't born into this, I would think it sounds like BS." Or was that simply how ancient people understood human-divine interaction? Eric suggested that "blood sacrifice spoke the language of the people; it was a symbol that spoke to them." So they would naturally interpret the cross as blood sacrifice (and some New Testament language bears this out). Matthew agreed. "I think all the sacrifices and scapegoating made *them* feel better, made them feel forgiven. They needed some kind of physical expression of it to make it real to them. Like when Moses went up on Sinai to meet with God, and the people made a golden calf to have a visible, tangible image of a god they could relate to."

Mark had done his homework. It was something he had wrestled with for some time. "I'm more in the Christus Victor camp: that in his death and resurrection Jesus shows his power over sin and death, and proclaims the love of God triumphs over it all." In evangelical circles, this is seldom ever heard. But for Mark, it was liberating. "Finding out that the Church for centuries didn't believe this Penal Substitutionary Atonement stuff—that it wasn't really promoted till the Reformation—that the Church held less ugly views of God, made me feel comfortable when I rejected this idea. I knew I wasn't on the outside. I was seeing God like the Church had for most of its existence."

At some point, I had to throw my own views into the mix, echoing part of what Kayla had said earlier: "For me, the cross is the symbol of God's love that says 'I love you so much, that you can kill me, and in my dying breath, I'll forgive you and still love you. Nothing can separate you from me, ever.' I need a theology that says that!" It had been a while since I'd read up on the various theologies of atonement, but I was more in line with the Moral Influence Theory.[28]

While we all knew that blood sacrifice was a prominent theme in the bible, so it would be natural to see the cross in those terms, someone made the important observation that it was only one of the many images the Apostle Paul used to describe the work of Christ. There were over a dozen different terms and images he borrowed from temple life, personal and familial relations, economic and commercial dealings, military and battle, and legal courts—from all aspects of Roman daily life. So big was the impact of the life and death of Jesus, that no single description could contain it.

But this single legal/sacrificial image, so driven into each of us since childhood by our home churches, had left its scar in some way on most of us in the group. The legacy of this popular Penal Substitutionary atonement theory? Matthew retold part of his story: "All that sin needing to be paid for by blood to appease God, because God hates sin and couldn't even look it, made me think for a long, long time that God hated me. ... I felt like God didn't love me, and I had to get rebaptized to get right. But sometimes I would just feel this love pulling me, like God saying even if I were rolling in the gutters, he would still love me. It was my fear that was keeping me from God." Jennifer summed up the importance of rethinking this issue and finding better explanations: "it's all about the fruit. What kind of fruit did that substitutionary atonement idea produce? Fear. We're afraid of God. That can't be right. But when I let go of those ideas, I feel the love of God; I don't feel afraid."

Amen!

Rethinking Sexual Ethics

We had touched on sexuality and sexual ethics in a couple of our sessions. In a group comprised of at least half LGBTQ people, this was to be expected. I had shared with the group members months earlier a post I had written which looked at sex in the bible.[29] It had been an attempt to rebut evangelical purity culture. The last group meeting of the year, we devoted exclusively to this topic.

Reading the Room

- Post-evangelicals should embrace a more healthy, sex-positive attitude

- "Fornication" in the bible did not mean what we were taught it means
- Sex is "moral" and ethical when it is mutually consensual, non-coercive, and non-exploitive
- Sex is deeply personal, powerfully connective, and is in inexplicable ways both a physical and spiritual act

Trigger Points

- Sex is only to be experienced within the bounds of heterosexual, single-spouse marriage
- Sex is primarily for the purpose of procreation
- Non-procreative sex is indulgence in the flesh, therefore sin
- Sex between members of the same gender is an abomination to God and expressly forbidden in the bible

Discussion

To launch our final discussion, I quoted a provocative Facebook post from a pastor friend. In it, he advised his gay spiritual sons, in somewhat graphic terms, to not allow their bodies to be used as "dumping grounds" for other men's pleasure, and to treat their bodies and their souls with respect.[30] I essentially agreed with the statement ... and was immediately checked by others in the group. Matthew, voicing his Gen Z, still-in-progress deconstruction of sex, responded, "I'd say [sex is fine] as long as it is mutually agreeable and non-coercive. Some sexual practices can *seem* abusive or non-respectful. Certain kinks or desires can be healing, can be a way of working through personal or sexual trauma. They can let a person experience intimacy in a way that is meaningful to them at that moment." Others made similar comments. Neill gave his opinion that, "It should be our own moral conscience, our conviction, that determines if the sex is 'moral,' not whether some church, or even biblical, standard says so."

As the conversation proceeded, I was reminded that I still had some unprocessed thinking of my own about sex. I wrote in my notes that evening, "My evangelical baggage even now makes me think of sex in dualistic terms, flesh versus spirit, which tends to only add shame and sees sex as sinful 'lust of the flesh' instead of viewing it in a holistic way. Why shouldn't physical sex be spiritual? Why is a physical connection between people inherently sinful just because they aren't committed?"

I had brought David Gushee's *After Evangelicalism* with me to the discussion, since he had a thoughtful chapter on post-evangelical views on sex. As a Baptist ethicist, his works, especially on LGBTQ inclusion in the church, had been making a splash in evangelical media. He argues basically from a place of human dignity, proposing a sexual ethic with "enthusiastic mutual consent as a floor and covenant marriage as its main norm." As it turned out, my Gen Z friends were already attuned to the fine points of sexual ethics: consent and respect. Addressing my lingering view of body/soul duality, Gushee insightfully writes, "Participating in kinds of sex that require disconnecting body and soul is a form of self-inflicted spiritual violence."[31] We are holistic beings.

We talked about whether marriage or any form of commitment was necessary or proper before engaging in sexual encounters. No one present thought so. And that clearly was not always the case in the bible: the patriarchs and heroes of the faith had multiple wives, concubines, Judah and Samson openly engaged prostitutes—all of which was legal and (more or less) socially acceptable in ancient Israel's culture. We discussed Paul's use of the two loaded and ambiguous terms for same-sex acts between men *(arsenokoitai* and *malakoi*—which most of the group was familiar with[32]) and their associations with temple prostitution, idolatry, and human trafficking for the first, and unhealthy self-indulgence or debauchery for the second. We looked at "fornication" *(porneia)* in the bible, where the word actually means prostitution and sexual exploitation, not premarital sex as most of us had been taught. And for those early Christians using Greek translations of the Hebrew Bible, it would naturally point back to the specific forms of forbidden familial and cultic sexual relations defined in Levitical law (hence, Paul's outrage over a man in the church in Corinth having sex with his stepmother, in 1 Cor 5). Distinct from "adultery" which is specifically condemned (at least for women!), nowhere in the bible does the word refer generically to sex outside of marriage.

We discussed polyamory, threesomes ("triads" and "throuples"—a popular portmanteau of "three" and "couple"), and whether we thought they were healthy and "moral." Matthew again set the tone. "Monogamy or a 'covenant' between two people isn't necessary for sexual intimacy to be ethical or moral. That's like the same standard that says sex must only be between a man and his wife—hetero marriage. It's artificial; it's a man-made rule." Neill added that he had performed a marital union between three partners in the church. "I have performed a blessing of a throuple before, and I would do it again—if they feel led by the Holy Spirit, that they are brought together by God. Otherwise, I'm imposing shame on them by denying church or pastoral recognition and blessing of their relationship."

We discussed what we thought should be the minimal criteria, and the ideas aligned with a morality of respectful treatment of ourselves and others, but strayed widely from traditional morality of heterosexual, monogamous marriage. Although still stinging from the gentle "rebuke" I'd received earlier, I suggested, "I think the standard should be whether it's mutually affirming, respectful; not abusive or exploitive. It can be a way of sharing a deeply personal connection with someone, not just a way 'getting your rocks off' with someone, basically just using them for your own pleasure."

We all came around to focusing primarily on three primary issues of mutual consent, non-coercion and non-exploitation; that sex shouldn't be exclusively about a one-sided satisfying of physical pleasure, but about enjoying a personal connection between those engaged. Sex, we all agreed, should be mutually affirming.

I walked away from the conversation still considering the implications of Matthew's words that "Sex can be a way to help process your emotions," that it could be a means of inner healing—and weighing whether someone choosing to act as a "dumpster" was necessarily acting unethically or immorally towards himself or God. It was a vibrant conversation, and a great way to end the year-long project.

The Group Experience

At the end of our 12-month ministry experiment, I wanted to evaluate the overall effect of the Discussion Group experience. This project addressed a very real and specific need in our church: to provide safe space for discussing and processing questions and doubts people had about their faith. Was it effective? Did it accomplish some of the ideals we had set forth for it? And importantly, could we define the specific group experience? For this, we return to phenomenology's basic analysis rubric—describing an experience rather than theologies. Based on the comments made by the participants about their group experience, the following is what we concluded.

Reading the Room

- The group was a safe space. With rare exception, participants felt comfortable to voice "unpopular" or "potentially scandalous" views, real thoughts and questions they were actually wrestling with
- The sense of "community" and "fellowship"—that participants were not alone in their wrestling—enhanced and catalyzed the D/R process on the individual level
- The group experience generally resulted in a closer sense of connection with both God and the faith group
- A "focused topic" approach with more active facilitation was generally more effective and appreciated by the participants

Discussion

The overall take-away from the group experience was that it was a positive and enjoyable experience for everyone involved. As previously noted, after one of our first meetings I had written in my notes and posted on Facebook, "Such beautiful, wonderful, and entertainingly neurotic, saints I get to hang out with. This morning, I feel incredibly blessed. And I thank God for bringing such a rich and diverse collection of people into my life. I am truly richer because of all you beautiful people." Or as Lauren, a straight Millennial from a fundamentalist background, wrote, "Sometimes you find your people in unexpected places … We certainly did." She wrote in an email that after leaving our discussions, "it feels like a bursting love. I leave feeling so grateful and full of life/energy." Eric echoed her sentiments, "Group has been a *wonderful* experience for me. I greatly look forward to it each time we have it and always regret those times where we've had to miss. ... From the first session, I felt this was a good place for us to plant roots."

For most of the participants, this was the first time they had experienced this type of open, free group discussion. After one particularly engaging conversation, Neill, one of the pastoral staff, told me, "In all the churches I've been a part of, I've never experienced anything like this group. This is how I know we're doing what God has called us to do [as a group]." Eric, a straight Gen X male, said several months later, "This group, this church, is the first place I feel free to ask questions and say what I really think without fear of being judged." In another context, Eric commented, "It's rare that people really talk about these kinds of topics within my background." Lauren wrote in response to a survey questionnaire, "I'd never experienced this before. Never had I heard people wrestle in this way and I was so interested in the differing perspectives. It challenged the rules and traditions, but it didn't challenge my faith." Kevin, another straight white male, noted, "I liked it [the group] because I was able to ask questions, pose a thesis about what I believe, with no fear of repercussion. No church group *ever* addressed the question[s] we did." After what I expected would be our most controversial session, on deconstructing sexual ethics and morality, Kayla surprised me, stopping me afterwards to say, "I've been involved in a number of Presbyterian and Episcopal churches in my life, and in all the churches I've been a part of, we've *never* had a conversation like that before." Like Neill, I took it as a positive sign that we were doing what God was leading us to do.

The fellowship of other seekers gave participants "permission" to indulge their questions. The fear of being ostracized, of being shunned as agents of doubt or discord, melted away in a new found sense of freedom and welcome. Eric wrote that in his former church, "it's almost heretical to consider that we might have been thinking about, teaching, preaching, or believing things 'wrong'. Questioning the dogma is tantamount to blasphemy." But in the group, he felt free. One of our gay Gen Z participants, Jordan, commented, "I think the main effect [of the group] is it made me more comfortable looking at God in unconventional ways. Being able to talk to a group of believers and say 'outlandish' things like 'maybe God doesn't have to be humanoid' or 'maybe God doesn't have to punish people eternally to be just'. Bottom line is I'm happier looking at God and being open to surprises." Lauren described her feelings about it: "This group allows me to do what I need to do at any given moment. It doesn't matter what head space I'm in, there is never judgment or pressure. Because of that, I find myself deconstructing more than I ever have and looking forward to conversations where I can dig even deeper."

A number of our sessions were free-flowing, unscripted, with no planned topic of discussion, and conversation "popcorned" around the room in a good-natured spirit of camaraderie. It was an opportunity for venting, for expressing random and sometimes frivolous thoughts that might not have found an outlet under other circumstances. When asked how the "no-holds-barred" discussion format felt, Eric, the Gen X, self-described deep thinker, commented, "Scary. Exhilarating. Hilarious. Safe. It's been a weird conflict at times. We've talked about all kinds of topics—both the gravely serious, and the absurd. ... I know at the end of the day, we're processing these things in community. We're searching the face of God, trying to find answers. Sometimes we find them, sometimes we don't. Both are OK." This style of conversation was favored by the younger participants. Jordan explained to me later that "this is how Gen Zs think." Michael, in particular, seemed to thrive in this type of discussion, and insisted, "Hey, I really liked those [popcorn] kind of conversations!"

However, this loose style grew tiresome to some after a few sessions, and they began wondering if they needed to participate any longer. In typical frank fashion, Jack, another Millennial, told me in private conversation, "You know I love getting together with everybody .... But I'm not sure who's in charge. Everybody is talking. There doesn't seem to be any direction sometimes, and I don't need to waste my time sitting on a couch just to listen to people bullshit about stuff that isn't interesting to me." Lauren, gracious as ever, said sometimes it "felt exhilarating—like we were on a ride and we weren't exactly sure where it was going or at what speed." Even Gen Z Jordan began to lose interest. "Yeah, I kinda thought that way, too, that they [the sessions] were becoming a waste of my time." The last few sessions, we changed tactics and began announcing planned topics in advance.

From a pastoral perspective, the group experience as a whole achieved the initial objectives of the project: normalizing the questioning/seeking process, and deepening a connection with God and community. Eric was one of the most extensive with his written reactions, and his thoughts will serve as a summary conclusion: "I was so impressed by the curiosity and the hunger to know God better. ... That hunger is infectious, and while I'm grappling with things, I realize it's OK. It's good, even. I don't have to have all the answers, but it's more about the journey. I'm so grateful for the Decon group." Responding to another survey question, he continued, "this group has me asking questions, both big ones and little ones. ... When we're talking through it within our faith communities, we're growing closer to Him and each other. God loves that, too."

A Composite Description of the Lived Experience of Faith Deconstruction & Reconstruction in the Evolving Faiths Discussion Group

The end goal of phenomenological research is to derive an exhaustive or composite description of the experience being studied. In heuristics, that summary description, called a "creative synthesis," often focuses on the self-expression of the researcher. In keeping with my adaptation of the methodology, the following is offered as a representative description of deconstruction based on my own D/R journey and participation in the Discussion Group common with the experiences of the other group participants.

> From the moment a person enters the evangelical faith community, one is immediately immersed in inflexible theology. We are entrenched in a system of absolutes, in black and white answers. We are steeped in the belief that we hold the one Truth, grounded in a literal reading of the bible, which is God's Eternal Word. Everyone else, including other Christian denominations, are in some way in error.
>
> We are taught that God is loving but just. He is righteous and holy, and cannot even look upon sin. Sin must be punished, it must be "paid for," and God's anger must be appeased. This can only be accomplished through sacrificial death, through blood. Only Jesus, as the divine and sinless Son of God, could be the perfect sacrifice to atone for our sins. By accepting that Jesus did this, we are saved.
>
> We are told, and taught to sing, "my heart was black with sin until the Savior came in. His precious blood, I know, will wash me whiter than snow. And in God's Word, I'm told, I'll walk the streets of gold. I'll

read my Bible and pray, and grow in him every day." That song encapsulates so many key themes: sinfulness, blood, salvation, God's Word, heaven, and the Christian duty to read the bible and pray. These, along with a "purity culture" of strict sexual morality, comprise much of the evangelical world.

The faith is "simple" and certain. This belief system is satisfying because it supplies absolute answers, and a person can remain in this "uncritical" state of Simplicity for years, embedded safely in like-minded community. But over time, as one breaks out of the evangelical bubble and is exposed to the broader reality of life and the differing beliefs of others, those rigid definitions can be tested. Questions and doubts may arise. One either responds by suppressing them or by exploring them.

Choosing to explore beyond evangelical boundaries, considering new ideologies, can trigger a crisis, sometimes called "Religious Disorientation Growth Syndrome." It can be world-shaking and personally devastating. Evangelical faith is built on sure foundations, and if those foundations are challenged, one's entire faith is in danger of collapsing. And because one's eternal security is based on certainty of correctness, daring to challenge sacred beliefs means potentially losing one's salvation and risking the fires of hell in the afterlife. Deconstructing often leads to being ostracized or marginalized by one's faith community, which compounds the sense of fear and isolation. The severity of one's mental and emotional trauma tends to be in proportion to the length of time spent saturated in evangelical culture, and seems to diminish in each succeeding generational cohort. Finding a new support system (a person or group) where questions are affirmed and encouraged is vital to surviving and thriving in this state of Shifting and Perplexity.

The Evolving Faiths Discussion Group provided that affirming, encouraging "safe space" for people transitioning out of fundamentalist and evangelical backgrounds. It provided a sense of camaraderie and community, while also providing stimulus and discussion for researching, rethinking, and exploring alternative theologies. It was a life-preserver to many in the group, providing shelter and a sense of stability that was missing after the person left the safety of evangelical circles. The year-long duration of the Group's calendar allowed a prolonged period of exposure and readjustment, which diminished the sense of immediate crisis and allowed a time of gradual acclimation, reorientation, and healing. This facilitated transition into a final state of Rebuilding, Reconstruction, or Harmony, characterized by a normalization of questioning and challenging as a valid (even biblical) spiritual way of life, an expanded perception of God, and a greater sense of community with the world at large.

6

Closing Thoughts

" 'The sacred' may be carried in individual minds, but it becomes real in conversations that can happen in sometimes unlikely places."

~ NANCY TATOM AMMERMAN[1]

Deconstruction usually ends in one of two ways. The person may end up questioning—and refuting—everything, with the result that he or she becomes agnostic or some variety of atheist. The other option is the goal of this pastoral intervention: the person reconstructs their faith virtually from the ground up, with a new-found freedom and joy, and ends up closer to God than they were before. The faith of this second group is typically marked by a more open, inclusive, pluralistic, culturally relevant, and decidedly more loving view of God and the world.

There are a host of reasons, some of which we have seen in the social context described in Chapter 2, why a person might become disillusioned with the Church and with their faith, and begin a D/R journey. Some of these cannot be resolved internally, such as the politicization of the Church or the abuse of power within it. But for those whose primary triggers were an internal discordance with inherited theology and doctrine, rethinking the foundations of evangelical belief is a necessary step on the journey toward wholeness and recovery.

There are no universal answers, as we saw in our group's discussions. What may satisfy one person may not necessarily be comfortable for another. And it is recognized that no amount of argument can ever persuade a heart. To some degree, personal revelation—some kind of "ah-ha" moment—must occur within the seeker to make her receptive to new, and often contradictory, insights. This was the situation in my case, as detailed in my "Hermeneutical Autobiography" in Chapter 1. In almost every case where significant change in perspective occurred relating to a foundational "truth" of my evangelical faith, it was instigated by a moment of personal revelation or clarity, often during prayer. This is especially true when it comes to reconfiguring one's cosmology, one's view of the essential nature of the Universe. As Raimon Panikkar, the renowned "apostle of inter-faith dialogue," once commented, "the real is not reducible to intelligibility."[2] That is, ultimate truth cannot be apprehended by intellect alone. Or, as Shakespeare famously penned in *Hamlet*, "There are more things in heaven and earth, Horatio, than are dreamt of in your philosophy." Inspiration, illumination, revelation or epiphany is often required.[3]

However, the topics—and resolutions—discussed in the previous chapter were of crucial concern for this pastor-researcher on his own journey and in the faith-processing of the participants in the Evolving Faiths Discussion Group. They were, of course, not the only topics one processes on their D/R journey. (Some of the most common being, the nature of the bible, eternal conscious torment (hell), penal substitutionary atonement, the problem of evil and suffering in the world, the abuses of the Church throughout history, and the lack of transcendent experience offered by the Church.[4]) Virtually everything that one has inherited as part of their life of faith becomes subject to rethinking, re-evaluation. Thankfully, once an initial major hurdle is cleared—typically by rethinking one of evangelicalism's hermeneutic keystones, like the existence of hell, the nature of the bible, or how one perceives God—there is much less resistance in challenging other secondary issues and theologies.

I want to draw pastoral notice, however, to the fact that theology is only one portion of a healthy spiritual life. Good theology in itself will not lead to improved spiritual experience and transformation. But bad theology *will* effectively block it. Our perspective and expectation will often determine what we experience. Our biggest hinderance to growth is often our own self-limiting hermeneutics. Thus, unhealthy theology which presents a stumbling block to deeper encounter with God needs to be addressed. This is the heart of the faith deconstruction and reconstruction journey.

The role of spiritual disciplines and practices cannot be overstated in shaping spiritual experience and creating a vibrant spiritual way of life. Some of our group discussions on the place of ritual and symbol in our spiritual practice were not only eye-opening but also palliative while dealing with reconstructing religious identity.[5] Eric mentioned how that was a new—and beneficial—insight for him during his process: "I was really moved by one [session] where we discussed the idea of using ritual/tradition/totems as a means of centering your mind/body/spirit on God. That whole scene is foreign to me ...[but] I lit a candle during service a few weeks ago. It brought about a peace I wasn't expecting." There is so much more to the spiritual life than simple "doctrinal belief" typified in evangelical circles.

And as we saw at the heart of this project, belonging to community is essential to our spiritual well-being as well. In facilitating this group as a safe space, I felt deeply gratified by comments about how much the group meant to the participants. Eric again: "I think small groups are where you create community. We never *really* had that before ... From the first session, I felt this was a good place for us to plant roots." Or, "we're processing these things in community. We're searching the face of God, trying to find answers [together]." Lauren wrote that being in the group "gave me room to start questioning all of the basics and understanding them better for myself, in ways I had never even thought to question." "I'd never experienced this before.... I think it hit a reset button and allowed me to start at the bottom and construct my way up."

This sense of community was mentioned as important by several in the group. A number of them had left more fundamental churches and told me one of the hardest parts of leaving was losing that sense of belonging, the warm embrace of fellowship. They felt its absence acutely. This is a common symptom in Escobar's "Severing" stage, that time when you know you have to leave for your own mental and emotional health (or are forced to leave), but the sudden separation leaves holes in your soul. Grieving that loss is normal. And finding a new community, a new spiritual tribe, is essential to the healing process. Jennifer told me this was particularly hard for her. She knew she and Mark had to leave their church, for their daughter's sake as well as their own. They didn't want her raised in a place that limited her role in the church, which wouldn't even let her read Scripture in public. And she teared up the Sunday we had her daughter read from the Gospels at The Abbey. They had to leave their former church; it was unhealthy and oppressive. And being welcomed and fully included in our humble faith community would hopefully be an important part of their recovery.

In another way, Jordan, a gay Gen Z recent graduate from a Christian college, blurted out one evening, "you realize that you guys are my only gay friends, the only gay people I actually hang out with at this point." He had processed accepting himself during his college years, but at that point still had no gay friends, and importantly, no gay *Christian* friends. Our group, composed as it was by about 60% LGBTQ people, and on some nights, 100% of those who showed up, was his primary support for a significant aspect of his personal identity.

It was as refreshing and encouraging for me as well, being part of a group of people who genuinely were seeking a deeper encounter with God while struggling with fundamental questions of faith. As recounted in Chapter 4, "The Act of Ministry," one of our early sessions fell on my birthday, and I remember so vividly that sense of joy and peace I felt being there among those goofy, irreverent, yet genuine people, exploring questions of faith; and I remember thinking I wouldn't want to be anywhere else. To be sure, there were times when the group felt like a burden, when I wondered if we had outlived our mission, particularly on those two occasions when it was just me and one other participant. But the overarching feeling during the entire year was that *this* was the culmination of my ministry. *This* is what I was called to do. This made sense of all the seemingly random streams of theological studies and experiences over the years. For such a time, a place, and a people as this, I was called.

Another bit of pastoral insight I gained from this experience. Too often pastors, particularly in the evangelical world, center their vocational life around the pulpit. This is our tradition, reflecting a Reformation mentality: the pulpit is center stage in most of our churches, the proclamation of the Word has replaced the altar as the focus of our worship. We can easily become paid preachers or teachers, professional liturgists. But we miss out on so much pastoral ministry—and genuine human interaction—by keeping distance from our congregants. Being part of a small group, especially one as personally impactful as the Evolving Faiths Discussion Group, is an important way of connecting with our faith communities on more than just a professional level.

There is a pastoral adage that says "they won't care what you know until they know that you care." Being in close proximity with people on a spiritual journey, sharing experiences and ideas, is a way of showing you care. Then, maybe—maybe—they'll be receptive to the "words of wisdom" you've gleaned over your lifetime. I'm reminded that there was a reason Jesus's disciples did not just listen to his sermons, but lived their lives with Jesus. Personal relationship is the means of spiritual transformation. And small groups, like this project, are ways of building such relationships.

Personal involvement in a person's D/R process shows that you (as pastor) are not simply concerned about doctrinal correctness or conformity but about the health and well-being of their souls, and that you care about their lives. In this sense, "being present" is a crucial act of ministry. Affirming their journey, and recognizing that no one has it exactly right (including the minister), allowing your people to make mistakes, to experiment, to find their way, however falteringly, is the normative path of spiritual growth. We need to be there, walking with them on that journey.

In the survey I emailed to each participant six months into the project, I asked in at least four different ways about the health of their relationship with God.[6] As much as I enjoyed the intellectual pursuits in our communal deconstruction process, as a pastor, this was my primary concern. The whole point was that their sense of connectivity with God, the perception of God in their lives, would expand. Sadly to me, no one reported experiencing angelic visitations or unexpected Christophanies. However, several indicated that their view of God had changed. Jordan, for example, related that the group "made me more comfortable looking at God in unconventional ways." "Bottom line is," he said, "I'm happier looking at God and being open to surprises." Lauren wrote at length about the change in her feelings toward God since being part of the group. "I find God more interesting than I used to. God had become another task and another person to disappoint. I walked around with Christian guilt all the time for not praying every day or reading my bible, etc. I think group has helped me see God in a different light. It feels like we are starting a new relationship—almost like dating someone for the first time. I think I originally thought it would feel like repairing an old relationship, but it doesn't feel that way at all. It feels like the God I was familiar with is no longer relevant for me, and I have this new God that I'm getting to know and actually like."

"Getting to know and actually like God"—that should make a pastor's heart smile.

Similar comments were made by others, that their *sense* of God, not just their intellectual way of thinking *about* God, had changed during the course of meeting session after session. For some, it was indescribable. How does one put into words the shift in feeling about God? But the growing impression was that God was pleased with their questions, that God delighted in their pursuit. For many of them, this was a *radical* change from the apprehension and alienation they had originally felt when they decided to reject certain evangelical "truths." Like the biblical patriarch Jacob wrestling with God, they are walking away differently, with a new sense of spiritual identity, and hopefully more blessed.

As group facilitator, the lived experience of the Discussion Group has had a profound effect on my sense of self and my spiritual calling, as much as it has on many of them. Whatever the next steps for this small group are in the coming year, whether we continue as a deconstruction-focused discussion and support group, morph into a religious book club, a bible study, or simply a fellowship/hang-out group, I know this has been one of the most spiritually formative and rewarding years of my life.

An Invitation to Change

This project from the beginning engaged in action research—that was the premise of my D.Min. thesis and the basis for this book. It was intended to discover whether the intervention of a church-sponsored series of encounters would meet the immediate spiritual crisis faced by a number of our congregants. The level of success would be measured by the "3 C's" in our people's lives: would they *continue* seeking and exploring as a spiritual life-style? Would they be more *comfortable* with those questions and lack of doctrinal certainty? And, importantly, was their sense of *connection* with God and the world around them enhanced? The evident answer to each of those questions seemed to be a resounding "Yes!"

The result of action research often leads to answering three general questions with regard to the specific context: What should we *stop* doing? What should we *continue* doing? What should we *start* doing? A few comments regarding these basic questions seems in order. These recommendations are offered not just to my local church but to evangelical (and post-evangelical) churches at large.

First, we must *stop* presenting ourselves or Christianity as having all the answers. We must stop presenting our doctrines as *the* correct way of viewing God and interacting with God. Our widely diverse denominational doctrines belie our conveyed certitude and prove that we do not possess any single answer to any question that satisfies everyone, even those sharing our evangelical worldview. And our certainty and closure is not only distasteful to those looking for broader answers, but will also stifle a healthy curiosity and deeper spiritual development. In short, far from securing one in the faith, an attitude of certainty actually impedes maturity.

Second, it is not enough to claim that our churches are safe spaces for questions, for seekers, or even for re-thinking and reforming (as many mainline churches are noted for). We must *start or continue* to actually provide a forum for those questions to be asked and explored, with others—we must create a sense of safe community. The forum need not be specifically a "deconstruction group," but there should be some kind of interactive, small-group activity where it is known to be place where the faith is explored freely, where questions are entertained, not simply "answered." This project confirmed the need for a regular time and place for these encounters to occur. Because "once is not enough." Deeply rooted questions will not be settled in one conversation. Repeated opportunity and engagement is needed.

These types of conversations can be life-changing, and our people's heart-felt questions are the front lines of faith in this generation. They are opportunities for encountering the holy. As Nancy Ammerman observes, "'The sacred' may be carried in individual minds, but it becomes real in conversations."[7] And, frankly, where else can people go? If our churches, our self-proclaimed "houses of God," do not offer hope, do not point the way, and do not encourage a deepening of the faith and a fresh vision, then we are effectively closing the doors in seekers' faces, forcing them to look for answers outside the church. And they will likely not return. On the other hand, churches of all varieties for decades have bemoaned the steady numeric decline and especially the exodus of the younger generations. Being known as a safe space for spiritual exploration may just result in a much desired "greening effect" in our rapidly graying congregations.

It may also prove beneficial—and more honest—if we *started* (or continued) claiming to offer *a way* of discovery for those soul-driven questions, rather than claiming to have found the final answers to everything. We don't have to surrender our confidence in our faith, we need not "water down" the gospel or diminish Christianity to be "just one of many paths to God." But we can say we offer Christ as the Way, we offer access to the Spirit who leads us along the Way and into all Truth. And the answers to specific questions we can release to the individual's walk with God.

We must present Christianity as a walk, a path, not an end-point. This will doubtless present opportunities for insecurity and alarm as we see our people making obvious mistakes, stumbling their way toward God—especially for those of us whose traditions for so long have been based on absolutes and "correct answers." But humans must learn to walk on their own, not be carried by their parents all their lives. And ultimately, isn't this what we really claim to have? As the Apostle Paul could say so confidently, "for I know in whom I have believed, and I am persuaded that *He* is able to keep that which I've committed unto Him until that day" (1 Tim 1:12). Let's stop trying to do the Spirit's job.

Along these lines, we must *start* viewing questioners as genuine seekers, not as rebels, challengers, or instigators of trouble. As I saw in this project so clearly, questions and deconstruction are not a sign of sickness to be cured or a problem to be solved, but a sign of a soul reaching out for something bigger and deeper than what they inherited.

And we must *start* or continue presenting a bigger God, one who is not intimidated or angered by questions or challenges. I believe the bible portrays God as one who invites and delights in engagement, a God constantly pushing the boundaries of our limited human perception. Surely the One who stretched forth the universe with a word cannot be confined to our tiny theological boxes. The God who called Abraham out of his tent and commanded him to "look up at the stars, and count them if you can," is surely calling us out of our tiny theological tents, inviting us to take in a more magnificent vista than what we had previously known. And perhaps, just perhaps, He is revealing himself in greater and more profound ways to those who pursue him with questions.

בָּרוּךְ אַתָּה, יְיָ אֱלֹהֵינוּ, מֶלֶךְ הָעוֹלָם, שֶׁהֶחֱיָנוּ וְקִיְּמָנוּ וְהִגִּיעָנוּ לַזְּמַן הַזֶּה.
Blessed are You, O LORD our God, King of the universe,
who has kept us alive, and sustained us, and brought us to
such a time as this!

Post Script

It's been 5 years since the Evolving Faiths Discussion Group project began. It has itself evolved, but is still meeting every other week. Now it's returned to more of a book discussion group, where the group reads works on theological and spiritual topics, typically one or two chapters per session, written by authors from a variety of perspectives. Names like N.T. Wright, Richard Rohr, David Benner, Marcus Borg, S. Abhayananda, and Elaine Pagels. We've discussed the Apostle Paul and his Jewish apocalyptic mysticism. We've read about the historical Jesus and the formation of the gospels. We've read about Christian and Sufi and Eastern mystics, and talked about the early Christian movement and the Gnostic Gospels. We've discussed the nature of humanity, ideas about the True Self and the False Self, and about methods of meditation and prayer. And we're considering exploring some so-called New Age spirituality writers, like Alan Watts and Ram Dass or Eckhart Tolle.

The specific books we select are less important than where they lead us and the questions and conversations they provoke. Because the questions we ask to a large extent influence the depth and shape of our spiritual lives.

This is no longer simply about Penal Substitutionary Atonement theories, the existence of Hell, or the inerrancy of the bible. Those crucial faith issues have long since been put to rest, even if not completely answered. The intensity level has diminished—the crisis of faith has passed—and we're now reading and discussing out of spiritual and intellectual curiosity.

Why? Because with an Infinite God, there's always more!

Our purpose now is to continue plumbing the richness of our faith and its history, but also to explore what others have encountered and believe about God, the Source, and the nature of Reality. To discover how others have reached out into that metaphysical realm of the Spirit, what they learned, and what they might have to share with us. And we're free to completely disagree and disregard whatever is not palatable to us at this point in our journeys. But surprisingly, after an initial shock and resistance, we often end up walking away with a nugget or two of new insight. We walk away richer than we were before. As one member who grew up Southern Baptist said this past week, "reading these different books shows me things I had no clue about."

And that's the point. We're still in a way deconstructing and reconstructing, though we no longer use that terminology. Now, we're simply exploring and expanding. Still asking questions, still comfortable with uncertainty, and still feeling our connection with God reaching into new areas and deepening in new ways. The old Wesleyan-Holiness writer on prayer, Leonard Ravenhill, once wrote that "a person with an experience of God is never at the mercy of a person with an argument." And we're finding this to be true. New ideas, new arguments, new theologies do not intimidate us. We are not cowed back into the safe corners of our evangelical or fundamentalist upbringings. We have no illusions about figuring it all out, and we sometimes walk away with more questions than when we started. There is a distinct sense of freedom in these explorations because we have a confidence in the goodness of God, the vastness of his Being, and the divine standing invitation to "come deeper."

The group membership has changed over the years. Many of the original participants have since moved on with their lives, some to other churches, some who have yet to find a spiritual home. And new members have joined who were not part of that original group, as I expect will be the case for as long as the group exists. The group, even as small as it is, still represents a cross-section of the generations, with representatives from the Boomer, Gen X, Millennial and Gen Z cohorts. I still function more or less as an older guide (though not the oldest!), the guy with the advanced theological degrees who can sometimes throw the spotlight on an overlooked point of interest or who can answer the occasional "Christian-related" question. And the others bring concerns and engaging points of view from their respective worlds, expressing their doubts or evolving convictions, each contributing something from their own experience and journey. The discussions are sometimes challenging, occasionally provocative, usually lively, and always entertaining. We meet now at a local coffee shop on alternating Wednesday evenings, but the group continues much in the same way as originally envisioned.

Interestingly, our group has actually outlived the church that birthed it. The Abbey was only a few months old when the D/R Discussion Group was initially launched, and like many new churches, survived only a few years. But the group's mission continues. In fact, after a meeting not long ago, one of the members pulled me aside and said that I should take it as a personal affirmation that for him this had been the most meaningful and impactful discussion we'd ever had. I can't even tell you what specifically we talked about; our conversation meandered through a variety of topics, as it normally does, using the current book as a launching pad. But it was a reminder that these kinds of conversations are desperately needed, even life-changing, and may indeed be the front lines of faith in our time. And though I'm now retired and no longer serve as a pastor, this ongoing "experiment" continues to be a high point in my life.

The future of the Church at large is still in question. We continue to watch the institutional church decline, especially in America, as more and more people find community and connection remotely, and as people sincerely hungry for spiritual reality, repulsed by the hypocrisy and corruption in established Christian organizations, eagerly explore alternative spiritual practices. No one knows what "doing church" will look like much further into the 21st century.

Perhaps tellingly, I am the only one of our group who continues to attend a traditional church. But as "Jordan," who is still with us, put it just recently, "this group *is* church to me." It addresses the need for community and regular fellowship, provides a steady stream of spiritual food for thought, and continues to be "a safe space to grow deeper."

Small groups like these, where people are free to ask questions and to explore their faith together without fear of critique or rebuke, may well be what that church future looks like.

Notes

Chapter 1 – Introduction: The Situation

[1] Wayne Teasdale, *The Mystic Heart: Discovering a Universal Spirituality in the World's Religions* (Novato, Calif: New World Library, 1999), 20.

[2] See, for example, David Kinnaman's *You Lost Me: Why Young Christians are Leaving Church and Rethinking Faith* (Grand Rapids: Baker Books, 2011), and David Kinnaman and Gabe Lyons's *UnChristian: What a New Generation Really Thinks About Christianity ... and Why it Matters* (Grand Rapids: Baker Books, 2007). Kristin Kobes Du Mez wrote a compelling and thorough examination of the toxic effect of White Christian nationalism, militant masculinity and misogyny on evangelicalism, and the culture of fear in the church for anything or anyone outside of white, cis hetero normativity, in her *Jesus and John Wayne: How White Evangelicals Corrupted a Faith and Fractured a Nation* (New York: Liveright Publishing, 2020).

[3] Tim Sensing, *Qualitative Research: A Multi-Methods Approach to Projects for Doctor of Ministry Theses* (Eugene, OR: Wipf & Stock, 2011), xix.

[4] The former denominations of regular attendees include Roman Catholic, Episcopal, United Methodist, Church of Christ, Nazarene, Mennonite, Southern Baptist, Assemblies of God, United Pentecostal Church, independent charismatic churches, and agnostic/atheist backgrounds.

[5] Lynn Butler-Kisber, *Qualitative Inquiry: Thematic, Narrative and Arts-Based Perspectives*, 2nd ed. (Los Angeles: Sage, 2018), 28.

[6] For a more detailed personal account of this reconciliation process and a theological defense of being both Christian and LGBTQ, see Stephen

Schmidt, "Being a Gay Evangelical," *Impact Magazine*, Dec 31, 2013, https://impactmagazine.us/2013/12/being-a-gay-evangelical/.
See also a similar autobiographical and apologetic work by Justin Lee, founder of the former Gay Christian Network online community, *Torn: Rescuing the Gospel from the Gays-vs.-Christians Debate* (New York: Jericho Books, 2012).

[7] Wayne Teasdale, *The Mystic Heart: Discovering a Universal Spirituality in the World's Religions* (Novato, Calif: New World Library, 1999).

[8] "Defining generations: Where Millennials end and Generation Z begins," Pew Research Center, Jan 17, 2019, https://www.pewresearch.org/fact-tank/2019/01/17/where-millennials-end-and-generation-z-begins/

[9] John Swinton and Harriet Mowat, *Practical Theology and Qualitative Research*, 2nd ed. (Norfolk, UK: SCM Press, 2016), 235-237.

[10] David Coghlan, "Seeking God in All Things: Ignatian Spirituality as Action Research," *The Way* 43/1 (Jan 2004), 99-100. Coghlan acknowledges drawing this classification from Peter Reason and Hillary Bradbury's *Handbook of Action Research* (London: Sage, 2001), 2.

[11] Max van Manen, *Researching Lived Experience: Human Science for an Action Sensitive Pedagogy*, 2nd ed. (New York: Routledge, 2015), 31, cited in John W. Creswell and Cheryl N. Poth, *Qualitative Inquiry & Research Design: Choosing Among Five Approaches*, 4th ed. (Los Angeles: Sage, 2018), 77.

[12] Coghlan, "Seeking God," 103.

[13] I should note that my thesis advisor urged me to adopt ethnography, or at least some aspects of it, because he felt it addressed my specific demographic group. Ethnography is particularly designed for the study of groups which share a significant degree of commonality, a specific shared culture. And the participants that joined the group were largely from one shared religious background: that of evangelical or Christian fundamentalism. In this regard, we were a homogenous group. We spoke the same language, we shared the same idioms, we had lived common religious experiences. In many ways, we shared the same worldview, despite some of our other demographic differences. Ethnography is also designed around direct immersion of the researcher into the life situation of the persons being studied—something that seemed especially to fit my role as pastor to many of the participants in a small church community. And it also addresses investigating central orienting themes and issues of the culture-sharing group. In some ways, it seemed an ideal match for what we were attempting to do. See Mary Clark Moschella, *Ethnography as a Pastoral Practice: An Introduction* (Cleveland: Pilgrim Press, 2008). But my initial

and primary interest was in exploring the *experience* of D/R and the potential therapeutic and spiritual effect of group discussion on people of faith, myself included. Heuristic phenomenology directly spoke to that interest.

[14] van Manen, *Researching Lived Experience*, 3, 2.

[15] John Swinton and Harriet Mowat, *Practical Theology and Qualitative Research*, 2nd ed. (Norfolk, UK: SCM Press, 2016), 102.

[16] van Manen, *Researching Lived Experience*, 9.

[17] Creswell and Poth, *Qualitative Inquiry*, 75-78, 115.

[18] Sensing, *Qualitative Research*, 180, emphasis added

[19] Elizabeth Brown Vallim Brisola and Vera Engler Cury, "Researcher Experience as an Instrument of Investigation of a Phenomenon: An Example of Heuristic Research." *Estudos de Psicologia* 33, no.1 (Jan-Mar 2016): 102. doi: https://doi.org/10.1590/1982-02752016000100010.

[20] van Manen, *Researching Lived Experience*, 163, quoted in Creswell and Poth, *Qualitative Inquiry*, 82.

[21] Clark Moustakas, *Heuristic Research: Design, Methodology, and Applications* (Newbury Park, CA: Sage, 1990), 14.

[22] Brisola and Cury, "Researcher Experience," 96, 98, 102.

[23] Moustakas, *Heuristic Research*, 9.

[24] Sandra M. Schneiders, "The Study of Christian Spirituality: Contours and Dynamics of a Discipline," in *Minding the Spirit: The Study of Christian Spirituality*, Elizabeth A. Dreyer and Mark S. Burrows, eds. (Baltimore: Johns Hopkins Univ Press, 2005), 18.

[25] Moustakas, *Heuristic Research*, 43.

[26] Schneiders, "Study of Christian Spirituality," 18.

[27] Creswell and Poth, *Qualitative Inquiry*, 78. Swinton and Mowat, *Practical Theology*, 106, describe bracketing as "the *suspension* of a person's beliefs and preconceptions in an attempt to look at the phenomenon 'as it is', that is, without any intrusion from the researcher. By adopting a stance of objectivity and neutrality, the phenomenon can be seen and understood for what it essentially is."

[28] Richard R. Osmer, *Practical Theology: An Introduction* (Grand Rapids: Eerdmans, 2008), 22.

[29] Moustakas, *Heuristic Research*, 90.

[30] Schneiders, "Study of Christian Spirituality," 18.

Chapter 2 – Deconstruction in American Christianity

[1] The quotation continues, "These people have an intuitive sense that there is more to Christianity than the rigid rules and theological constructs of the past"—which proved an accurate description of those I encountered in the group. They all sensed there was more. David M. Felten and Jeff Procter-Murphy, *Living the Questions: The Wisdom of Progressive Christianity* (New York: HarperOne, 2012), xii.

[2] Kurtis Vanderpool, "The Age of Deconstruction and the Future of the Church." *Relevant*, April 7, 2021. https://www.relevantmagazine.com/faith/the-age-of-deconstruction-and-future-of-the-church/

[3] Charles Taylor, in his landmark work, *A Secular Age*, describes this "enchanted" worldview as, "the world of spirits, demons, and moral forces which our ancestors lived in. ... People who live in this kind of world don't necessarily believe in God ... But in the outlook of [pre-modern] European peasants ..., beyond all the inevitable ambivalences, the Christian God was the ultimate guarantee that good would triumph or at least hold the plentiful forces of darkness at bay" (Charles Taylor, *A Secular Age* (Cambridge, MA: The Belknap Press of Harvard University Press, 2007), 26).

[4] Ryan P. Burge, *The Nones: Where They Came From, Who They Are, and Where They Are Going* (Minneapolis: Fortress Press, 2021), 38.

[5] Pew Research Center, "When Americans Say They Believe in God, What Do They Mean?" Religion & Public Life, Apr 25, 2018, https://www.pewforum.org/2018/04/25/when-americans-say-they-believe-in-god-what-do-they-mean/

[6] Taylor agrees with this sentiment. In defining what he means by "secular," he dismisses the idea that "science killed belief." Rather, especially in light of America's entrenched religiosity, he proposes a sense of secularity in which belief is but one of a plurality of options rather than a social or cultural given. (Taylor, *Secular Age*, 3-4.)

[7] Becka A. Alper, "Why America's 'Nones' Don't Identify with a Religion," Pew Research Center, Aug 8, 2018, https://www.pewresearch.org/fact-tank/2018/08/08/why-americas-nones-dont-identify-with-a-religion/

[8] Thomas Keating, *Open Mind, Open Heart*, 20th Anniversary Ed. (New York: Continuum, 2006), 7.

[9] Taylor, *Secular Age*, 1-2, 26-27.

[10] Striking a familiar tone of inspiring fear in the faithful for political cause, the *New England Paladin* wrote in 1800, "Should the infidel Jefferson be elected to the Presidency, the *seal of death* is that moment set on

our holy religion, our churches will be prostrated and some infamous prostitute, under the title of the Goddess of Reason, will preside in the Sanctuaries now devoted to the worship of the Most High" (Quoted in Paul Johnson, *A History of the American People* (New York: HarperCollins, 1997), 206-207).

[11] The words of Kenneth Kantzer, an early leader of evangelicalism, dean of Trinity Evangelical Divinity School, and editor of *Christianity Today* from 1978 to 1982, in John Woodbridge and Wendy Murray Zoba, "Standing on the Promises: Former CT editors Carl Henry and Kenneth Kantzer evaluate evangelicalism in light of its twentieth-century developments," *Christianity Today*, Sep 16, 1996, https://www.christianitytoday.com/ct/1996/september16/6ta028.html.

[12] Randall Balmer, *Bad Faith: Race and the Rise of the Religious Right* (Grand Rapids: Eerdmans, 2021), Preface. See also, Randall Balmer, "The Real Origins of the Religious Right," *Politico Magazine*, May 27, 2014, https://www.politico.com/magazine/story/2014/05/religious-right-real-origins-107133/

[13] Falwell preached at least two sermons against civil rights in 1964 and 1965, and Blacks were prohibited from membership in his church until 1968. His "whites only" Christian academy was opened in 1967, the same year Lynchburg public schools desegregated. (Seth Dowland, *Family Values and the Rise of the Christian Right* (Philadelphia: Univ of Pennsylvania Press, 2015), 27.)

[14] Balmer, "Real Origins of the Religious Right."

[15] Balmer, *Bad Faith*, especially Part Two: "The Abortion Myth and the Rise of the Religious Right."

[16] Du Mez, *Jesus and John Wayne*, 12.

[17] Dowland, *Family Values*, throughout.

[18] Kinnaman and Lyons, *UnChristian*, 27.

[19] Kinnaman, *You Lost Me*, 8. More broadly, religious historian Julia Corbett Hemeyer states that religion and church are seen by younger generations as largely irrelevant to their lives, and too focused on money, rules, and power (Julia Corbett Hemeyer, *Religion in America*, 7th ed. (New York: Routledge, 2016), 31).

[20] Rachel Held Evans, "Why Millennials are Leaving the church," *CNN Belief Blog*, July 27, 2013, http://religion.blogs.cnn.com/2013/07/27/why-millennials-are-leaving-the-church/. This sentiment is reported by Kinnaman as well: "They are not disillusioned with tradition; they are frustrated with slick or shallow expressions of religion. ... They

want a more traditional faith, rather than a hip version of Christianity" (Kinnaman, *You Lost Me*, 78).

[21] David Kinnaman and Mark Matlock, *Faith for Exiles: 5 Ways for a New Generation to Follow Jesus in Digital Babylon* (Grand Rapids: Baker Books, 2019). As a pastor with a vested interest in shepherding this generation of Nones and spiritual seekers, I found Kinnaman's focus on technology as the latest villain and his attachment to worn-out evangelical tropes (such as his "four-chapter Christian story: creation-fall-redemption-restoration") to be disappointingly out of touch. This is an author who could stand some "deconstruction" in his theological perspectives.

[22] Kinnaman and Lyons, *UnChristian*, 15.

[23] Ryan P. Burge, "The 2020 Vote for President by Religious Groups—Christians," *Religion in Public*, Mar 29, 2021, https://religioninpublic.blog/2021/03/29/the-2020-vote-for-president-by-religious-groups-christians/. "Religion and the 2024 Presidential Election," Public Religion Research Institute, Nov 8, 2024, https://prri.org/spotlight/religion-and-the-2024-presidential-election/

[24] David P. Gushee, *After Evangelicalism: The Path to a New Christianity* (Louisville: Westminster John Knox, 2020), 27.

[25] Bob Smietana, "Matt Chandler, megachurch pastor and ACTS 29 leader, placed on leave," *Religion News Service*, Aug 29, 2022. https://religionnews.com/2022/08/29/matt-chandler-megachurch-pastor-and-acts-29-leader-placed-on-leave-for-unhealth-instagram-messages-woman/

[26] *Hillsong: A Megachurch Exposed*, directed by Dan Johnstone, performance by Troy Dillinger, Michael G. Gabel, and Marie Finch (Breaklight Pictures, 2022), *Discovery+*, https://www.discoveryplus.com/show/hillsong-a-megachurch-exposed-us

[27] David Crampton, "New Zealand Authorities Investigating Nation's Largest Megachurch," *Christianity Today*, Aug 24, 2022, https://www.christianitytoday.com/news/2022/august/arise-church-new-zealand-investigation-intern-abuse.html

[28] Julie Roys, "Pastor Resigns from Houston Megachurch After Admitting Affair," *The Roys Report*, Jan 3, 2022, https://julieroys.com/jeremy-foster-houston-megachurch-hope-city-affair-resignation/

[29] Sarah Pulliam Bailey, "Southern Baptist leaders covered up sex abuse, kept secret database, report says," *Washington Post*, May 22, 2022, https://www.washingtonpost.com/religion/2022/05/22/southern-baptist-sex-abuse-report/

[30] The full report of Guidepost Solutions independent investigation of the cover-up is available here: https://www.sataskforce.net/updates/guidepost-solutions-report-of-the-independent-investigation

[31] The resultant church environment was described by former staff as a "set of longstanding problems with Driscoll's cut-throat and autocratic management style, anger, and personal hubris." See Valerie Tarico, "Christian right mega-church minister faces mega-mutiny for alleged abusive behavior," *Salon*, Apr 3, 2014, https://www.salon.com/2014/04/03/christian_right_mega_church_minister_faces_mega_muntiny_for_abusive_behavior_partner/. See also coverage in evangelical *Christianity Today*, such as Morgan Lee's "Mark Driscoll Steps Down While Mars Hill Investigates Charges," Aug 24, 2014, https://www.christianitytoday.com/news/2014/august/mark-driscoll-steps-down-while-mars-hill-investigates-charg.html

[32] See the 2022 Hulu documentary, *God Forbid: The Sex Scandal that Brought Down a Dynasty*, directed by Billy Corbin, with Jerry Falwell, Jr., Giancarlo Granda, Sam Myerson (Rakontur, 2022), *Hulu*, https://www.hulu.com/movie/god-forbid-the-sex-scandal-that-brought-down-a-dynasty-d0c5802f-05ec-4826-9390-f9ceca67f3e0

[33] As a point of reference, these are not just random names pulled from a scandal sheet. As someone born, raised, and steeped in the evangelical world, I am personally familiar with most of these minsters and ministries. In fact, one of the victims of sexual assault at Hillsong College in Sydney, who appeared in the *Hillsong: A Megachurch Exposed* documentary, is the daughter of a former friend from seminary.

[34] Elle Hardy, "The Sexual Abuse Scandal That's Engulfed the Evangelical Movement," *New Republic*, Sep 20, 2024, https://newrepublic.com/article/185907/ evangelical-movement-sexual-abuse-scandal, and Tracy DeLatte, "Gateway Church founder Robert Morris released from Oklahoma jail," KDFW Fox 4 News, Mar 31, 2026, https://www.fox4news.com/news/gateway-church-founder-robert-morris-released-from-oklahoma-jail

[35] Mike Hixenbaugh and Elizabeth Chuck, "Assemblies of God churches shielded accused predators — and allowed them to keep abusing children," NBC News, Oct 20, 2025, https://www.nbcnews.com/news/us-news/assembly-god-church-shield-predators-child-sex-abuse-allegations-rcna240213

[36] Ann Marie Shambaugh, "Former staff at Life.Church describe toxic work culture and an alleged assault by Pastor Craig Groeschel," *The Roys Report*, Apr 23, 2026, https://roysreport.com/former-staff-life-church-toxic-

work-culture-alleged-assault-by-groeschel/. One of the witnesses the report is based upon is personally known to me. Another former insider commented, "What's crazy is that the most egregious things I know personally aren't even in this report."

[37] Brian D. McLaren, "Thank God that More People are Deconstructing their Faith," *Premier Christianity*, Aug 1, 2022, https://www.premierchristianity.com/opinion/thank-god-that-more-people-are-deconstructing-their-faith/13570.article

[38] Emma Copper, "Anything But Christian: Why Millennials Leave the Church," *Medium*, Jan 30, 2019, https://medium.com/@EmmaCopper/anything-but-christian-why-millennials-leave-the-church-ccae210dfb06.

[39] As sociologist Nancy Tatom Ammerman writes, "... in the United States, a perception of declining 'religion' and growing 'spirituality' implies that as there is less of one, there will more of the other. It also implies a commonsense wisdom that 'religion' is organized, traditional, and communal, while 'spirituality' is improvised and individual. But ... there is actually a good deal of overlap between the two domains" (Nancy Tatom Ammerman, *Sacred Stories, Spiritual Tribes: Finding Religion in Everyday Life* (New York: Oxford Univ. Press, 2014), 4).

[40] Josh Packard and Casper ter Kuil, "Gen Z is Keeping the Faith. Just Don't Expect to See Them at Worship," *Religion News Service*. Sep 23, 2021. https://religionnews.com/2021/09/23/gen-z-is-keeping-the-faith-just-dont-expect-to-see-them-at-worship/

[41] Hemeyer, *Religion in America*, 32. This corresponds with what Ammerman calls a "rising religious individualism" (Ammerman, *Sacred Stories, Spiritual Tribes*, 3).

[42] Ryan P. Burge, "Most 'Nones' Still Keep the Faith." *Christianity Today*, Feb 24, 2021, https://www.christianitytoday.com/news/2021/february/nones-religious-unaffiliated-faith-research-church-belief.html

[43] Gregory A. Smith, "About Three-in-Ten U.S. Adults Are Now Religiously Unaffiliated," Pew Research Center, Dec 14, 2021, https://www.pewresearch.org/religion/2021/12/14/about-three-in-ten-u-s-adults-are-now-religiously-unaffiliated/. These numbers are flexible depending on how the survey question is asked. For example, Gallop puts the Nones at 21% of the population (roughly 2 in 10) in 2022, but their question—"What is your religious preference—are you Protestant, Roman Catholic, Mormon, Jewish, Muslim, another religion or no religion?"—defines None as "no religion," versus Pew's somewhat looser definition which includes atheists, agnostics and "nothing in particular." (Frank Newport, "Slowdown in the Rise of Religious Nones," Gallup, Polling Matters,

Dec 4, 2022, https://news.gallup.com/opinion/polling-matters/406544/slow-down-rise-religious-nones.aspx

[44] Burge, *The Nones*, 50, 67.

[45] Burge, *The Nones*, 41.

[46] Kinnaman and Matlock, *Faith for Exiles*, 24-28.

[47] Burge, *The Nones*, 66, emphasis added.

[48] Burge, *The Nones*, 29.

[49] Pew Research Center, "When Americans Say"; Burge, *The Nones*, 129.

[50] Springtide Research Institute, "Gen Z and Religion—What the Statistics Say," Sep 29, 2022, https://www.springtideresearch.org/post/gen-z-and-religion-what-the-statistics-say

[51] Smith, "Three-in-Ten U.S. Adults."

[52] Burge, "'Nones' Still Keep the Faith."

[53] Church of England, "Younger people more likely to pray than older generations, survey finds," Aug 28, 2022, https://www.churchofengland.org/media-and-news/press-releases/younger-people-more-likely-pray-older-generations-survey-finds

[54] Jonathan Evans, et al, "Many Religious 'Nones' Around the World Hold Spiritual Beliefs," Pew Research Center, Sep 4, 2025, https://www.pewresearch.org/religion/2025/09/04/many-religious-nones-around-the-world-hold-spiritual-beliefs/

[55] Barna Group, "Meet the 'Spiritual but Not Religious,'" Faith & Christianity, Apr 6, 2017, https://www.barna.com/research/meet-spiritual-not-religious/

[56] Springtide Research Institute, "Ask Josh: What is the difference between being religious and being spiritual?", Oct 4, 2022, https://www.springtideresearch.org/post/ask-josh-what-is-the-difference-between-being-religious-and-being-spiritual

[57] Ammerman, *Sacred Stories, Spiritual Tribes*, 288-293.

[58] Barna Group, "Meet the 'Spiritual but Not Religious.'" Barna divided SBNRs into two groups: in SBNR #1 were those who still identified with a religion but did not view that faith as important; and SBNR #2 comprised atheists, agnostics and the unaffiliated. Forty-one percent of SBNR #1 and 36% of SBNR #2 did not practice any of these.

[59] Barna Group, "Meet the 'Spiritual but Not Religious.'"

[60] Heather Green, "Study: Gen Z doubles down on spirituality, combining tarot and traditional faith," *Religion News Service*, Aug 11, 2021, https://religionnews.com/2021/08/11/study-gen-z-doubles-down-on-spirituality-combining-tarot-and-traditional-faith/. See also, Packard and ter Kuil, "Gen Z is Keeping the Faith."

[61] Green, "Gen Z doubles down on spirituality." Of those who practiced in fortune telling, 17% practice daily, 25% weekly, 27% at least once a month, and 31% less than once a month.

[62] Mat Blasio, "Seeking Safe Havens," Springtide Research Institute, Voices of Young People, Oct 21, 2021, https://www.springtideresearch.org/post/sap-blog-leaving-religion

[63] Blasio, "Seeking Safe Havens."

[64] See Molly Hanson, "Could neo-paganism be the new 'religion' of America?" *Big Think*, Sep 30, 2019, https://bigthink.com/the-present/modern-paganism/

[65] Brian D. McLaren, *A New Kind of Christianity: Ten Questions that are Transforming the Faith* (New York: HarperOne, 2010), 33.

[66] Jon Bloom, "What Does 'Deconstruction' Even Mean?" *Desiring God*, Feb 15, 2022, https://www.desiringgod.org/articles/what-does-deconstruction-even-mean

[67] Phyllis Tickle, *The Great Emergence: How Christianity is Changing and Why* (Grand Rapids: Baker Books, 2008), 79.

[68] McLaren, *New Kind of Christianity*, 22, 55.

[69] James McGrath offers "Jengafication" as a colorful candidate, if it weren't a trademark infringement. Like the game, where players remove wooden blocks one at a time from an 18-story tower while trying to keep the tower from collapsing, so deconstructors identify and remove pieces of their faith tradition that can no longer remain comfortably ... often until the tower crashes down. (*Beyond Deconstruction: Building a More Expansive Faith* (Grand Rapids: Eerdmans, 2026), 1).

[70] Carl R. Trueman, "Josh Harris's Message Remains the Same," *First Things*, Aug 12, 2021, https://www.firstthings.com/web-exclusives/2021/08/josh-harriss-message-remains-the-same

[71] See, for example, his use of this paradigm in Paul Ricoeur, *The Symbolism of Evil*, trans. Emerson Buchanan (Boston: Beacon, 1969), particularly the conclusion.

[72] Mark Gregory Karris, *Religious Refugees: (De)Constructing Toward Spiritual and Emotional Healing* (Orange, CA: Quoir, 2020), 18.

[73] Karris, *Religious Refugees*, 18-19.

[74] Peter Enns, *The Sin of Certainty: Why God Desires our Trust More than our "Correct" Beliefs* (San Francisco: HarperOne, 2016), 157.

[75] See, for example, Richard Rohr, *The Universal Christ: How a Forgotten Reality Can Change Everything We See, Hope for, and Believe* (New York: Convergent Books, 2019), 243-248.

[76] Tyler Huckabee, "Reminder: 'Deconstruction' Does not Mean 'Deconversion,'" *Relevant*, Dec 6, 2021. https://www.relevantmagazine.com/faith/church/reminder-deconstruction-does-not-mean-deconversion. This was in response to a well-distributed video clip that week (Dec 2021) of evangelical mega-pastor Matt Chandler equating deconstruction with abandoning the faith.

[77] Walter Brueggemann, *Praying the Psalms: Engaging Scripture and the Life of the Spirit*, 2nd ed (Eugene, OR: Cascade Books, 2007), 3; quoted in Zahnd, *When Everything's on Fire*, 140.

[78] Brian D. McLaren, *Faith After Doubt. Why Your Beliefs Stopped Working and What to Do About It* (New York: St Martin's Essentials, 2021), 223-235.

[79] Morgan S. Peck, *The Different Drum: Community Making and Peace* (New York: Touchstone, 1987).

[80] Kathy Escobar, *Faith Shift: Finding Your Way Forward When Everything You Believe is Coming Apart* (New York: Convergent, 2014).

[81] Escobar, *Faith Shift*, 146.

[82] Karris, *Religious Refugees*, 53-74; quotation is from 54. He somewhat colloquially identifies them as: Station One: Feeling at Home; Station Two: Splinterhood; Station Three: "To Be or Not To Be"; Station Four: Returning Home Different; Station Five: Disorientation; Station Six: Angstville; Station Seven: Farewell and Goodbye; and lastly, Station Eight: Extreme Makeover—Home Edition.

[83] Generally inclusive of McLaren, Peck, Ricoeur, and famously delineated by James Fowler in his *Stages of Faith: The Psychology of Human Development and the Quest for Meaning* (San Francisco: Harper, 1981).

[84] Tickle, *Great Emergence*, 91-96; quotation is from 96.

[85] The Word of Faith movement, popularized by Kenneth E. Hagin, Sr. (1917–2003), is sometimes imprecisely called the "prosperity" or "health and wealth gospel" because of its emphasis on manifesting physical healing and material prosperity through faith, particularly through "positive confession." This "name it and claim it" teaching has been

criticized as an oversimplification of God's will and an attempt to manipulate God's power for one's personal (selfish) desires. Tithing and "seed-faith" giving were a principal means of activating God's power to one's benefit, which sadly reinforced a transactional view of one's relationship with God. However valid some critique of its doctrines and excesses may be, the teachings have been a revitalizing force in many people's faith. They also continue to be a strong influence in neo-pentecostal churches and a particularly powerful driving force in church expansion in Latin America and Africa. I believe Derek Vreeland is correct when he states, "Word of faith teaching is not a heresy to be obliterated, but a theologically premature movement that needs significant reconstruction" (Derek E Vreeland, "Reconstructing Word of Faith Theology," paper presented at the Society for Pentecostal Studies, Jan 2001, reprinted at https://www.hopefaithprayer.com/word-of-faith/reconstructing-word-of-faith-theology/).

[86] Gregory A. Smith, et al, "Decline of Christianity in the U.S. Has Slowed, May Have Leveled Off," *Religious Landscape Study*, Pew Research Center, Feb 26, 2025, https://www.pewresearch.org/religion/2025/02/26/decline-of-christianity-in-the-us-has-slowed-may-have-leveled-off/

[87] Story related in Cynthia Bourgeault, *Centering Prayer and Inner Awakening* (Lanham, MD: Cowley, 2004), 56-57.

Chapter 3 – A Biblical Theology of Deconstruction

[1] Bloom, "What Does 'Deconstruction' Even Mean?"

[2] Nahum M. Sarna, *Genesis, The JPS Torah Commentary* (Philadelphia: Jewish Publication Society, 1989), 227.

[3] James L. Kugel, *The Bible as It Was* (Cambridge, MA: Belknap Press of Harvard Univ Press, 1997), 227.

[4] Quoted in Kugel, *Bible as It Was*, 228.

[5] Kugel, *Bible as It Was*, 228-229.

[6] Kugel, *Bible as It Was*, 229, emphasis added.

[7] Ellen F. Davis, *Getting Involved with God: Rediscovering the Old Testament* (Cambridge, MA: Cowley, 2001), 121-143.

[8] Davis, *Getting Involved with God*, 133.

[9] For text, translation, and commentary, see Rabbi Aviva Hellman, "Baba Metzia 59b: *Tanur Shel Akhnai," Sefaria*, https://www.sefaria.org/sheets/144163?lang=bi.

[10] See Romans 3:21-22, 28. "For now a righteousness from God, apart from law, has been made known ... For we maintain that a man is justified by faith apart from observing the law." This was a revolutionary idea.

[11] The National Association of Evangelicals defined four key statements of faith to which one must agree in order to be legitimately called an evangelical. The fourth statement reads, "Only those who trust in Jesus Christ alone as their Savior receive God's free gift of eternal salvation" ("NAE, LifeWay Research Publish Evangelical Beliefs Research Definition," https://www.nae.org/evangelical-beliefs-research-definition/).

[12] See related comments in Joseph A. Fitzmyer, *The Acts of the Apostles, The Anchor Bible* (New York: Doubleday, 1998), 453-473.

[13] A plain reading of the text, the *peshat*, is the simplest, yet just one of multiple, ways of extracting meaning from Scripture, according to Jewish hermeneutics. "Insofar as biblical interpretation is concerned, there is not one set of conventions; ... interpreters had often widely divergent methods and goals, and they produced readings of the same text which were 'as far as east from west'" (James L. Kugel and Rowan A. Greer, *Early Biblical Interpretation* (Philadelphia: Westminster Press, 1986), 28. See also, Rabbi Lawrence Kushner, *Jewish Spirituality: A Brief Introduction for Christians* (Woodstock, VT: Jewish Lights Publishing, 2001), 49-51, where he describes 4 levels of interpreting Scripture: the simple/superficial reading *(peshat),* allusion *(remez),* implication *(derash),* and secret/mysterious meaning *(sod).*

[14] This is a key argument, for example, when addressing with evangelicals LGBTQ+ inclusion in the church, and related arguments about "biblical definitions" of sex and marriage. If singleness and celibacy are too burdensome a yoke for straight people not blessed with that charism, why/how should they be imposed on people with same-sex attraction? (See Schmidt, "Gay Evangelical.")

[15] For a compelling description of Saul/Paul as a Jewish apocalyptic mystic and zealot, and the implications of his multi-year deconstruction and reconstruction process in Damascus, Arabia, and Tarsus, see N.T. Wright's *Paul: A Biography* (San Francisco: HarperOne, 2018), especially Part One: Beginnings.

[16] Historian Donald Akenson comments somewhat candidly that Paul "truly got on people's nerves. Even his fellow believers found him impossible at times. Saul and the brother of Yeshua ... were often at loggerheads. Jesus' brother was the head of the believers in Jerusalem after Yeshua's death, and he and Saul carried on a decades-long negotiation about what was the ambit of true faith. Brilliant, god-drunk, and unpredictable, Saul,

who had never met Yeshua of Nazareth in the flesh, was convinced that he knew him better than those who had" (Donald Harman Akenson, *Saint Saul: A Skeleton Key to the Historical Jesus* (New York: Oxford Univ Press, 2000), 8).

[17] Describing the thorough-going reworking of Paul's worldview caused by his divine encounter, A.D. Nock writes, "For him [Paul] to become a Christian meant in the first instance a complete change of face ... He brought to it not merely a fresh enthusiasm but also an imperious inner need to discover an interpretation and reconciliation of the old and the new in his religious life." (A.D. Nock, *Conversion: The Old and the New in Religion from Alexander the Great to Augustine of Hippo* (Oxford: Clarendon, 1933), 191, quoted in Fitzmyer, *Acts of the Apostles*, 422). That "enthusiasm" and "inner need" are characteristic of faith deconstruction.

[18] Akenson, *Saint Saul*, 203.

[19] This approach is painfully common among pop theologians and pastors eager to prove a point. For example, Baptist pastor Terry Austin, "Jesus and Deconstruction," *Baptist News Global*, Nov 22, 2021; or Brandan Robertson, in his otherwise wonderful work, *True Inclusion: Creating Communities of Radical Embrace* (St Louis, MO: Chalice Press, 2018), 69 ff, where he declares the word "literally translates as 'to expand one's mind'" (71). Even emergent movement sage Brian McLaren approaches Jesus's words from a Greek philosophical perspective: "'Repent' means literally, become pensive again or have a change of mind and heart" (*New Kind of Christian*, 138). At the risk of being clumsily reductionist, rabbinic Judaism was much more pragmatic and grounded in real-life in its worldview, as the debate over the oven of Akhnai mentioned earlier exemplifies.

[20] As the great Israeli historian and scholar on Jesus and Paul, Joseph Klausner, attests quite explicitly in his classic work, *Jesus of Nazareth*, "Jesus of Nazareth was a product of Palestine alone, a product of Judaism unaffected by any foreign admixture. ... Jesus spoke Aramaic and there is no hint that he knew Greek—none of his sayings shows any clear mark of Greek literary influence. Without any exception he is wholly explainable by the scriptural and Pharisaic Judaism of his time" (Joseph Klausner, *Jesus of Nazareth*, trans. Herbert Danby (Boston: Beacon Press, 1964), 363). There are other schools of thought which contend that Hebrew was a living language at the time, not solely reserved for Torah reading and preaching or Temple ritual, but no reputable scholar presumes that Jesus preached or conversed in Greek.

[21] The Mishnah records Rabbi Joshua ben Qorhah explaining, "Why does the section, 'Hear, O Israel' precede 'And if you will obey my

commandments'? This is in order that one may first accept the yoke of the Kingdom of heaven and afterwards the yoke of the commandments" (m.Ber 2.2). See Geza Vermes, *The Religion of Jesus the Jew* (Minneapolis: Fortress Press, 1993), especially the chapter on "Jesus and the Kingdom of God," 120-151.

22 Vermes, *Religion of Jesus*, 146. To be sure, NT teaching contains elements of both the present and eschatological aspects of the Kingdom (as do references in the Hebrew Bible, intertestamental literature, rabbinic and early church literature), but Jesus is more concerned with its immediate presence, especially as inaugurated in his person.

23 E.P. Sanders, "The Life of Jesus" in *Christianity and Rabbinic Judaism: A Parallel History of Their Origins and Early Development*, Hershel Shanks, ed. (Washington DC: Biblical Archeology Society, 1992), 71. J.W. Doeve, in his classic work, *Jewish Hermeneutics in the Synoptic Gospels and Acts* (Assen: Van Gorcum, 1954) likewise argues against a special divine "consciousness of vocation" as the basis of Jesus's authority to challenge traditional readings of Scripture. "The method of expounding Scripture used by Jesus and the earliest Christians was none other than the method used in the Synagogue. ... The fact that both for Jesus and for his contemporaries, Scripture contained *the word of God*, and that they were possessed of a particular method for understanding this divine utterance in Scripture" (140-141).

24 David Daube, *The New Testament and Rabbinic Judaism* (1956; repr., Peabody, MA: Hendrickson, 1994), 57.

25 Klausner explains, "the Pharisees and the *Tannaim*—even the earliest of them—did, indeed, 'pile up the measure' of the ceremonial laws, and they overlaid the original nucleus with a multiplicity of detail and minutiae as unwittingly to obscure the divine purpose of these laws. This habit Jesus rightly opposes..." (Klausner, *Jesus of Nazareth*, 371).

26 The National Association of Evangelicals adopted what's been called the "Evangelical Quadrilateral," developed by historian David Bebbington, identifying the four primary characteristics of the evangelical faith: Conversionism, Biblicism, Activism, Crucicentrism (see Appendix D: The Evangelical Quadrilateral). The cornerstone is the first principle, Conversionism: "the belief that lives need to be transformed through a 'born-again' experience and a life-long process of following Jesus" (https://www.nae.org/what-is-an-evangelical/). Religious historian Randall Balmer, however, prefers a three-part ("trinitarian"!) definition: belief in the bible as God's revelation, the centrality of spiritual conversion, and a commitment to evangelism. (Balmer, *Bad Faith*, "Definitions and Terms.")

[27] The gospel writer's choice of ἄνωθεν, which may legitimately be translated either "again" or "from above," seems a deliberate wordplay to tease the dialogue between Jesus and Nicodemus. This wordplay would only work in Greek; there is no Hebrew or Aramaic equivalent with similar dual temporal and spatial connotations. (Raymond Brown, *The Gospel According to John, The Anchor Bible*, vol 1 (Garden City, NY: Doubleday, 1980), 130-141.) Regardless of which meaning is preferred, both lead to the same conclusion of physical impossibility and spiritual necessity.

[28] See, Yevamot 62a, "And Reish Lakish said ... a convert who just converted is like that of a child new born (גֵּר שֶׁנִּתְגַּיֵּיר כְּקָטָן שֶׁנּוֹלַד דָּמֵי)."

[29] McLaren, *New Kind of Christianity*, 28.

[30] Sanders, "Life of Jesus," 63-64. "Behind *hamartoloi* stands, almost beyond question, the Hebrew word *resha'im* ... *Resha'im* [רְשָׁעִים] is virtually a technical term. It is best translated 'the wicked', and it refers to those who sinned willfully and heinously and who did not repent. ... Certainly the term would include professional sinners such as usurers..." (E. P. Sanders, *Jesus and Judaism* (Philadelphia: Fortress, 1985), 174-211; quotation is from 177).

[31] Shabbat 31a

[32] As David Daube explains, "by the time of Jesus most Rabbis held that the entire religion was implied in a small number of first principles, or even a single one ... yet they never ceased to insist on the absolute and independent validity of each particular commandment" (Daube, *Rabbinic Judaism*, 251).

[33] Baba Metzia 59b:5

[34] This is the case in the "Oven of Akhnai" debate recounted above, when Rabbi Joshua refutes Rabbi Eliezer's miraculous signs, referencing Scripture that "after the majority must one incline" (Exod. 23:2)—where in context it actually reads, "You *shall not* follow a majority in wrongdoing..."

[35] Daube, *Rabbinic Judaism*, 428.

[36] See Mathew J. Distefano for his discussion and helpful itemization of this list in his joyously irreverent yet extremely beneficial work for deconstructors, *Heretic! An LGBTQ-Affirming, Divine Violence-Denying, Christian Universalist's Responses to Some of Evangelical Christianity's Most Pressing Concerns* (Orange, CA: Quoir, 2018), 34-37. See also, Joseph Fitzmyer, *The Gospel According to Luke. The Anchor Bible*, vol 1 (New York: Doubleday, 1985), 667-668.

[37] Distefano, *Heretic!*, 38; Fitzmyer, *Luke*, 667.

[38] Fitzmyer, *Luke*, 667.

[39] See, for example, Romans 15:9 quoting Psalm 18:49, but excluding surrounding context of Ps 18:41-42, 46-47. Or the selective use in Rom 15:10 of Dt 32:43 with the omission of any mention of divine retribution. Or the reworking of Dt 21:23 in Galatians 3:13 to omit God's curse; or in itemizing the "Armor of God" in Eph 6, where the writer draws from Is 59:17-18, but again chooses not to include Isaiah's "garments of vengeance," "fury as a mantle," repayment, wrath and requital to his enemies. (See Distefano, *Heretic!*, 44-51.)

[40] Paul Ricoeur, *Interpretation Theory* (1976), 31-32; quoted in Sandra M. Schneiders, *Written That You May Believe: Encountering Jesus in the Fourth Gospel*, rev & expanded ed. (NY: Herder & Herder, 2003), 185.

[41] John 14:7,9; Col 1:15, 2:9; 2 Cor 4:4; Heb 1:3, etc.

[42] On this theme, see Bradley Jersak, *A More Christlike God: A More Beautiful Gospel* (Pasadena: CWRpress, 2015).

[43] This highlights the important distinction between hermeneutics and critical exegesis. Where exegesis tasks itself with reconstructing the text's meaning within its historical context and uncovering the author's intent, hermeneutics deals with the reader's activity in discovering truth in the text for him- or herself.

Chapter 4 – The Act of Ministry

[1] Rachel Held Evans, "Is Doubt an STD?," *Rachel Held Evans*, Apr 12, 2013, https://rachelheldevans.com/blog/doubt-std-keller

[2] The Gospel Coalition, a union of evangelical and Reformed churches founded by Timothy Keller and D.A. Carson, had just released an article viewing deconstruction as a "problem" and "sickness" in the church to be cured, and it had generated a wave of critical reactions and responses on social media and in the blogosphere. The article in question was Joshua Ryan Butler's "4 Causes of Deconstruction," *The Gospel Coalition*, Christian Living, Nov 9, 2021, https://www.thegospelcoalition.org/article/4-causes-deconstruction/.

[3] According to Andy Stanley, pastor of the Atlanta-based evangelical megachurch, North Point Community Church, built on the basis of small groups, one of the key principles in creating a successful small group ministry is "to provide a predictable environment where participants experience authentic community and spiritual growth." And one of the components of that stability is that groups are best when closed—that is, when

they have regular, consistent participants. We could not enforce that, but it was a working idea. (Andy Stanley and Bill Willits, *Creating Community: 5 Keys to Building a Small Group Culture* (Colorado Springs: Multnomah Books, 2004), 182-184.)

[4] Celebrate Recovery, "Small Group Guidelines," https://celebraterecovery.com/resources/cr-tools/guidelines.

[5] John Baker, Johnny Baker, and Mac Owen, *Celebrate Recovery 365 Daily Devotional: Healing from Hurts, Habits, and Hang-Ups* (Grand Rapids: Zondervan, 2021), "Day 1: The First Step."

[6] Celebrate Recovery, "Small Group Guidelines.

[7] "10 Fundamental Components of Recovery," NAMI Thurston/Mason, https://namitm.org/10fcr/

[8] Mary Moschella, referencing Margaret Kornfeld's *Cultivating Wholeness: A Guide to Care and Counseling in Faith Communities* (2000), in Moschella, *Ethnography as Pastoral Practice*, 34.

[9] Margaret J. Wheatley, *Finding Our Way: Leadership for an Uncertain Time* (San Francisco: Berrett-Koehler, 2005), 26.

[10] Personal conversation with David Gormong, via Skype, Nov 5, 2021.

[11] Margaret Wheatley agrees that "conversation is the natural way humans think together. ... Human beings know how to talk to each other—we've been doing this ever since we developed language. We're not [re]inventing conversation in the 21st century, we're reclaiming it from earlier human experience." In group conversations, she suggests reminding oneself that "everyone here has something to teach me" ... and, importantly, "we expect it to be messy at times" (*Turning to One Another: Simple Conversations to Restore Hope to the Future.* 2nd ed. (San Francisco: Berrett-Koehler, 2009), 34,36).

[12] Stanley and Willits discuss this as one of their "group essentials" to promote group participation. "More than sharing the right answers, we want people to share their lives" (Stanley and Willits, *Creating Community*, 157).

[13] Moschella, *Ethnography as Pastoral Practice*, 142, 145. See also, Stanley and Willits, *Creating Community*, 157.

[14] This idea of "comfort with uncertainty" would come up again and again, and was, in fact, one of the three initial goals of the group's formation, one of the "Three C's": becoming *comfortable* with questions. (The other two C's were that they would *continue* the D/R process, with resulting enhanced *connection* with God.) At least 4 of the group had read Peter

Enns's *The Sin of Certainty* (San Francisco: HarperOne, 2016), which made repeated appearances in our conversations and finally compelled me to buy and read the book myself just to stay up!

[15] See related comments in Appendix C: Significant Statements under Theme: Crisis Level.

[16] The disappointment, however, was placed in better perspective when I reread Stanley and Willits's reminder that every group had its own natural life-cycle. Every group eventually reshapes or breaks up over time. It was *not* a sign of failure but an organic part of the nature of groups. (Stanley and Willits, *Creating Community*, 109.)

[17] Lynn Butler-Kisber, *Qualitative Inquiry: Thematic, Narrative and Arts-Based Perspectives*, 2nd ed. (Los Angeles: Sage Publications, 2018), 29.

[18] See Appendix B: Touching Bases Questionnaire.

[19] Moustakas, *Heuristic Research*, 47.

[20] Bishop Robert Barron, "Bishop Barron Q&A on Discernment," *Word on Fire,* podcast 311, aired Nov 22, 2021, audio 24:10, https://www.wordonfire.org/videos/wordonfire-show/episode311/

[21] Text message from group participant Lauren to myself and co-pastor.

[22] Matthew, for example, talked favorably about his Wicca and Tarot-reading friends; and Lauren adopted some ritual activities to deepen her connection with nature, which her husband Eric (jokingly?) referred to as "her witchy ways." Others considered more contemplative practices customarily associated with Catholicism more than with their native evangelicalism.

[23] See, for example, Karris's "Religious Disorientation Growth Syndrome" *(Religious Refugees)* or Escobar's "Faith Shift" paradigm *(Faith Shift)* discussed in Chapter 2, "Deconstruction in American Christianity."

[24] This was true of Jordan, Michael, and Grace (Gen Zs); Jack and Kayla (Millennials); and Dan (Gen X). Dan may have been unique in that he was not raised religious. His family was Catholic, but as he put it, "wasn't that serious about it."

Chapter 5 – Deconstructing Theologies & the Group Experience

[1] Diana Butler Bass, *Grounded: Finding God in the World. A Spiritual Revolution* (San Francisco: HarperOne, 2015), 21.

[2] Moustakas, *Heuristic Research*, 27-32.

[3] Moustakas, *Heuristic Research*, 28.

[4] Moustakas, *Heuristic Research*, 28.

[5] Moustakas, *Heuristic Research*, 30.

[6] Moustakas, *Heuristic Research*, 31.

[7] Creswell and Poth, *Qualitative Inquiry*, 93; Moschella, *Ethnography as a Pastoral Practice*, 27.

[8] Two of the three "C" goals outlined in the Introduction: *continue* in a lifestyle of questioning, *comfort* with uncertainty, and a closer *connection* with God and the world.

[9] Moustakas, *Heuristic Research*, 32.

[10] Creswell and Poth, *Qualitative Inquiry*, 79-80.

[11] Like a "thick description" in ethnography (Moschella, *Ethnography as a Pastoral Practice*, 198).

[12] Creswell and Poth, *Qualitative Inquiry*, 201.

[13] Creswell and Poth, *Qualitative Inquiry*, 201.

[14] As mentioned in Chapter 1, "The Introduction," the difference between "post-evangelical" and "exvangelical," is largely intuitive and subjective. The former tends to mark some distance and evolution in thought, but not a complete break from some of the foundational ideals of evangelicalism, while the latter implies some degree of hostility and an absolute departure from all things evangelical.

[15] Wayne Grudem, *Systematic Theology: An Introduction to Biblical Doctrine* (Grand Rapids: Zondervan, 2000).

[16] Millard J. Erickson, *Christian Theology*, 3 vols (Grand Rapids: Baker, 1983-1985).

[17] "Assemblies of God 16 Fundamental Truths: #1 The Scripture Inspired," https://ag.org/Beliefs/Statement-of-Fundamental-Truths; Southern Baptist Convention's "Baptist Faith & Message 2000: I. The Scriptures," https://bfm.sbc.net/bfm2000/; NAE's "Statement of Faith," https://www.nae.org/statement-of-faith/. Or see Appendix E: NAE Statement of Faith.

[18] "Baptist Faith & Message 2000: I. The Scriptures," https://bfm.sbc.net/bfm2000/. It is noteworthy that the term "inerrant" is now missing from the Statements of Faith of the National Association of Evangelicals, the SBC and AG. The NAE and AG SOF still include the words "inspired, infallible, and authoritative," while Southern Baptists

insist on "totally true," but the word "inerrant"—still so central in any in-person argument—seems to have been studiously avoided. Note that both Grudem's *Systematic Theology* and Erickson's *Christian Theology* each devote a full chapter to Inerrancy.

[19] Grudem, *Systematic Theology*, 100. Erickson writes, "If he [God] is omnipotent, he is able to so affect the biblical author's writing that nothing erroneous enters into the final product" (*Christian Theology*, 225). This was the kind of naïve, simplistic reasoning most of us had grown up with. "Being wholly and verbally God-given, Scripture is without error or fault in all its teaching, no less in what it states about God's acts in creation, about the events of world history, and about its own literary origins under God, than in its witness to God's saving grace in individual lives" (The Evangelical Theological Society, "The Chicago Statement on Biblical Inerrancy, 1978," Statement #4, https://www.etsjets.org/files/documents/Chicago_Statement.pdf; See Appendix F.)

[20] Grudem, *Systematic Theology*, 202, 205, 206; Erickson, *Christian Theology*, 284-289.

[21] Grudem, *Systematic Theology*, 509, emphasis in the original.

[22] "The prayers of his people clearly affect how God acts" (Grudem, *Systematic Theology*, 377).

[23] See Erickson's discussion on "Providence and Prayer" (*Christian Theology*, 405-406).

[24] These negative descriptions are less a product of evangelical teaching than they are born out of personal real-life frustration. Grudem, for example, offers three reasonable explanations for prayer: to express our trust and dependence on God; to bring us into deeper fellowship with God; and allows us to be involved in activities of eternal import. "When we pray, the work of the kingdom is advanced" (Grudem, *Systematic Theology*, 376-377).

[25] Grudem, *Systematic Theology*, 510.

[26] Grudem, *Systematic Theology*, 579. See Erickson, *Christian Theology*, 819.

[27] Grudem, *Systematic Theology*, 579-580. "The penal-substitution theory confirms the biblical teaching of the total depravity of all humans" (Erickson, *Christian Theology*, 822).

[28] The Christus Victor (or Ransom) theory was the predominant view of the Church for the first thousand years. Other major views include the Recapitulation theory, the Satisfaction theory, Moral Influence theory, and of course the evangelical favorite, Penal Substitution. For some

helpful perspectives on various atonement (and other) theories, see Mark D. Baker and Joel B. Green, *Recovering the Scandal of the Cross: Atonement in New Testament and Contemporary Contexts*, 2nd ed. (Downers Grove: IVP Academic, 2011).

[29] Stephen Schmidt, "What's So Wrong with Being a Christian Slut?" *Impact Magazine*, July 10, 2021, https://impactmagazine.us/2021/07/whats-so-wrong-with-being-a-christian-slut-2/.

[30] Quotation is included in Appendix C: Significant Statements, under Theme: Sexuality & Sexual Ethics.

[31] Gushee, *After Evangelicalism*, 119, 132

[32] Many of the group had read books relating to the "clobber passages," like the classic *What the Bible Really Says About Homosexuality*, by Daniel Helminiak (Alamo Square Press, 2000 [1994]), Justin Lee's *Torn: Rescuing the Gospel from the Gays-vs.-Christians Debate* (New York: Jericho Books, 2012), or the popular, though less scholarly, *God and the Gay Christian* by Matthew Vines (New York: Convergent Books, 2014).

Chapter 6 – Closing Thoughts

[1] Ammerman, *Sacred Stories, Spiritual Tribes*, 302.

[2] Raimon Panikkar, *The Rhythm of Being: The Gifford Lectures* (Maryknoll, NY: Orbis Books, 2010), 216, in a discussion on the difficulty of Westerners embracing the idea of *advaita*.

[3] My case, while far from unique, may not be universal. Group participant Mark, for example, stated that the primary instrument of his deconstruction was logic and reasoning. He had questions, and his intellect was the door through which possible answers came.

[4] See, for example, popular writer of theology, Keith Giles, who lists what he sees as the six most common issues: the Bible, Eternal Torment (Hell), Penal Substitutionary Atonement, Suffering in the World, The End-Times Hype, and lastly the failures of the Church. (Keith Giles, "The 6 Pillars of Religious Deconstruction," *Patheos*, Keith Giles, Aug 27, 2019, https://www.patheos.com/blogs/keithgiles/2019/08/the-6-pillars-of-religious-deconstruction/.)

[5] See, for example, some of the comments in Appendix C: Significant Statements under Theme: Life as Sacramental; Ritual & Symbol.

[6] See Appendix B: Touching Bases Questionnaire

[7] Ammerman, *Sacred Stories, Spiritual Tribes*, 302.

Bibliography

Akenson, Donald Harman. *Saint Saul: A Skeleton Key to the Historical Jesus.* New York: Oxford Univ Press, 2000.

Alper, Becka A. "Why America's 'Nones' Don't Identify with a Religion." Pew Research Center. Aug 8, 2018. https://www.pewresearch.org/fact-tank/2018/08/08/why-americas-nones-dont-identify-with-a-religion/

Ammerman, Nancy Tatom. *Sacred Stories, Spiritual Tribes: Finding Religion in Everyday Life.* New York: Oxford Univ. Press, 2014.

Baker, Mark D. and Joel B. Green. *Recovering the Scandal of the Cross: Atonement in the New Testament and Contemporary Contexts.* 2nd ed. Downers Grove, IL: IVP Academic, 2011.

Balmer, Randall. *Bad Faith: Race and the Rise of the Religious Right.* Grand Rapids: Eerdmans, 2021.

———. "The Real Origins of the Religious Right." *Politico Magazine.* May 27, 2014. https://www.politico.com/magazine/story/2014/05/religious-right-real-origins-107133/

Barna Group. "Meet the 'Spiritual but Not Religious.'" *Faith & Christianity.* Apr 6, 2017. https://www.barna.com/research/meet-spiritual-not-religious/

Barron, Bishop Robert. "Bishop Barron Q&A on Discernment." *Word on Fire.* Podcast 311. Aired Nov 22, 2021. https://www.wordonfire.org/videos/wordonfire-show/episode311/

Blasio, Mat. "Seeking Safe Havens." Springtide Research Institute. Oct 21, 2021. Voices of Young People. https://www.springtideresearch.org/post/sap-blog-leaving-religion

Bloom, Jon. "What Does 'Deconstruction' Even Mean?" *Desiring God.* Feb 15, 2022. https://www.desiringgod.org/articles/what-does-deconstruction-even-mean

Bourgeault, Cynthia. *Centering Prayer and Inner Awakening.* Lanham, MD: Cowley, 2004.

Brisola, Elizabeth Brown Vallim and Vera Engler Cury. "Researcher Experience as an Instrument of Investigation of a Phenomenon: An Example of Heuristic Research." *Estudos de Psicologia* 33, no.1 (Jan-Mar 2016): 95-105. doi: https://doi.org/10.1590/1982-02752016000100010

Brown, Raymond. *The Gospel According to John. The Anchor Bible.* 2 vols. Garden City, NY: Doubleday, 1980-1981.

Burge, Ryan P. "The 2020 Vote for President by Religious Groups—Christians." *Religion in Public.* Mar 29, 2021. https://religioninpublic.blog/2021/03/29/the-2020-vote-for-president-by-religious-groups-christians/

———. "America Got a Little More Religious. No, Really." *Graphs About Religion.* Mar 28, 2026. https://www.graphsaboutreligion.com/p/america-got-a-little-more-religious

———. "Most 'Nones' Still Keep the Faith." *Christianity Today.* Feb 24, 2021. https://www.christianitytoday.com/news/2021/february/nones-religious-unaffiliated-faith-research-church-belief.html

———. *The Nones: Where They Came From, Who They Are, and Where They Are Going.* Minneapolis: Fortress Press, 2021.

Butler, Joshua Ryan. "4 Causes of Deconstruction." *The Gospel Coalition*, Christian Living, Nov 9, 2021. https://www.thegospelcoalition.org/article/4-causes-deconstruction/.

Butler-Kisber, Lynn. *Qualitative Inquiry: Thematic, Narrative and Arts-Based Perspectives.* 2nd ed. Los Angeles: Sage, 2018.

Church of England. "Younger people more likely to pray than older generations, survey finds." Aug 28, 2022. https://www.churchofengland.org/media-and-news/press-releases/younger-people-more-likely-pray-older-generations-survey-finds

Coghlan, David. "Seeking God in All Things: Ignatian Spirituality as Action Research." *The Way.* 43/1 (Jan 2004): 97-108.

Copper, Emma. "Anything But Christian: Why Millennials Leave the Church." *Medium,* Jan 30, 2019. https://medium.com/@Emma-Copper/anything-but-christian-why-millennials-leave-the-church-ccae210dfb06.

Creswell, John W. and Cheryl N. Poth. *Qualitative Inquiry & Research Design: Choosing Among Five Approaches.* 4th ed. Los Angeles: Sage, 2018.

Davis, Ellen F. *Getting Involved with God: Rediscovering the Old Testament.* Cambridge, MA: Cowley, 2001.

Daube, David. *The New Testament and Rabbinic Judaism.* 1956. Reprint, Peabody, MA: Hendrickson, 1994.

DeLatte, Tracy. "Gateway Church founder Robert Morris released from Okla-homa jail." KDFW Fox 4 News. Mar 31, 2026. https://www.fox4news.com/news/gateway-church-founder-robert-morris-released-from-oklahoma-jail

Distefano, Matthew J. *Heretic! An LGBTQ-Affirming, Divine Violence-Denying, Christian Universalist's Responses to Some of Evangelical Christianity's Most Pressing Concerns.* Orange, CA: Quoir, 2018.

———. *Heretic Too! An LGBTQ-Celebrating, Divine Violence-Denying, Post-Christian Universalist's Responses to More of Evangelicalism's Concerns.* Chico, CA: Quoir, 2024.

Doeve, J.W. *Jewish Hermeneutics in the Synoptic Gospels and Acts.* Assen: Van Gorcum, 1954.

Dowland, Seth. *Family Values and the Rise of the Christian Right.* Philadelphia: University of Pennsylvania Press, 2015.

Du Mez, Kristin Kobes. *Jesus and John Wayne: How White Evangelicals Corrupted a Faith and Fractured a Nation.* New York: Liveright Publishing, 2020.

———. "Jesus and John Wayne and the Evangelical Reckoning." Public lecture and panel discussion. University of Oklahoma, Norman, OK. Sep 8, 2022.

———. "There are No Real Evangelicals. Only Imagined Ones." *Religion News Service.* Feb 6, 2019. https://religionnews.com/2019/02/06/there-are-no-real-evangelicals-only-imagined-ones/

Enns, Peter. *The Bible Tells Me So: Why Defending Scripture Has Made Us Unable to Read It.* San Francisco: HarperOne, 2015.

———. *How the Bible Actually Works.* New York: HarperOne, 2019.

———. "Protestantism and Biblical Criticism: One Perspective." In *The Bible and the Believer: How to Read the Bible Critically & Religiously*, edited by Marc Zvi Brettler, Peter Enns, and Daniel Harrington, 126–175. New York: Oxford Univ Press, 2012.

———. *The Sin of Certainty: Why God Desires our Trust More than our "Correct" Beliefs.* San Francisco: HarperOne, 2016.

Erickson, Millard J. *Christian Theology.* 3 vols. Grand Rapids: Baker, 1983-1985.

Escobar, Kathy. *Faith Shift: Finding Your Way Forward When Everything You Believe is Coming Apart.* New York: Convergent, 2014.

Evangelical Theological Society. "The Chicago Statement on Biblical Inerrancy, 1978." https://www.etsjets.org/files/documents/Chicago_Statement.pdf

Evans, Jonathan, et al, "Many Religious 'Nones' Around the World Hold Spiritual Beliefs," Pew Research Center, Sep 4, 2025, https://www.pewresearch.org/religion/2025/09/04/many-religious-nones-around-the-world-hold-spiritual-beliefs/

Evans, Rachel Held. "How Evangelicals Won a Culture War and Lost a Generation." *CNN Belief Blog.* Mar 31, 2014. https://religion.blogs.cnn.com/2014/03/31/how-evangelicals-won-a-culture-war-and-lost-a-generation/

———. "How to Win a Culture War and Lose a Generation." *Rachel Held Evans.* May 9, 2012. https://rachelheldevans.com/blog/win-culture-war-lose-generation-amendment-one-north-carolina

———. "Why Millennials are Leaving the church." *CNN Belief Blog.* July 27, 2013. http://religion.blogs.cnn.com/2013/07/27/why-millennials-are-leaving-the-church/

Felten, David M. and Jeff Procter-Murphy. *Living the Questions: The Wisdom of Progressive Christianity.* New York: HarperOne, 2012.

Fitzmyer, Joseph A. *The Acts of the Apostles. The Anchor Bible.* New York: Doubleday, 1998.

———. *The Gospel According to Luke. The Anchor Bible.* 2 vols. New York: Doubleday, 1985.

Fowler, James W. *Stages of Faith: The Psychology of Human Development and the Quest for Meaning.* San Francisco: Harper, 1981.

Giles, Keith, ed. *Before You Lose Your Mind: Deconstructing Bad Theology in the Church.* Oak Glen, CA: Quoir, 2021.

———. "Finding a Firm Foundation for Reconstruction." *Patheos.* Keith Giles. Sept 20, 2019. https://www.patheos.com/blogs/keithgiles/2019/09/finding-a-firm-foundation-for-reconstruction/.

———. "The 6 Pillars of Religious Deconstruction." *Patheos*. Keith Giles. Aug 27, 2019. https://www.patheos.com/blogs/keithgiles/2019/08/the-6-pillars-of-religious-deconstruction/.

Green, Heather, "Study: Gen Z doubles down on spirituality, combining tarot and traditional faith." *Religion News Service*. Aug 11, 2021. https://religionnews.com/2021/08/11/study-gen-z-doubles-down-on-spirituality-combining-tarot-and-traditional-faith/

Grudem, Wayne. *Systematic Theology: An Introduction to Biblical Doctrine*. Grand Rapids: Zondervan, 2000.

Gushee, David P. *After Evangelicalism: The Path to a New Christianity*. Louisville: Westminster John Knox, 2020.

Haidt, Jonathan. *The Anxious Generation: How the Great Rewiring of Childhood is Causing an Epidemic of Menal Illness*. New York: Penguin, 2024.

Hanson, Molly. "Could neo-paganism be the new 'religion' of America?" *Big Think*. Sep 30, 2019. https://bigthink.com/the-present/modern-paganism/

Hardy, Elle. "The Sexual Abuse Scandal That's Engulfed the Evangelical Movement." New Republic. Sep 20, 2024, https://newrepublic.com/article/185907/ evangelical-movement-sexual-abuse-scandal

Hellman, Rabbi Aviva. "Baba Metzia 59b: *Tanur Shel Akhnai." Sefaria*. https://www.sefaria.org/sheets/144163?lang=bi.

Helminiak, Daniel. *What the Bible Really Says About Homosexuality*. Millenium Edition, Updated and Expanded. Alamo Square Press, 2000 [1994].

Hemeyer, Julia Corbett. *Religion in America*. 7th ed. New York: Routledge, 2016.

Hixenbaugh, Mike and Elizabeth Chuck. "Assemblies of God churches shielded accused predators — and allowed them to keep abusing children." NBC News. Oct 20, 2025. https://www.nbcnews.com/news/us-news/assembly-god-church-shield-predators-child-sex-abuse-allegations-rcna240213

Hübner, Jamin Andreas. *Deconstructing Evangelicalism: A Letter to a Friend and a Professor's Guide to Escaping Fundamentalist Christianity*. Kindle edition. Rapid City, SD: Hills Publishing Group, 2020.

Huckabee, Tyler. "Reminder: 'Deconstruction' Does not Mean 'Deconversion.'" *Relevant*, Dec 6, 2021. https://www.relevantmagazine.com/faith/church/reminder-deconstruction-does-not-mean-deconversion/.

Jersak, Bradley. *A More Christlike God: A More Beautiful Gospel.* Pasadena: CWRpress, 2015.

———. *A More Christlike Way: A More Beautiful Faith.* Pasadena: CWRpress, 2019.

Johnson, Paul. *A History of the American People.* New York: HarperCollins, 1997.

Karris, Mark Gregory. *Religious Refugees: (De)Constructing Toward Spiritual and Emotional Healing.* Orange, CA: Quoir, 2020.

Keating, Thomas. *Open Mind, Open Heart.* 20th Anniversary Ed. New York: Continuum, 2006.

Kinnaman, David. *You Lost Me. Why Young Christians are Leaving Church and Rethinking Faith.* Grand Rapids: Baker Books, 2011.

Kinnaman, David and Gabe Lyons. *UnChristian: What a New Generation Really Thinks About Christianity ... and Why it Matters.* Grand Rapids: Baker Books, 2007.

Kinnaman, David and Mark Matlock. *Faith for Exiles: 5 Ways for a New Generation to Follow Jesus in Digital Babylon.* Grand Rapids: Baker Books, 2019.

Klausner, Joseph. *From Jesus to Paul.* Trans. William Stinespring. New York: Macmillan Co., 1944.

———. *Jesus of Nazareth.* Trans. Herbert Danby. Boston: Beacon Press, 1964.

Kugel, James L. *The Bible as It Was.* Cambridge, MA: Belknap Press of Harvard Univ Press, 1997.

Kugel, James L. and Rowan A. Greer. *Early Biblical Interpretation.* Philadelphia: Westminster Press, 1986.

Kushner, Rabbi Lawrence. *Jewish Spirituality: A Brief Introduction for Christians.* Woodstock, VT: Jewish Lights, 2001.

Lee, Justin. *Torn: Rescuing the Gospel from the Gays-vs.-Christians Debate.* New York: Jericho Books, 2012.

McGrath, James F. *Beyond Deconstruction: Building a More Expansive Faith.* Grand Rapids: Eerdmans, 2026.

McLaren, Brian D. *Do I Stay Christian? A Guide for the Doubters, the Disappointed, and the Disillusioned.* New York: St. Martin's Essentials, 2022.

———. *Faith After Doubt. Why Your Beliefs Stopped Working and What to Do About It.* New York: St Martin's Essentials, 2021.

———. *Finding Our Way: The Return of the Ancient Practices.* Nashville: Thomas Nelson, 2008.

———. *The Great Spiritual Migration: How the World's Largest Religion is Seeking a Better Way to be Christian.* New York: Convergent, 2016.

———. *A New Kind of Christianity: Ten Questions that are Transforming the Faith.* New York: HarperOne, 2010.

———. "Thank God that More People are Deconstructing their Faith." *Premier Christianity.* Aug 1, 2022. https://www.premierchristianity.com/opinion/thank-god-that-more-people-are-deconstructing-their-faith/13570.article

Moschella, Mary Clark. *Ethnography as a Pastoral Practice: An Introduction.* Cleveland: Pilgrim Press, 2008.

Moustakas, Clark. *Heuristic Research: Design, Methodology, and Applications.* Newbury Park, CA: Sage, 1990.

National Association of Evangelicals. "NAE LifeWay Research Evangelical Beliefs Research Definition." Oct 15, 2015. http://research.lifeway.com/wp-content/uploads/2015/11/NAE-LifeWay-Research-Evangelical-Beliefs-Research-Definition-Methodology-and-Use.pdf

———. "What is an Evangelical?" Accessed Oct 15, 2022. https://www.nae.org/what-is-an-evangelical/

Osmer, Richard R. *Practical Theology: An Introduction.* Grand Rapids: Eerdmans, 2008.

Packard, Josh and Casper ter Kuile. "Gen Z is Keeping the Faith. Just Don't Expect to See Them at Worship." *Religion News Service.* Sep 23, 2021. https://religionnews.com/2021/09/23/gen-z-is-keeping-the-faith-just-dont-expect-to-see-them-at-worship/

Parker, Kim and Ruth Igielnik, "On the Cusp of Adulthood and Facing an Uncertain Future: What We Know About Gen Z So Far." Pew Research Center. May 14, 2020. https://www.pewresearch.org/social-trends/2020/05/14/on-the-cusp-of-adulthood-and-facing-an-uncertain-future-what-we-know-about-gen-z-so-far-2/

Pew Research Center. "In U.S., Decline of Christianity Continues at Rapid Pace." Oct 17, 2019. https://www.pewresearch.org/religion/2019/10/17/in-u-s-decline-of-christianity-continues-at-rapid-pace/

———. "Modeling the Future of Religion in America." Sep 13, 2022. https://www.pewresearch.org/religion/2022/09/13/modeling-the-future-of-religion-in-america/

———. "When Americans Say They Believe in God, What Do They Mean?" Religion & Public Life. Apr 25, 2018. https://www.pewforum.org/2018/04/25/when-americans-say-they-believe-in-god-what-do-they-mean/

Public Religion Research Institute. "Religion and the 2024 Presidential Election." Nov 8, 2024. https://prri.org/spotlight/religion-and-the-2024-presidential-election/

Robertson, Brandan. *True Inclusion: Creating Communities of Radical Embrace*. St. Louis, MO: Chalice Press, 2018.

Rohr, Richard. *Falling Upward: A Spirituality for the Two Halves of Life*. San Francisco: Jossey-Bass, 2011.

———. *Immortal Diamond: The Search for Our True Self.* San Francisco: Jossey-Bass, 2013.

———. *The Universal Christ: How a Forgotten Reality Can Change Everything We See, Hope for, and Believe*. New York: Convergent Books, 2019.

Roys, Julie. "Pastor Resigns from Houston Megachurch After Admitting Affair." *The Roys Report*. Jan 3, 2022. https://julieroys.com/jeremy-foster-houston-megachurch-hope-city-affair-resignation/

Sanders, E. P. *Jesus and Judaism*. Philadelphia: Fortress, 1985.

———. "The Life of Jesus." In *Christianity and Rabbinic Judaism: A Parallel History of Their Origins and Early Development*. Hershel Shanks, ed. 41–84. Washington DC: Biblical Archeology Society, 1992,

Sarna, Nahum M. *Genesis. The JPS Torah Commentary*. Philadelphia: Jewish Publication Society, 1989.

Schmidt, Stephen. "Being a Gay Evangelical." *Impact Magazine*. Dec 31, 2013. https://impactmagazine.us/2013/12/being-a-gay-evangelical/

———. "What's So Wrong with Being a Christian Slut?" *Impact Magazine*. July 10, 2021. https://impactmagazine.us/2021/07/whats-so-wrong-with-being-a-christian-slut-2/.

———. "When Your Faith is Bigger than the Bible ..." *Impact Magazine.* June 12, 2015. https://impactmagazine.us/2015/06/when-your-faith-is-bigger-than-the-bible/.

Schneiders, Sandra M. "The Study of Christian Spirituality: Contours and Dynamics of a Discipline." In *Minding the Spirit: The Study of Christian Spirituality.* Elizabeth A. Dreyer and Mark S. Burrows, eds. 5–24. Baltimore: Johns Hopkins Univ Press, 2005.

———. *Written That You May Believe: Encountering Jesus in the Fourth Gospel.* Rev & Expanded ed. NY: Herder & Herder, 2003.

Sensing, Tim. *Qualitative Research: A Multi-Methods Approach to Projects for Doctor of Ministry Theses.* Eugene, OR: Wipf & Stock, 2011.

Shambaugh, Ann Marie. "Former staff at Life.Church describe toxic work culture and an alleged assault by Pastor Craig Groeschel." *The Roys Report.* Apr 23, 2026. https://roysreport.com/former-staff-life-church-toxic-work-culture-alleged-assault-by-groeschel/

Smietana, Bob. "Deconstruction or reconstruction? Pastors discuss a reboot of evangelicalism," *Religion News Service.* Oct 25, 2022. https://religionnews.com/2022/10/25/evangelicals-hope-to-reconstruct-a-healthier-version-of-their-faith/

———. "Matt Chandler, megachurch pastor and ACTS 29 leader, placed on leave." *Religion News Service.* Aug 29, 2022. https://religionnews.com/2022/08/29/matt-chandler-megachurch-pastor-and-acts-29-leader-placed-on-leave-for-unhealth-instagram-messages-woman/

Smith, Gregory A. "About Three in Ten U.S. Adults Are Now Religiously Unaffiliated." Pew Research Center. Dec 14, 2021. https://www.pewresearch.org/religion/2021/12/14/about-three-in-ten-u-s-adults-are-now-religiously-unaffiliated/

Smith, Gregory A., et al. "Decline of Christianity in the U.S. Has Slowed, May Have Leveled Off." *Religious Landscape Study.* Pew Research Center. Feb 26, 2025. https://www.pewresearch.org/religion/2025/02/26/decline-of-christianity-in-the-us-has-slowed-may-have-leveled-off/

Springtide Research Institute. "Ask Josh: What is the difference between being religious and being spiritual?" Oct 4, 2022. https://www.springtideresearch.org/post/ask-josh-what-is-the-difference-between-being-religious-and-being-spiritual

———. "Does Gen Z Believe in a Higher Power?" Nov 30.2022. https://www.springtideresearch.org/post/does-gen-z-believe-in-a-higher-power

———. "Gen Z and Religion—What the Statistics Say." Sep 29, 2022. https://www.springtideresearch.org/post/gen-z-and-religion-what-the-statistics-say

———. "Gen Z is Less Religious or Spiritual Than Older Generations? That's a Myth." Nov 3, 2022. https://www.springtideresearch.org/post/gen-z-is-less-religious-or-spiritual-thats-a-myth

———. "An Inside Look at Gen Z's Spiritual Practices." Nov 29, 2022. https://www.springtideresearch.org/post/an-inside-look-at-gen-zs-spiritual-practices

———. *The State of Religion & Young People 2021: Navigating Uncertainty.* Oct 2021. https://springtideresearch.org/the-state-of-religion-2021-digital-edition/

Stanley, Andy and Bill Willits. *Creating Community: 5 Keys to Building a Small Group Culture.* Colorado Springs: Multnomah Books, 2004.

Swinton, John and Harriet Mowat. *Practical Theology and Qualitative Research.* 2nd ed. Norfolk, UK: SCM Press, 2016.

Taylor, Charles. *A Secular Age.* Cambridge, MA: The Belknap Press of Harvard University Press, 2007.

Teasdale, Wayne. *The Mystic Heart: Discovering a Universal Spirituality in the World's Religions.* Novato, Calif: New World Library, 1999.

Van Manen, Max. *Researching Lived Experience: Human Science for an Action Sensitive Pedagogy.* 2nd ed. New York: Routledge, 2015.

Van Voorhis, Aaron. *A Survival Guide for Heretics.* Eugene, OR: Wipf and Stock, 2016.

Vanderpool, Kurtis. "The Age of Deconstruction and the Future of the Church." *Relevant.* April 7, 2021. https://www.relevantmagazine.com/faith/the-age-of-deconstruction-and-future-of-the-church/.

Vermes, Geza. *Jesus the Jew.* Philadelphia: Fortress Press, 1973.

———. *The Religion of Jesus the Jew.* Minneapolis: Fortress Press, 1993.

Vines, Matthew. *God and the Gay Christian.* New York: Convergent Books, 2014.

Vreeland, Derek E. "Reconstructing Word of Faith Theology," Paper presented at the Society for Pentecostal Studies, Jan 2001, reprinted at https://www.hopefaithprayer.com/word-of-faith/reconstructing-word-of-faith-theology

Wagner, Meagan Ruby. "Deconstruction's Critics are Those with Much to Lose." *Red Letter Christians.* Nov 17, 2021. https://www.redletterchristians.org/deconstructions-critics-are-those-with-much-to-lose/.

Wheatley, Margaret J. *Finding Our Way: Leadership for an Uncertain Time.* San Francisco: Berrett-Koehler, 2005.

———. *Turning to One Another: Simple Conversations to Restore Hope to the Future.* 2nd ed. San Francisco: Berrett-Koehler, 2009.

Wilensky-Lanford, Brook. "Gen Z's Religious Affiliation Stats are Confusing ... But Only When Viewed from a Christian-Centric Perspective." *Religion Dispatches.* July 27, 2021. https://religiondispatches.org/gen-zs-religious-affiliation-stats-are-only-confusing-if-you-view-them-from-a-christian-centric-perspective/.

Witherington, Ben, III. *The Acts of the Apostles: A Socio-Rhetorical Commentary.* Grand Rapids: Eerdmans/Paternoster, 1998.

Wolsey, Roger. *Kissing Fish: Christianity for People Who Don't Like Christianity.* Lexington, KY: Xlibris, 2011.

Woodbridge, John and Wendy Murray Zoba. "Standing on the Promises: Former CT editors Carl Henry and Kenneth Kantzer evaluate evangelicalism in light of its twentieth-century developments." *Christianity Today,* Sep 16, 1996. https://www.christianitytoday.com /ct/1996/september16/6ta028.html.

Wright, N.T. *Paul: A Biography.* San Francisco: HarperOne, 2018.

Zahnd, Brian. "Deconstruction or Restoration?" *Brian Zahnd.* April 27, 2016. https://brianzahnd.com/2016/04/deconstruction-or-restoration/

———. *When Everything's on Fire: Faith Forged from the Ashes.* Downers Grove, IL: IVP, 2021.

Appendices

Appendix A
Letter of Information and Consent
The Abbey Church

Letter of Information and Consent from Pastor Steve
Faith Deconstruction/Reconstruction Discussion Group

Introduction

1. You are being asked to participate in a research study that is one part of Pastor Steve's Doctor of Ministry project thesis at the Virginia Theological Seminary.
2. Part of this study will focus on the Faith Deconstruction/Reconstruction discussion group at The Abbey Church, and you have been selected because you are participating in the group.

Purpose of the Study

3. The purpose of the study is to explore the spiritual experience of people in the process of faith deconstruction and reconstruction—or, simply put, what it feels like to go through the questioning and reframing of one's faith.
4. It is designed to explore the richness and diversity of the lives of people in the process of reshaping their beliefs, and to listen for common themes and experiences.
5. Ultimately, this research will be incorporated into a doctoral thesis and other material resulting from this study. Your participation may also assist in shaping worship and discipleship programs at The Abbey, and may benefit other people seeking a deeper connection with God.

Description of the Study Procedures

6. If you agree to participate in this study, you may be asked to share in a group setting your experiences of spiritual development, your questions and changing views about God and Christianity and/or other issues of faith, and offer an evaluation of what has been meaningful to you.
7. I may make notes after each group meeting, recording observations, impressions and highlights of our conversations together. All notes will be anonymous and respect your privacy.
8. I am also inviting you, if you are willing, to participate beyond the group discussion, and to record your own reactions and responses during the process, and to talk about your experience. This may be done through conversations/interviews along the way, or by texts or emails to Pastor Steve journaling your thoughts and feelings.

Confidentiality

9. Any information you share during the group discussion or follow-up communications will remain **confidential**, and any comments noted from the discussions will be cited anonymously.
10. Your comments may be anonymously quoted in the final written report and in other material resulting from the study. In all cases, **your identity will not be revealed and your privacy will be protected.**

Consent

11. Participation in this discussion group and study is strictly voluntary. If you agree to participate, please sign the consent statement below.
    If you have any questions or comments, please do not hesitate to speak with me, or contact me by email ([redacted]) or on Facebook ([redacted]).

I, ____________________, have consented to participate in this research project, and understand the parameters of participation and confidentiality as outlined above.

____________________ ______________

Signature Date

Appendix B
Touching Bases Email Questionnaire

Hey everyone,
First, thanks for doing this. Here are some basic questions we'll be talking about during our one-on-one interviews, for those who'd like to participate. I'd love to have some written responses of your memorable experiences, too, if you like expressing yourself in writing. And again, your responses will be kept confidential. We'll have a group session later where you can share your thoughts to the degree you're comfortable (although based on our experience, I don't think anybody's been shy about sharing their thoughts!).
[So be aware whether you're hitting the "Reply" or the "Reply All" button!]

Basically, I'd like you to describe your experience of the faith Deconstruction/Reconstruction (D/R) process from 3 angles:

1. from a personal angle (what has your personal journey/process been like?)
2. from the "group" angle (what was it like participating with the group, processing out loud, publicly?)
3. how did the group experience contribute (help/hinder/totally f-up) your personal process?

So here are some questions to ponder. Feel free to answer or skip any.

General

1. At this stage in your life, <u>how important to you</u> is your faith / relationship with God?
   a. How does this compare with other times in your life? (more, less, same)
   b. In a sentence or two, how would you describe your relationship with God?

Personal Experience

2. In what ways have you been going thru the Deconstruction/Reconstruction (D/R) process in your life?
    a. Can you think of a specific area or question you find/found challenging?
    b. How did asking these questions or dealing with these issues make you feel?
        i. Did they make you question your connection with God? With the church? With other Christians?
        ii. Was the process comfortable to you, or did you experience some kind of conflict or crisis (internally or with others) in the process? Feel free to explain.
3. How has the personal experience of going thru D/R affected your relationship with God?

Group Experience

4. What is your overall experience of participating in our Group discussions?
    a. general feelings or impressions
    b. Overall, how did it feel to have such a wide range of questions about faith be explored like this (our kind of "no-holds-barred" discussion format)?
5. Was there a particularly memorable or meaningful group session or topic that stands out to you or was important/significant to you?
    a. What was it about?
    b. Why did it stick out to you?
    c. What impact has the discussion had on you?
    d. Has it changed your perspective about God, life, the church? How?
    e. How did you feel? What were you thinking? What went thru your mind when the discussion was going on? (Was it a moment of new perspective or insight; or was it a challenge or conflict to your faith or beliefs?)

Group/Personal

6. Has our Group experience affected your relationship with God? How?
7. Has this Group experience made you more comforta-ble with uncertainty and questions in your faith?
8. Has this process (personal and in group) affected your Connection/relationship with, or understanding of, God? How?
9. Has this process (personal and in group) changed your perspective or relationship with the faith community? How?
10. How has participating in this Group contributed to your own D/R process? (Helped, hindered, etc)

Feel free to add any other comments you'd like to share with me personally.

Thanks again for taking the time to work through this with me.

I love all y'all!
Steve

Appendix C
Significant Statements, Themes, and Interpretations

The following statements are culled from Group Discussions, interviews, personal texts, emails, and conversations about Deconstruction and Reconstruction. Occasional comments from engaged conversations in social media public forums focused on Deconstruction are included for added perspective and are marked as anonymous. Participant's generational cohort is indicated where relevant to topic. Editorial comments for clarity are added in square brackets.

Theme: Group Experience

- "This conversation was one of our best. This is what I look forward to: a group of people to really talk about spiritual ideas and explore, share our experiences and thoughts. A place to grow and share. In the all the churches I've been a part of, I've never experienced anything like this group. That this is how I know we're doing what God has called us to do."
  ~ Neill, March 10, After group discussion.

- "This group, this church, is the first place I feel free to ask questions and say what I really think without fear of being judged."
  ~ Eric, Sep 8, Personal conversation. (Mark agreed.)

- "You realize that you guys are my only gay friends, the only gay people I actually hang out with at this point...." [Realizing that this mixed group, where about half are LGBTQ, is essential for his normalization/socialization as a gay Christian man.]
  ~ Jordan, Sep 16, After group discussion

- "We had our 'Decon/Recon' Discussion/Support group meeting last night. And this morning all that is going thru my head is that Pauline prayer about 'the glorious riches in the inheritance in the saints.' Such beautiful, wonderful, and entertainingly neurotic, saints I get to hang out with. This morning, I feel incredibly blessed. And I thank God for bringing

such a rich and diverse collection of people into my life. I am truly richer because of all you beautiful people."
~ Steve, Nov 5, Project Notes & Facebook post

- "Sometimes you find your people in unexpected places. If you've been hurt by churches before, I hope you find an inclusive and healing place to land. ❤ We certainly did."
  ~ Lauren, Feb 20, Social Media post

- "Group has been a WONDERFUL experience for me. I greatly look forward to it each time we have it and always regret those times where we've had to miss. While worship service is good, I think small groups are where you create community. We never REALLY had that before ... From the first session, I felt this was a good place for us to plant roots."
  ~ Eric, May 13, Survey Questionnaire

- [How does the no-holds-barred discussion format make you feel?] "Scary. Exhilarating. Hilarious. Safe. It's been a weird conflict at times. We've talked about all kinds of topics—both the gravely serious, and the absurd. At times I wish we were a little more of the other, but I know at the end of the day, we're processing these things in community. We're searching the face of God, trying to find answers. Sometimes we find them, sometimes we don't. Both are OK."
  ~ Eric, May 13, Survey Questionnaire

- "In a way, we found our people. Once we started the Deconstruction group, the volume on that was turned WAY up. Between the group there, and the addition of Jordan, Michael, Sebastian, Matthew, and Kayla, I was so impressed by the curiosity and the hunger to know God better. ... That hunger is infectious, and while I'm grappling with things, I realize it's OK. It's good, even. I don't have to have all the answers, but it's more about the journey. I'm so grateful for the Decon group. It's really forced me to think and to study"
  ~ Eric, May 13, Survey Questionnaire

- "It's rare that people really talk about these kinds of topics within my background. It's almost heretical to consider that we might have been thinking about, teaching, preaching, or believing things "wrong". Questioning the dogma is tantamount to blasphemy."

~ *Eric, May 13, Survey Questionnaire*

- "This group has me asking questions, both big ones and little ones. When we're studying, we're growing closer to Him. When we're talking through it within our faith communities, we're growing closer to Him and each other. God loves that, too."

  ~ *Eric, May 13, Survey Questionnaire*

- "The Decon group has been a perfect next step for us on our journey. It's allowed us to question ourselves, each other, and to think and grow. It's what I've needed for a long time, even though I didn't know it. I'm so very grateful to be a part of it."

  ~ *Eric, May 13, Survey Questionnaire*

- "It feels like a bursting love. I leave feeling so grateful and full of life/energy."

  ~ *Lauren, May 16, Survey Questionnaire*

- [About the wide range of questions:] "It felt exhilarating--like we were on a ride and we weren't exactly sure where it was going or at what speed. The way that shame was left out of it allowed for a rich process that felt so freeing and fun."

  ~ *Lauren, May 16, Survey Questionnaire*

- "We talked about prayer and I remember leaving feeling awestruck. I had imagined we would deconstruct controversial topics (homosexuality, abortion, etc), but I never dreamed we could touch something as sacred and universal as prayer. When we did that, it opened everything up. It gave me room to start questioning all of the basics and understanding them better for myself, in ways I had never even thought to question."

  ~ *Lauren, May 16, Survey Questionnaire*

- "I'd never experienced this before. Never had I heard people wrestle in this way and I was so interested in the differing perspectives. It challenged the rules and traditions, but it

didn't challenge my faith--I think it hit a reset button and allowed me to start at the bottom and construct my way up."
~ Lauren, May 16, Survey Questionnaire

- "This group allows me to do what I need to do at any given moment. It doesn't matter what head space I'm in, there is never judgment or pressure. Because of that, I find myself deconstructing more than I ever have and looking forward to conversations where I can dig even deeper."
~ Lauren, May 16, Survey Questionnaire

- "[Because of the group,] I find God more interesting than I used to. As I stated previously, God had become another task and another person to disappoint. I walked around with Christian guilt all the time for not praying every day or reading my Bible, etc. I think group has helped me see God in a different light. It feels like we are starting a new relationship--almost like dating someone for the first time. I think I originally thought it would feel like repairing an old relationship, but it doesn't feel that way at all. It feels like the God I was familiar with is no longer relevant for me, and I have this new God that I'm getting to know and actually like."
~ Lauren, May 16, Survey Questionnaire

- "I liked it [the group] because I was able to ask questions, pose a thesis about what I believe, with no fear of repercussion. No church group EVER addressed the question we did on prayer. There were always assumptions/baselines of faith. Questions about 'how' we prayed were okay, but to challenge the idea of needing to pray or the purpose of prayer ... that would be unthinkable."
~ Kevin, May 17, Personal conversation

- "I think the main effect [of the group] is it made me more comfortable looking at God in unconventional ways. Being able to talk to a group of believers and say 'outlandish' things like 'maybe God doesn't have to be humanoid' or 'maybe God doesn't have to punish people eternally to be just'. Bottom line is I'm happier looking at God and being open to surprises."
~ Jordan, May 17, Survey Questionnaire

- "My overall experience of group discussion was positive... I definitely felt like I wasn't the most profound one in the group, but it meant that I could listen to more perspectives. The free range of questions was overall good, even if it meant that we'd get into ghosts and aliens and the Bible. The serious discussions led to those moments of realization that I was narrow-minded about God, and the less serious days were more relationship-building with everyone involved."
  ~ Jordan, May 17, Survey Questionnaire

- [About the wide range of questions:] "I really appreciated the range. In the fundamentalist side of my upbringing, a lot of these questions would feel blasphemous and there would be a sense of shame for asking them. In the mainline, more "liberal" side of my past, doctrine and fundamental beliefs like this were rarely discussed in group settings."
  ~ Kayla, May 14, Survey Questionnaire

- "I felt reassured. When we don't talk about our questions on matters like prayer, it's easy to think everyone else has perfect faith or thinks the same way except me, but being honest about the struggle helps build authenticity and deeper community."
  ~ Kayla, May 14, Survey Questionnaire

- "[The group has] helped me think about the big topics that many of us are taught as Christians, and identify some of the ones that we are most likely to challenge in today's world. In some cases, I've been questioning the topic for a long time, but didn't really acknowledge it or realize to what degree I questioned it until we all discussed it aloud."
  ~ Kayla, May 14, Survey Questionnaire

- "I love the conversations, but sometimes I feel like I get sidelined, like I'm not smart enough to participate. Sometimes you guys talk about stuff I don't know about, and when I talk about my past, I feel like I'm stupid."
  ~ Neill, Oct 5, Personal conversation

- "You know I love getting together with everybody and talking about stuff that's going on in our heads. But I'm not sure who's in charge. Everybody is talking. There doesn't seem to

be any direction sometimes, and I don't need to waste my time sitting on a couch (at the clubhouse) just to listen to people bullshit about stuff that isn't interesting to me."
~ Jack, Oct 5, Personal conversation

- [After our session on sexual ethics and morality]: "I've been involved in a number of Presbyterian and Episcopal churches in my life, and in all the churches I've been a part of, we've never had a conversation like that before"
~ Kayla, Oct 19, Group discussion

- [Is the group done?] "I felt like we tackled the most significant topics the first couple of weeks of our group sessions. Now, I'm kinda 'post-deconstruction.'"
~ Jordan, Nov 2, Group discussion

- [About the lack of organization and "popcorn" conversation style] "Yeah, I kinda thought that way, too, they were becoming a waste of my time."
~ Jordan, Nov 2, Group discussion

- "Hey, I really liked those [popcorn] kind of conversations!—but the last few haven't been that way. They've been focused, and I really liked them."
~ Michael, Nov 2, Group discussion

- [On group duration; on taking July/August hiatus off next year:] "Yes, that's actually a great idea. It will give people the chance to remember why the group is important to them. Everybody needs some time off. And, instead of once a month [another proposal for next year], maybe make it a fixed number of sessions and doing it intensely, like a 5-week course. Gives people a definite time frame."
~ Michael, Nov 2, Group discussion

Theme: Personal D/R Experience

- "I kept feeling the pull of love, wrapping around me. I couldn't escape it. And I threw out everything I used to believe and rebuilt everything from that. What didn't fit, I let go of."
~ Matthew, June 3, Group discussion

- [in response to being asked by Noel by text message: "So Pastor Steve, what DOES is feel like to go thru the questioning and reframing of your faith? Was just wonderin"]
  "For me, it's a really cool experience -- that questioning/reframing faith thing. I feel like being a gay man forced me to deal with God on a level I wouldn't have had to if I were str8. So, it's opened up a bunch of doors to see God differently. Of course, it opens even more questions, but ... it's a good thing." [Noel's text response: "I don't think anything in the History of Everything has ever made more sense than just that, Pastor Steve"
  ~ Steve (Gen X), Nov 4, Text conversation with Sebastian (group participant)

- "The image of the God of creation shatters paradigms. God is too big for any limited theology. It was ideas like that, like how big God is, that helped me accept being gay and break out of those limited paradigms."
  ~ Kayla (Millennial), Dec 2, Group discussion

- "For most of my adulthood, we were faithful members of the Church of Christ. Lauren and I both grew up in that faith tradition.... A few years ago, her brother came out as gay, which at the time, I strongly believed was a sin. A few years later, he told us he was going to transition into a woman. This, for sure, flew into the face of what I've grown up accepting as Gospel Truth™. Similarly, a good friend of mine from High School, transitioned into a woman, and I knew her well enough to know her heart. I worked with good people who were also in the LGBTQ+ community, ... That forced me into a long pause, and I needed to figure some things out. At the same time, seeing the treatment of African Americans/Hispanic Americans/Immigrants in our country sparked another "crisis of faith" in my mind. In the wake of the George Floyd murder, the minister at our church gave a "watered down" sermon on a Sunday morning where he echoed the rallying cry that "Black Lives Matter" and was called out on the carpet for it ... and it INFURIATED me that he was "in trouble" over this. Furthermore, he engaged in people on Social Media about this topic as well as LGBTQ+ rights, causing additional pressure. In fact, he was asked to apologize from the pulpit at church for those comments. At that moment, I knew I had to find a church body that shared my views."

~ Eric (Gen X), May 13, Survey Questionnaire

- "After years and years of ascribing to a dogma, it's really hard to tug at those strings ... and once I start pulling the thread, it's scary worrying just how far that will take me."

  ~ Eric (Gen X), May 13, Survey Questionnaire

- [How did asking questions make you feel?] "Scared. Worried. Am I buying into to societal norms versus God's word? Am I buying into false prophets? ..., and I've wondered at times if I'm buying into the thoughts of a person rather than that mind of God. ... it makes me wonder if I'm falling for wolves in sheep's clothing. At times, Steve, I've questioned that about you (and Neil). Am I bringing damnation upon my soul? Those are fleeting thoughts, but they do bubble into my consciousness."

  ~ Eric (Gen X), May 13, Survey Questionnaire

- [How is D/R affecting your relationship with God?] "You [Steve] said something pretty early on that's really resonated with me. Paraphrasing, but the essence is that, 'God wants us to question Him.' We're MUCH better off asking questions than accepting everything on its face. God wants us thinking about, grappling with, and sorting out Him and His nature. Israel wrestled with God, and was marked for life because of it. In a former life, I accepted everything and didn't really stew on Godly matters. The preacher guy said it, and I believed it—end of story. I find myself digging into God's word a lot more now than I did then. That's a good thing."

  ~ Eric (Gen X), May 13, Survey Questionnaire

- "For me, 'deconstruction' was part of my identity formation. There's been no real 'crisis' in my life, just a constant evolution."

  ~ Kevin (Millennial), May 17, Personal conversation

- "In my senior year of college, my small group read through the book *The Sin of Certainty* by Peter Enns. ... What I left with from that book was a frightening idea that perhaps the

Bible isn't actually full of accurate historical accounts. This was pressed further in my time with the D/R group. I found this thinking pivotal, because it left me feeling vulnerable, yet oddly ok with being unsure.... It was terrifying at first, because it was looking completely counter to 22 years of being taught otherwise by my family and old churches. In a way, ... it gave me peace in knowing that God doesn't have to be one perfect standard that little sinful me can't meet."

~ *Jordan (Gen Z), May 17, Survey Questionnaire*

- "I've been going through the D/R process in my prayer life, in my perception of God, including how they do or don't relate to the world, and in my view of Scripture."

  ~ *Kayla (Millennial), May 14, Survey Questionnaire*

- "Many aspects of the process are joyous and liberating, but it's also uncomfortable. I used to think I had a common faith foundation with almost all other Christians that would allow me to communicate and work alongside, ... but it's getting harder to find that common ground. That's partly because of how I see other people's views causing harm sometimes, but also because I know they think my views cause harm."

  ~ *Kayla (Millennial), May 14, Survey Questionnaire*

- "[Deconstruction has] expanded my thinking about God. My favorite metaphor for it has been the sense that I spent most of my youth splashing around in a small estuary thinking, 'So this is God.' Then something made me look up at the wider ocean and a voice inside said, 'No, *that* is God.'"

  ~ *Kayla (Millennial), May 14, Survey Questionnaire*

- "For me, it [Deconstruction] is about getting closer to Jesus and getting away from what the guy at the front of the church is saying. My faith isn't about knowing the answers. It's about trust, knowing Jesus and who the I AM is."

  ~ *Patrick (Millennial), Sep 21, Personal conversation*

- "I think I'm ready to reconstruct, but I have no idea how or where to begin. I don't even really know what I fully believe anymore. All I know is that I've felt this "pull" from God. Like an urge to reconnected with Them and to experience their love in my own unique way. I don't fully know how to explain

this feeling. Again, I don't know where to start. I know I don't want to/can't go back to the non-denominational/Evangelical world/belief system I was in before. I don't believe a lot of the things I used to. I even stopped believing that God cares for personal relationships until I started to feel this "pull" like they're inviting me to sit with them. I know this probably sounds so weird & Evangelical and maybe I'm imagining things??? Long story short, how do I begin reconstructing?"
~ *Anonymous (LN), Sep 28, social media public forum*

- [About lack of D/R crisis:] "I'd been processing being gay for so long, and came to the conclusion that all the religious conflict was from a faith I inherited, not my own real faith, that I guess all these other theological issues were already dismissed in the same way. They were inherited issues, not really my own anyway."
~ *Jordan (Gen Z), Nov 2, Group discussion*

- [About lack of D/R crisis] "I grew up Catholic, and my family wasn't that serious about it. I had to memorize answers from the catechism for confirmation, but I was never good with memorization, so most of it never stuck with me. So, these strict theological dogmas were never a problem with me."
~ *Dan (Gen X), Nov 2, Group discussion*

- "Does anyone else feel just very exhausted by the whole deconstruction process? It's one thing to know what you DON'T believe any more, but to pick up those pieces and know where to go from there, that feels like the most tiring point. ... I just don't even have the energy to try and pick up the pieces of my Christianity, though I do authentically love Jesus and have zero doubts about Him. I've been on this journey since 2020, and I'm tired of trying to reframe my faith. I just want to like ... live if that makes sense."
~ *Anonymous (TNE), Dec 28, social media public forum*

Theme: Crisis Level

- "I'm totally comfortable. [No crisis. I asked why?] Because I've always put my faith and my sense of connection with God, in

Jesus, not in the church and not in theology. So any questions I have do not disrupt my connection with Jesus at all."
~ Patrick (Millennial), June 17, Personal conversation

- "I didn't really have a crisis of faith in God. It was more about rejecting organized Christianity. That's why I came to The Abbey. I saw the [Facebook] ad about "Got Questions", and it looked like a safe place for questions."
  ~ Kayla (Millennial), Jan 6, Group discussion

- "My old church was demoralizing to me. It made me feel negative about myself. And it was too confining. God was put in a restrictive box, too narrow, too judgmental, too exclusive. So I essentially walked away from God ... I don't "know" intuitively that there is a God, but I choose to believe there is one." [So for him, there was a crisis event and a returning]
  ~ Matthew (Gen Z), Jan 6, Group discussion

- "I don't have any real crisis—then or now."
  ~ Jordan (Gen Z), Jan 6, Group discussion

- "Different generations have different questions. I really don't have a crisis level."
  ~ Jack (Millennial), Jan 20, Group discussion

- "I don't think I have a crisis level, either. I'm more looking for a community of acceptance for LGBT, minority, diversity ... I just wanted to learn more about God, especially during recovery—but not a crisis level."
  ~ Sebastian (Gen Z), Jan 20, Group discussion

- "Exposure to different backgrounds helps me understand, think through my faith better" [no crisis level]
  ~ Michael (Gen Z), Jan 20, Group discussion

- "Most of us are not motivated by a deep sense of crisis."
  ~ Michael (Gen Z), Jan 20, Group discussion

- "We all have questions, but we never felt isolated from God. None of us, except maybe Matthew, had had any kind of crisis."
  ~ Michael (Gen Z), Jan 20, Group discussion

- "Some people just want the text book answers. Want a life manual. They don't want an expanding spiritual relationship with God."
  ~ *Michael (Gen Z), Jan 20, Group discussion*

- "Millennials and I-gen, they don't want to be indoctrinated. And I'm with them. We want something more organic. And we want to see it lived out in the people who teach it. And we want community, life together."
  ~ *Barb (Gen X), Jan 29, Personal conversation*

- "For me, 'deconstruction' was part of my identity formation. There's been no real 'crisis' in my life, just a constant evolution."
  ~ *Kevin (Millennial), May 17, Personal conversation*

Theme: Comfort Level with Questioning & Uncertainty

- "I'm totally comfortable. [I asked why?] Because I've always put my faith and my sense of connection with God, in Jesus, not in the church and not in theology. So any questions I have do not disrupt my connection with Jesus at all."
  ~ *Patrick (Millennial), June 17, Personal conversation*

- "Questioning and wrestling is an act of worship. We are not challenging God, we are expanding our understanding, seeking to know God better. The hubris is in thinking we have the answers."
  ~ *Steve (Gen X), June 17, Personal conversation*

- "We have no right saying we know all about God—God is infinite and we are such limited humans, our limited brains cannot possibly grasp understanding God."
  ~ *Patrick (Millennial), June 17, Personal conversation*

- "Eric loves this stuff; it makes him feel closer to God. But for me, I feel like the whole thing is unraveling, and sometimes I feel like I just don't believe any of it anymore. It's not really making me feel closer to God. I feel like all the unraveling is moving me farther away from God."
  ~ *Lauren (Millennial), Sep 14, Group discussion*

- [Has the group helped you feel comfortable with questions?] "Definitely. That's not my nature usually and walking out of Decon group, I usually have more questions that I did walking in. Hearing perspectives from others as we kinda "popcorn" around the room, it's a lot of me thinking 'I've never considered that.' and 'Wow, that's insightful.' I almost wish I could record it and review it again later. But, seeing and hearing God-loving people express diametrically differing views on all these topics shows me that we can have these differences and still be in community. It's rare that people really talk about these kinds of topics within my background. It's almost heretical to consider that we might have been thinking about/teaching/preaching/believing things 'wrong'. Questioning the dogma is tantamount to blasphemy."
  ~ Eric (Gen X), May 13, Survey Questionnaire
- "This group has me asking questions, both big ones and little ones. When we're studying, we're growing closer to Him. When we're talking through it within our faith communities, we're growing closer to Him and each other. God loves that, too."
  ~ Eric (Gen X), May 13, Survey Questionnaire
- "I felt really 'out there'. It felt like I had gotten lost in the world and didn't feel tethered anymore to certainty. I also felt like a child--I think other's reactions to these thoughts made me feel immature (aww...she's so cute. She'll figure it out and come back around)."
  ~ Lauren (Millennial), May 16, Survey Questionnaire
- [How did asking questions make you feel?] "It became really undoing for me and created an internal conflict that I mostly cut off and ignored. I had talked with my dad about all my thoughts and questions and he basically told me that I was becoming a Universalist and that it didn't make sense. He really challenged me on how "wrong" those people are and, again, made me feel like I was simple-minded or immature for not seeing through that line of thinking."
  ~ Lauren (Millennial), May 16, Survey Questionnaire

- "[When] we talked about prayer and I remember leaving feeling awe struck.... I never dreamed we could touch something as sacred and universal as prayer. When we did that--it opened everything up. It gave me room to start questioning all of the basics and understanding them better for myself, in ways I had never even thought to question."
  ~ *Lauren (Millennial), May 16, Survey Questionnaire*

- [Has the group helped you feel comfortable with questions?] "Absolutely. Not only do I feel comfortable, I feel ENCOURAGED to do so. I find myself thinking about possible questions and teasing things apart in ways I never did before. I also feel allowed to be apathetic. It no longer feels wrong, but more so, a part of the process that I can have until it changes."
  ~ *Lauren (Millennial), May 16, Survey Questionnaire*

- "I've been asking questions my whole life ... like, 'why is the story I've been told the truth?' 'Why this truth?' Where do you stop asking questions? It's like peeling an onion, one layer at a time. When do we stop? When we reach the point of personal satisfaction. If my goal is to find truth, there is NO stopping point."
  ~ *Kevin (Millennial), May 17, Personal conversation*

- "I will always be striving for an equilibrium, for balance between knowing and not knowing. I'm pretty comfortable with the unknown."
  ~ *Kevin (Millennial), May 17, Personal conversation*

Theme: Previous Experience in Church

- "The experience at my old church was demoralizing to me. It made me feel negative about myself. And it was too confining. God was put in a restrictive box, too narrow, too judgmental, too exclusive. So I essentially walked away from God, and became an ethical humanist."
  ~ Matthew (Gen Z), Jan 6, Group discussion

- "I've been questioning since I was 18 [she's now in her 30s], and my main issues were also about the narrow view of God, and the lack of pluralism. God is bigger than any one religion or perception. It's like standing in an estuary or stream, enjoying the water, and thinking that is God, and then seeing the ocean, and seeing now that that is God. Both are true."
  ~ Kayla (Millennial), Jan 6, Group discussion

- "At a baby's baptism, the priest charges the whole congregation with their spiritual wellbeing and health... And when I went through RCIA, I needed a sponsor. Why don't evangelicals have "god parents" for new converts and seekers? Evangelicals are too self-focused, don't really care about other people. Like, with Sister Jenny. Her evangelical church doesn't help her at all, they ignore her needs. But the Catholics are helping her ... the Knights of Columbus, the Society of Saint Vincent DePaul.... Why don't we see faith sponsors in the evangelical world?"
  ~ Jack (Millennial), Jan 20, Group discussion

- "Faith growing up was pedantic. Specific doctrines, positions, faith claims. Post-modernism was a trap of the devil. Asking questions was frowned on."
  ~ Kevin (Millennial), May 17, Personal conversation

- "A few summers ago, my daughter was at church camp, and they had some kind of scripture reading competition. We were so proud of her. She read with such feeling and expression, and she won the competition. It made me really sad to realize that she would never be allowed to read Scripture in our church. ... That was one of the reasons we decided to leave the Church of Christ."
  ~ Jennifer (Gen X), May 7, Personal conversation

- "... seeing the treatment of African Americans/Hispanic Americans/Immigrants in our country sparked another "crisis of faith" in my mind. In the wake of the George Floyd murder, the minister at our church gave a "watered down" sermon on a Sunday morning where he echoed the rallying cry that "Black Lives Matter" and was called out on the carpet for it ... and it INFURIATED me that he was "in trouble" over this.

Furthermore, he engaged in people on Social Media about this topic as well as LGBTQ+ rights, causing additional pressure. In fact, he was asked to apologize from the pulpit at church for those comments. At that moment, I knew I had to find a church body that shared my views."

~ Eric (Gen *X), May 13, Survey Questionnaire*

Theme: Scripture

- [On women in ministry] "I was taught every word in the bible is carved in stone. You don't think the Holy Spirit dictated that specifically?"

  ~ Matthew, June 15, Personal conversation

- "That was Paul's opinion, his own judgment. He was talking about a situation. But not every single word is inspired by the Holy Spirit; some were written just by man." [ie, basically, the bible isn't inerrant]

  ~ Neill, June 15, Personal conversation

- "If scripture is God-breathed, so is humanity -- God breathed the breath of life into us -- so are we infallible, or is scripture as fallible as we are?"

  ~ Michael, Apr 7, Group discussion

- "Just because the Bible says something, does that make it the ultimate authority on reality, on the nature of the universe, the sole source of Truth about God...?"

  ~ Kevin, May 17, Personal conversation

- [On discussing "praying in the spirit", using Paul's explanation in 1 Cor 14]: "At the end of that very same chapter Paul forbids women from speaking. I not sure I care what he has to say about the matter."

  ~ Mark, Aug 4, Group discussion

- "The bible is full of contradictions. You can't use it to prove anything. Peter Enns [*Bible Tells Me So*] gave an example of two verses in Proverbs that directly contradict each other, and there they are, side by side."

  ~ Eric, Aug 4, Group discussion

- "It took me a long time to be able to let myself say "the bible is not inerrant, it is not infallible". Once I did, I fell in love with the Bible, and things started making more sense for me."
  ~ *Mark, Sep 8, Personal conversation*

- "I think we have to hold the Bible loosely in our hands, and not try to force it to be all consistent, all one point of view. If we hold it too tightly or too literally, we can prevent it from speaking to us and it loses its power."
  ~ *Jennifer, Sep 14, Group discussion*

- "The Bible is not one book, even though we tend to think so. It's a library. It's got sections of law, poetry, song, history, mythology … written across a few thousand years. 'The Bible' doesn't '*say*' any one thing."
  ~ *Mark, Sep 14, Group discussion*

- "The Bible is a history of man getting it wrong about God."
  ~ *Mark, Sep 14, Group discussion*

- [Mark expanding] "The bible is a story of people's perceptions and interactions with God. It's a history of them continually saying 'this is who god is' and him correcting their thinking. It's adventures in missing the point. 'God wants us to conquer and kill our neighbors!' Not really. 'God favors us and dislikes others!' Nope, try again. Part of the miracle of Christ is God taking human form to show us who God really is—and people killed him because they couldn't take it. We see today that people continue to misunderstand who God is"
  ~ *Mark, Sep 20, Text message*

- "Treating the Bible as an absolutely and inviolably inerrant and infallible transcription of the words of God is to make an idol of it that quenches the voice of the Holy Spirit in the soul"
  ~ *Anonymous (RhD), FB Oct 1*

- "When I was deconstructing I needed reassurance that God was the God of the bible. I thought by reading the bible my faith would strengthen. But as I read the bible my deconstruction sped up. Reading the bible actually caused me to doubt it even more." [In response to being asked "Did your deconstruction lead you to a more in-depth relationship with God or did it lead you to not believe in God at all?", he said] "It led me to not know."

~ Anonymous (BD), Oct 1, social media public forum

- "I see it [Scripture] more as God giving us a framework in which we make decisions, and those decisions determine our outcomes. My view of the Bible is changing, moving from 'guidebook' to maybe a book of 'best practices' to outline a good life, to loving our neighbor."

  ~ Eric, Oct 5, Group discussion

Theme: Prayer

- "Things that I ask myself: If God answers prayers, why do every other religion with prayer feel as though their prayers are just as answered? Is prayer just confirmation bias and a placebo effect?"

  ~ Kevin, Oct 26, Email

- "I don't know if I really believe in prayer anymore. Isn't it just "confirmation bias"? If a prayer gets answered, God gets glory, but if it's not answered, it must not have been God's will? Isn't that intellectually dishonest; aren't we just kidding ourselves?"

  ~ Kevin, Nov 18, Group discussion

- "Does prayer change things or the situation, or does it change us? We can be so outcomes-focused!"

  ~ Jordan, Nov 18, Group discussion

- "Our faith is what sustains us to move the mountain, one stone at a time. I heard someone say, 'Faith doesn't mean the mountain will move all at once. Maybe it's that faith that sustains us to move the mountain one stone at a time.'"

  ~ Kevin, Nov 18, Group discussion

- "Prayer can be a tool for empathy with other people, and for consolation for us. Isn't it more about communing with God, and maybe a way to relate to people, forming bonds with people."

  ~ Jack, Nov 18, Group discussion

- "We can't treat prayer, God, like a genie in a bottle."
  ~ *Jack, Nov 18, Group discussion*

- "We have to watch our attitude. Expectation can lead to frustration. Anticipation that God will do something is different than expectation of specific outcomes. With prayer, we invite God into our situations, but we don't tell him what to do or how to do it."
  ~ *Steve, Nov 18, Group discussion*

- "Prayer is more about us than about God. It's cathartic."
  ~ *Eric, Nov 18, Group discussion*

Theme: Images of God

- "God is bigger than any one religion or perception. It's like standing in an estuary or stream, enjoying the water, and thinking that is God, and then seeing the ocean, and seeing now that that is God. Both are true."
  ~ *Kayla, Jan 6, Group discussion*

- "[At my former church,] God was put in a restrictive box, too narrow, too judgmental, too exclusive. So I essentially walked away from God, and became an ethical humanist."
  ~ *Matthew, Jan 6, Group discussion*

- "God is like an Italian grandmother. 'Oh, if you liked that, if you liked the new taste you got from that movement, why did you stop there? Why not keep trying something new?' God is bigger than any perception, and is constantly drawing us on to more."
  ~ *Matthew, Jan 6, Group discussion*

- "God is love, everything else is up to question."
  ~ *Neill, Jan 20, Group discussion*

- "Been thinking about the interaction of God, as slow, gradual influence versus intervention. That's the phrase that occurred to me on the drive down: 'Involvement more than intervention.' God does occasionally intervene, break in, but most often it's a constant/continual involvement, a subtle influence

over time."
~ Steve, Oct 5, Group discussion

- "I'm beginning to see God as being there all along, but you have to look to find him—like Jesus's whole 'ask, seek, knock' thing. I think that a faith of questions leads us to look ... and find."
  ~ Steve, Oct 5, Group discussion

Theme: Sexuality & Sexual Ethics

- [in response to a comment about whether having sex with five different people in one week bad. Person was going through a breakup and a sexual awakening simultaneously] "Good or bad are reductive. Does it grow you and meet your needs? Is it life-affirming or is it a crutch? Sex and intimacy is sooo lovely. But it can be addictive and take over, like lots of other fun things. As long as you're being mindful and not using it to avoid working through your shit."
  ~ Anonymous (BU), July 3, social media public forum
- "Even in your horny moments, don't let anybody treat you like a dumping ground for their semen. It's not a hole, it's your body, & it deserves better than that! And so does your soul."
  ~ Anonymous (RPW), Oct 11, social media public forum
- "My evangelical baggage even now makes me think of sex in dualistic terms, flesh versus spirit, which tends to only add shame and sees sex as sinful "lust of the flesh" instead of viewing it in a holistic way. Why shouldn't physical sex be spiritual? Why is a physical connection between people inherently sinful just because they aren't committed?"
  ~ Steve, Oct 19, Group discussion
- "I was taught in church (UPC) that, yes, there is pleasure in marital sex, but it should only be done for procreation."
  ~ Matthew, Oct 19, Group discussion
- "I have performed a blessing of a throuple [threesome] before, and I would do it again -- if they feel led by the Holy Spirit, that they are brought together by God. Otherwise, I'm imposing shame on them by denying church or pastoral recognition

and blessing of their relationship."
~ Neill, Oct 19, Group discussion

- "It should be our own moral conscience, our conviction, that determines if the sex is 'moral,' not whether some church, or even biblical, standard says so."
  ~ Neill, Oct 19, Group discussion

- [When asked about his current sexual ethic] "I don't have a lot of experience in this area, but when I get in that situation in the future, I'd want to treat her the way her father would want her to be treated."
  ~ Michael, Oct 19, Group discussion

- "I think the standard should be whether it's mutually affirming, respectful; not abusive or exploitive. It can be a way of sharing a deeply personal connection with someone, not just a way 'getting your rocks off' with someone, basically just using them for your own pleasure."
  ~ Steve, Oct 19, Group discussion

- "I'd say as long as it is mutually agreeable and non-coercive. Some sexual practices can seem abusive or non-respectful. Certain kinks or desires can be healing, can be a way of working through personal or sexual trauma. They can let a person experience intimacy in a way that is meaningful to them at that moment."
  ~ Matthew, Oct 19, Group discussion

- "Monogamy or 'covenant' between two people isn't necessary for sexual intimacy to be ethical or moral. That's like the same standard that says sex must only be between a man and his wife—hetero marriage. It's artificial; it's a man-made rule."
  ~ Matthew, Oct 19, Group discussion

- "Fornication in the bible isn't about premarital sex. The word specifically refers to sexual activities forbidden in the Books of Moses, like incest, bestiality and other 'unclean' practices. It's about sex within close family relations and certain pagan

practices. Nowhere in the bible is marriage used as the defining factor."
~ *Steve, Oct 19, Group discussion*

- "You commodify people when you put your expectations on dating or a relationship—we use people for our purposes instead of appreciating them for who they are."
~ *Kayla, Oct 19, Group discussion*
- "According to Sternberg's Triangular Love theory, 'consummate love' is made up of commitment, intimacy, passion. Those three components form a healthy, lasting relationship."
~ *Matthew, Oct 19, Group discussion*
- [After our session on sexual ethics and morality]: "I've been involved in a number of Presbyterian and Episcopal churches in my life, and in all the churches I've been a part of, we've never had a conversation like that before"
~ *Kayla, Oct 19, Group discussion*
- "Sex can be a way to help process your emotions"
~ *Matthew, Oct 19, Group discussion*

Theme: Life, Life After Death, Judgment, Heaven & Hell

- "I don't live to die. I live to live." [Ie: we're not supposed to live with a constant fear of judgment in the next life.]
~ *Matthew, Dec 2, Group discussion*
- "Take care of the pennies and the dollars will take care of themselves." [Meaning, focus on what's at hand, living now, doing justice, love mercy now, and don't even consider/worry about the "dollars", the eternal outcome or reward.]
~ *Eric, Dec 2, Group discussion*
- "Take care of the pennies, and the dollars don't matter."
~ *Michael, Dec 2, Group discussion*
- "Judgment day—I see it more as a place of healing, of being 'fixed', restored. That fits more with the Hebrew idea of justice: restoration and healing, not necessarily punishment."
~ *Steve. Dec 2, Group discussion*

- [About "Judgment Day"] "If we can have compassion on the worst criminals or pedophiles by getting to know them, how much more would God, who knows us so intimately, be compassionate, not punishment-oriented."
  ~ *Lauren, Dec 2, Group discussion*

- "I see judgment more in terms of justice, like how the Old Testament prophets saw it, as restoration. Returning things back to how they should have been. I don't see it being so much about punishment."
  ~ *Kayla, Dec 2, Group discussion*

- "As an agnostic, I do not deny that the gospels could possibly be true. I would welcome the reality of a loving God looking after me, directing my life. In all honestly, I hope I am wrong! ... But a MASSIVE part that causes me to not believe is the doctrine of hell. I cannot fathom tormenting my kids if they'd messed up."
  ~ *Anonymous (BD), Oct 3, social media public forum*

- "I cannot reconcile the idea of hell with the loving presence of God I know and experience. And all that evangelical talk about God NOT actually sending people to hell but merely respecting OUR choice to go there seems like nonsense. If there is a "hell," it's gotta be some kind of image of the self-torment and destruction we bring upon ourselves in this life. In the next life, I believe there is only healing, restoration and wholeness—all thru the embrace of eternal love."
  ~ *Steve, Oct 3, response to Anonymous (BD)*

- "I could no longer reconcile that I could have such compassion for [people's] history/behaviors/circumstances, yet God couldn't possibly understand their context enough to keep them out of Hell."
  ~ *Lauren, May 16, Survey Questionnaire*

- "The very notion that the same God who says "Love your enemies" and forgave his *while* they were crucifying him, would then later torture them in hell forever, is as nonsensical as it gets."
  ~ *Anonymous (AVV), Dec 27, social media public forum*

Theme: Life as Sacramental; Ritual & Symbol

- "Rituals are tools, they help us focus and direct us even when we're not feeling it."
  ~ Eric, Dec 2, Group discussion
- "Symbols can condense so much meaning into something so small."
  ~ Jordan, Dec 2, Group discussion
- "Symbols interconnect us"
  ~ Eric, Dec 2, Group discussion
- "Symbols provide us a common language for our spirituality"
  ~ Steve, Dec 2, Group discussion
- "Symbols can be a language, a common ground, for on-going discovery and exploration."
  ~ Jordan, Dec 2, Group discussion
- "Symbols can be powerful ways of connecting with God and power. They can help us make real the invisible."
  ~ Steve, Feb 3, Group discussion
- "Praying the rosary is a lot like meditation."
  ~ Dan, Feb 3, Group discussion
- [Talking about praying the rosary at the Celebration of the Immaculate Conception, Dec 8] "With all those people praying so fervently, it was the closest I've felt to the presence of God ... even more than in my Pentecostal days."
  ~ Jack, Feb 3, Group discussion
- [Speaking of "rhythms, rituals and religion"] "Millennials *love* and are drawn to rituals to find depth and meaning. Maybe it's in reaction to their parents' generation where everything was simplified and almost iconoclastic."
  ~ Barb, Mar 22, Personal conversation
- "... I was really moved by one [meeting] where we discussed the idea of using ritual/tradition/totems as a means of centering your mind/body/spirit on God. That whole scene is foreign

to me, but hearing the various differing opinions brought that into focus from me. In my upbringing, those were viewed as substitutes for God, and a problem. If you need a crucifix or shrine or a candle, then you're going about things wrong, and it becomes less about God and more about the physical thing, whatever it may be. ... but hearing how they help others re-framed my thinking about. God wants us to be near him. If that's what it takes for you, God is perfectly fine with that. It's also caused me to be more tuned into that when I see others doing it. I lit a candle during service a few weeks ago. It brought about a peace I wasn't expecting. It was as if I had given that thing over to God. It wasn't just mine anymore."
~ Eric, May 13, Survey Questionnaire

Theme: The Cross: Atonement, sacrifice, etc

- "If we can have compassion on the worst criminals or pedophiles by getting to know them, how much more would God, who knows us so intimately, be compassionate, not punishment-oriented."
  ~ Lauren, Dec 2, Group discussion
- "The cross IS grace."
  ~ Lauren, Feb 18, Group discussion
- "Blood sacrifice spoke the language of the people; it was a symbol that spoke to them."
  ~ Eric, Feb 18, Group discussion
- "We focus so much on the death, but it seems the resurrection is more important."
  ~ Michael, Feb 18, Group discussion
- "Love, compassion, is triumphant. If we see the cross as justice, then we will model "justice" in our lives—it's all about paying our dues. But if we see the cross as love and compassion, then the practical implications for our real lives is that we model love and compassion, undeserved. There are real, practical ethical implications to our theology."
  ~ Kayla, Feb 18, Group discussion

- "God creates people with sin. Even if we don't believe in original sin, there's no doubt that there's inevitable sin. Perfection was never on the table. Then he has to sacrifice himself to himself to save us from the sin we were doomed to have from creation ... which he created? I just don't understand it. ... The idea of having to sacrifice myself to myself to save the people, sounds almost mythical. If I weren't born into this, I would think it sounds like BS."
  ~ *Lauren, Sep 13, Personal text*

- "I think all the sacrifices and scapegoating made THEM feel better, made them feel forgiven. They needed some kind of physical expression of it to make it real to them. Like when Moses went up on Sinai to meet with God, and the people made a golden calf to have a visible, tangible image of a god they could related to."
  ~ *Matthew, Sep 14, Group discussion*

- [effect of bad theology] "All that sin needing to be paid for by blood to appease God, because God hates sin and couldn't even look it, made me think for a long, long time that God hated me. Even when I was preaching in my other church, I felt like God didn't love me, and I had to get rebaptized to get right. But sometimes I would just feel this love pulling me, like God saying even if I were rolling in the gutters, he would still love me. It was my fear that was keeping me from God."
  ~ *Matthew, Sep 14, Group discussion*

- "I'm more in the Christus Victor camp: that in his death and resurrection Jesus shows his power over sin and death, and proclaims the love of God triumphs over it all."
  ~ *Mark, Sep 14, Group discussion*

- "Finding out that the Church for centuries didn't believe this Penal Substitutionary Atonement stuff—that it wasn't really promoted till the Reformation—that the Church held less ugly views of God, made me feel comfortable when I rejected this idea. I knew I wasn't on the outside. I was seeing God like the Church had for most of its existence."
  ~ *Mark, Sep 14, Group discussion*

- [the result of our theology] "it's all about the fruit. What kind of fruit did that subst. atonement idea produce? Fear. We're afraid of God. That can't be right. But when I let go of those ideas, I feel the love of God; I don't feel afraid."
  ~ *Jennifer, Sep 14, Group discussion*

- "For me, the Cross is the symbol of God's love that says 'I love you so much, that you can kill me, and in my dying breath, I'll forgive you and still love you. Nothing can separate you from me, ever.' I need a theology that says that!"
  ~ *Steve, Sep 14, Group discussion*

- "The sad truth is, when I look at most Christians, I see people who don't truly value themselves for the insanely beautiful masterpieces they are. I see people who see themselves as innately evil and worthy of terrible destinies. That's called self-hatred, and it breeds nothing but projected hatred. Is it any wonder that Christians are deemed by most non-Christians as the most judgmental people on earth?"
  ~ *Anonymous (MM), Sep 17, social media public forum*

Appendix D
The Evangelical (or Bebbington) Quadrilateral

Evangelicals are a vibrant and diverse group, including believers found in many churches, denominations and nations.
Our community brings together Reformed, Holiness, Anabaptist, Pentecostal, Charismatic and other traditions. As noted in the statement "Evangelicals — Shared Faith in Broad Diversity,"[1] our core theological convictions provide unity in the midst of our diversity. The NAE Statement of Faith[2] offers a standard for these evangelical convictions.
Historian David Bebbington also provides a helpful summary of evangelical distinctives, identifying four primary characteristics of evangelicalism:

Conversionism
the belief that lives need to be transformed through a "born-again" experience and a life-long process of following Jesus

Biblicism
a high regard for and obedience to the Bible as the ultimate authority

Activism
the expression and demonstration of the gospel in missionary and social reform efforts

Crucicentrism
a stress on the sacrifice of Jesus Christ on the cross as making possible the redemption of humanity

These distinctives and theological convictions define us — not political, social or cultural trends. In fact, many evangelicals rarely use the term "evangelical" to describe themselves, focusing simply on the core convictions of the triune God, the Bible, faith, Jesus, salvation, evangelism and discipleship.

Source: National Association of Evangelicals
[1] https://www.nae.org/sharedfaith/
[2] https://www.nae.org/statement-of-faith/

Appendix E
NAE | National Association of Evangelicals Statement of Faith

- **We believe** the Bible to be the inspired, the only infallible, authoritative Word of God.
- **We believe** that there is one God, eternally existent in three persons: Father, Son and Holy Spirit.
- **We believe** in the deity of our Lord Jesus Christ, in His virgin birth, in His sinless life, in His miracles, in His vicarious and atoning death through His shed blood, in His bodily resurrection, in His ascension to the right hand of the Father, and in His personal return in power and glory.
- **We believe** that for the salvation of lost and sinful people, regeneration by the Holy Spirit is absolutely essential.
- **We believe** in the present ministry of the Holy Spirit by whose indwelling the Christian is enabled to live a godly life.
- **We believe** in the resurrection of both the saved and the lost; they that are saved unto the resurrection of life and they that are lost unto the resurrection of damnation.
- **We believe** in the spiritual unity of believers in our Lord Jesus Christ.

The NAE intentionally has not copyrighted its Statement of Faith so that it may be used widely. If including the NAE Statement of Faith on your website, include: "As adopted by the National Association of Evangelicals."

Source: https://www.nae.org/statement-of-faith/

Appendix F
The Chicago Statement on Biblical Inerrancy 1978

A SHORT STATEMENT

1. God, who is Himself Truth and speaks truth only, has inspired Holy Scripture in order thereby to reveal Himself to lost mankind through Jesus Christ as Creator and Lord, Redeemer and Judge. Holy Scripture is God's witness to Himself.
2. Holy Scripture, being God's own Word, written by men prepared and superintended by His Spirit, is of infallible divine authority in all matters upon which it touches: it is to be believed, as God's instruction, in all that it affirms, obeyed, as God's command, in all that it requires; embraced, as God's pledge, in all that it promises.
3. The Holy Spirit, Scripture's divine Author, both authenticates it to us by His inward witness and opens our minds to understand its meaning.
4. Being wholly and verbally God-given, Scripture is without error or fault in all its teaching, no less in what it states about God's acts in creation, about the events of world history, and about its own literary origins under God, than in its witness to God's saving grace in individual lives.
5. The authority of Scripture is inescapably impaired if this total divine inerrancy is in any way limited or disregarded, or made relative to a view of truth contrary to the Bible's own; and such lapses bring serious loss to both the individual and the Church.

ARTICLES OF AFFIRMATION AND DENIAL

Article I

We affirm that the Holy Scriptures are to be received as the authoritative Word of God.

We deny that the Scriptures receive their authority from the Church, tradition, or any other human source.

Article II
We affirm that the Scriptures are the supreme written norm by which God binds the conscience, and that the authority of the Church is subordinate to that of Scripture.

We deny that Church creeds, councils, or declarations have authority greater than or equal to the authority of the Bible.

Article III
We affirm that the written Word in its entirety is revelation given by God. We deny that the Bible is merely a witness to revelation, or only becomes revelation in encounter, or depends on the responses of men for its validity.

Article IV
We affirm that God who made mankind in His image has used language as a means of revelation.

We deny that human language is so limited by our creatureliness that it is rendered inadequate as a vehicle for divine revelation. We further deny that the corruption of human culture and language through sin has thwarted God's work of inspiration.

Article V
We affirm that God' s revelation in the Holy Scriptures was progressive.

We deny that later revelation, which may fulfill earlier revelation, ever corrects or contradicts it. We further deny that any normative revelation has been given since the completion of the New Testament writings.

Article VI
We affirm that the whole of Scripture and all its parts, down to the very words of the original, were given by divine inspiration.

We deny that the inspiration of Scripture can rightly be affirmed of the whole without the parts, or of some parts but not the whole.

Article VII
We affirm that inspiration was the work in which God by His Spirit, through human writers, gave us His Word. The origin of Scripture is divine. The mode of divine inspiration remains largely a mystery to us.

We deny that inspiration can be reduced to human insight, or to heightened states of consciousness of any kind.

Article VIII
We affirm that God in His Work of inspiration utilized the distinctive personalities and literary styles of the writers whom He had chosen and prepared.

We deny that God, in causing these writers to use the very words that He chose, overrode their personalities.

Article IX
We affirm that inspiration, though not conferring omniscience, guaranteed true and trustworthy utterance on all matters of which the Biblical authors were moved to speak and write.

We deny that the finitude or fallenness of these writers, by necessity or otherwise, introduced distortion or falsehood into God's Word.

Article X
We affirm that inspiration, strictly speaking, applies only to the autographic text of Scripture, which in the providence of God can be ascertained from available manuscripts with great accuracy. We further affirm that copies and translations of Scripture are the Word of God to the extent that they faithfully represent the original.

We deny that any essential element of the Christian faith is affected by the absence of the autographs. We further deny that this absence renders the assertion of Biblical inerrancy invalid or irrelevant.

Article XI
We affirm that Scripture, having been given by divine inspiration, is infallible, so that, far from misleading us, it is true and reliable in all the matters it addresses.

We deny that it is possible for the Bible to be at the same time infallible and errant in its assertions. Infallibility and inerrancy may be distinguished, but not separated.

Article XII
We affirm that Scripture in its entirety is inerrant, being free from all falsehood, fraud, or deceit.

We deny that Biblical infallibility and inerrancy are limited to spiritual, religious, or redemptive themes, exclusive of assertions in the fields of history and science. We further deny that scientific hypotheses about earth history may properly be used to overturn the teaching of Scripture on creation and the flood.

Article XIII
We affirm the propriety of using inerrancy as a theological term with reference to the complete truthfulness of Scripture.

We deny that it is proper to evaluate Scripture according to standards of truth and error that are alien to its usage or purpose. We further deny that inerrancy is negated by Biblical phenomena such as a lack of modern technical precision, irregularities of grammar or spelling, observational descriptions of nature, the reporting of falsehoods, the use of hyperbole and round numbers, the topical arrangement of material, variant selections of material in parallel accounts, or the use of free citations.

Article XIV
We affirm the unity and internal consistency of Scripture.

We deny that alleged errors and discrepancies that have not yet been resolved vitiate the truth claims of the Bible.

Article XV
We affirm that the doctrine of inerrancy is grounded in the teaching of the Bible about inspiration.

We deny that Jesus' teaching about Scripture may be dismissed by appeals to accommodation or to any natural limitation of His humanity.

Article XVI
We affirm that the doctrine of inerrancy has been integral to the Church's faith throughout its history.

We deny that inerrancy is a doctrine invented by Scholastic Protestantism, or is a reactionary position postulated in response to negative higher criticism.

Article XVII
We affirm that the Holy Spirit bears witness to the Scriptures, assuring believers of the truthfulness of God's written Word.

We deny that this witness of the Holy Spirit operates in isolation from or against Scripture.

Article XVIII
We affirm that the text of Scripture is to be interpreted by grammatico-historical exegesis, taking account of its literary forms and devices, and that Scripture is to interpret Scripture.

We deny the legitimacy of any treatment of the text or quest for sources lying behind it that leads to relativizing, dehistoricizing, or discounting its teaching, or rejecting its claims to authorship.

Article XIX
We affirm that a confession of the full authority, infallibility, and inerrancy of Scripture is vital to a sound understanding of the whole of the Christian faith. We further affirm that such confession should lead to increasing conformity to the image of Christ.

We deny that such confession is necessary for salvation. However, we further deny that inerrancy can be rejected without grave consequences both to the individual and to the Church.

Source: The Evangelical Theological Society, https://www.etsjets.org/files/documents/Chicago_Statement.pdf

Made in the USA
Coppell, TX
16 May 2026

77235151R00154